LITERACIES, SEXUALITIES, AND GENDER

Offering diverse and wide-ranging perspectives on gender, sexualities, and literacies, this volume examines the intersection of these topics from preschool to adulthood. With a focus on current events, race, and the complex role of identity, this text starts with an overview of the current research on gender and sexualities in literacies and interrogates them from a range of multimodal contexts. Not restricted to any gender identity or age group, these chapters provide a much-needed and original update to the ways representations and performances of gender and sexualities through literacy practices are viewed in educational and sociocultural contexts. Scholars share their insights and transformative visions that respect and embrace difference while creating space for new and deeper understandings of contemporary issues.

Barbara J. Guzzetti is a Professor of English and English Education in the New College of Interdisciplinary Arts and Sciences and Affiliated Faculty with the Mary Lou Fulton Teachers College and the Center for Gender Equity in STEM at Arizona State University, USA.

Thomas W. Bean is a Professor of Reading/Literacy and the Rosanne Keeley Norris Endowed Chair at Old Dominion University, USA.

Judith Dunkerly-Bean is an Assistant Professor of Literacy at Old Dominion University, USA.

LITERACIES, SEXUALITIES, AND GENDER

Understanding Identities from Preschool to Adulthood

Edited by
Barbara J. Guzzetti
Thomas W. Bean
Judith Dunkerly-Bean

Routledge
Taylor & Francis Group

NEW YORK AND LONDON

First published 2019
by Routledge
711 Third Avenue, New York, NY 10017

and by Routledge
2 Park Square, Milton Park, Abingdon, Oxon, OX14 4RN

Routledge is an imprint of the Taylor & Francis Group, an informa business

© 2019 Taylor & Francis

The right of the Barbara J. Guzzetti, Thomas W. Bean, and Judith Dunkerly-Bean to be identified as the authors of the editorial material, and of the authors for their individual chapters, has been asserted in accordance with sections 77 and 78 of the Copyright, Designs and Patents Act 1988.

Library of Congress Cataloging-in-Publication Data
Names: Guzzetti, Barbara J., editor. | Bean, Thomas W., editor. | Dunkerly-Bean, Judith, editor.
Title: Literacies, sexualities, and gender : understanding identities from preschool to adulthood / edited by Barbara J. Guzzetti, Thomas W. Bean, Judith Dunkerly-Bean.
Description: New York : Routledge, 2019. | Includes bibliographical references and index.
Identifiers: LCCN 2018028841 | ISBN 9781138311985 (hbk) | ISBN 9781138312012 (pbk) | ISBN 9780429458514 (ebk) | ISBN 9780429857959 (eISBN) | ISBN 9780429857966 (eISBN) | ISBN 9780429857942 (eISBN)Subjects: LCSH: Literacy—Social aspects. | Literacy—Sex differences. | Identity (Psychology) | Gender identity.
Classification: LCC LC149 .L48 2019 | DDC 370.15/1—dc23
LC record available at https://lccn.loc.gov/2018028841

ISBN: 978-1-138-31198-5 (hbk)
ISBN: 978-1-138-31201-2 (pbk)
ISBN: 978-0-429-45851-4 (ebk)

Typeset in Bembo
by Swales & Willis Ltd, Exeter, Devon, UK

We dedicate this book to the late Helen Harper, our treasured colleague and friend whose feminist scholarship on gender continues to inspire and inform us.

CONTENTS

PART IV
Gender, Sexualities, and Adult Literacies 167

FOREWORD

Creating a Pedagogy of Ambulatory Reflection

If we were able to search through all written texts, observe artworks, and return to the origins of what each of us consider our own civilization's past, it would be a futile task to find gender-free works. Gender has been an un-articulated center of human focus for as long any records have existed. Not in the sense of the obvious, but of the unstated-but-emphasized realities that surround histories . . . indeed, it is often what we don't read or see, but what is implied, in historical gender emphasis. Through absence, we understand gender, in the most literal sense, and gender has been articulated as male . . . and everyone else. Audre Lorde called this notion the mythical norm, that which has been posited, and re-posited from the beginnings of time, and accepted as what was, what is, and what will continue to be. Comprehending the vulgarity of how dominant powers have existed and continued to exist at the expense of gender articulation, gender rights, and gender differences is an effort in which the authors of this book engage. To understand this is to begin to understand how gender is included within the complexities of intersectionality.

We are in a germinal stage as we enter into an intersectional way of being, knowing, and living. Our understanding of habitus in regard to the lived reality of every human being must include how we function within, without, beyond gender and Lorde's mythical norms.

As we walk up and down the corridors of linguistic scrimmaging attempting to capture exactly how gender-ish stuff can be expressed, we crash into walls, peer through adjoining windows, and climb over societal obstacles in order to address the preferences, politics, and particularities of individuals. Observed simultaneously from the panopticon of political correctness introducing confusion over what is and is not appropriate and who speaks for how gender is articulated, we have an impasse in getting through the hall. And this is our work with literacy; we encounter history, etymology, the ways of language becoming, and then where it is going. As literacy educators, we attempt to move away from the word and in a Freirean sense read the world, while still creating new and equitable knowledges.

As we interrogate, define, and re-define gender, my thought is that it is ever-becoming and tentative. Our literacy pedagogy of gender must be humble, and aware of how words act as catalysts and agents of change, and/or how they harm and restrain. Our methodologies must be fluid, and as educators we listen to the needs of those whose lives depend on this fluidity. Indeed, humility is the pedagogical requirement for our emancipatory work, and certainly, in this context, gender deserves this. As we do work, we must look behind ourselves, reflect on where we began, have been, are, and are going. And, with a pureness of intent we continually process our journey, listen to those who are continually before, in, or just out of the passage. As we are all gendered/gendering/un-gendering/genderists/becoming in some way in or out of a classification or designation, we eliminate any essentialist inclination as to what/who/or how gender is. That is, we remain immersed in fluidity and on a vagabond transmigration.

What could be more complex than attempting to reside within pedagogies of literacy that are often fixed in curricular basements? The ability to critically move and re-move original and traditional ways to interpret gender (or to insist on a gender) becomes a constant in the emerging intersectional sphere. Through our tentative research, theory, narrative, and lived worlds, we are able to move within a pedagogical space acknowledging and repudiating those mythical norms and Western needs to define and stop the sojourn. Our acts of teaching reflect and embody those ways in which we know and live; and, how we include the ways of others. This is more than being sensitive, reflective, or "open-minded," it falls upon us to walk this walk with students, colleagues, friends, and unknown persons who fall within or without particular gender expectations or identities. There is no right, but we find there are many wrongs . . . those words and contexts that harm and define; and we continually attempt to return to that corridor and retrace the steps.

This volume offers ways in which to begin to enter a conversation on and with intersectionality as we navigate with care. The authors recount research and theoretical rambles along with switchbacks, short and long cuts, and dead ends. As we grow with the multiplicity of gender, we remind ourselves that the only hurry is to ensure that everyone makes the trek of their own choosing, in their own way. My hope is that this respectful and unpretentious walk is continual, self-conscious, and sincere.

Shirley R. Steinberg
University of Calgary

PREFACE

As we composed this edited volume with some of the best international scholars in the world, we were mindful of social difference and the potential for progressive gender policies in the United States and abroad, as well as discriminatory policies that persist in this arena. Issues as important as gender-neutral bathrooms, LGBTQIA+ rights of those who identify as lesbian, gay, bisexual, transgender, queer or questioning, intersex, asexual, or other orientations; anti-bullying; and a host of other transformative practices have been featured in the daily news. In addition, the current political and social climate is drawing increased attention to issues in gender and sexualities. Almost daily, members of the press report women's stories of sexual assault and harassment, ranging from those in the film industry in Hollywood to those in Congress in Washington, DC (Davies, 2017). These incidents have fostered the #MeToo movement on social media to encourage women to speak up, share their stories, and have their voices heard to stimulate social change. The news media are also advancing conversations about gender issues and gender identity, highlighting experiences of being transgender, such as the *New York Times'* report of a federal injunction against President Trump's proposed ban on transgender military troops (Phillips, 2017).

Professional organizations are recognizing the importance of advancing an agenda of gender and sexualities in literacy research and practice. For example, the Literacy Research Association (LRA) Board of Directors approved the establishment of a standing committee, Gender and Sexualities. The National Council of Teachers of English (NCTE) has established a Lesbian, Gay, Bisexual, Transgender, and Queer Advisory Committee. The International Literacy Association (ILA) blog highlights books for transgender teens (Hayn, Klemmons, & Langley, 2015).

It is up against this complex array of policy and power that the scholars in this volume seek to address and offer a counterpoint to discriminatory practices and policies. This volume is essential reading for a host of audiences including literacy educators and researchers across the lifespan, higher education faculty, classroom teachers, media specialists, communication scholars, technology educators, and policy makers. In addition, this volume will be important to leaders outside of education concerned with issues of gender justice and social justice.

Article 2 of the United Nations' Declaration of Human Rights (UNDHR) ensures the just and equal treatment of all and speaks against discriminatory practices (p. 6). Yet, despite being ratified by nearly every nation on earth, discriminatory policies and practices persist globally. Stereotyping abounds related to gender and expression of gender across the lifespan. The scholars in this volume offer insight and transformative vision that respects and embraces differences while creating space for resistance.

Organization

This volume addresses a host of gender-related issues across the life span. In doing so, the chapters are organized into four sections: Gender and Early Literacies; Gender and Childhood Literacies; Gender and Adolescent Literacies; and Gender and Adult Literacies.

Part I: Gender, Sexualities, and Early Childhood Literacies

These chapters focus on young children's literacies from birth to the primary grades. In Chapter 1, "Navigating Gender and Social Influences on Early Literacy Development," Jacqueline Lynch describes social influences on young children's development in relation to gender. In Chapter 2, "Preschool-Aged Children's Gender Identity Development: Exploring Gender Through Multicultural Literature," Rebekah Piper examines children's literature that introduces gender issues to identify how parents, caregivers, teachers, and others can use literature centered on gender identity to engage children in critical conversations related to gender. In Chapter 3, "Child's Play: Reading and Remaking Gendered Action Texts with Toys," Karen Wohlwend draws on sociocultural theory and gender theory to examine preschooler's pretend play, uncovering the literacies that children use to make stories with their bodies, toys, puppets, and props that represent "doing boy" or "doing girl."

Part II: Gender, Sexualities, and Childhood Literacies

These chapters focus on the literacies of children who are past the primary grades and were considered as older children by the chapter authors. In Chapter 4, "A Literacy of Resistance: Girlhood and Domestic Violence," Tracey Pyscher describes a teenage girl with history of trauma and domestic violence to reframe how this teen flipped the typical script of trauma and domestic violence through resistance. In Chapter 5, "Gender in the Making: Literacies and Identities in Girls' Self-Initiated Making Activities," Elizabeth Gee and Priyanka Parekh explore how girls' self-initiated making activities within a science, technology, engineering, and mathematics (STEM) context provided a means to alter their gender scripts and identities. In Chapter 6, "Understanding How Indigenous Latinx Children Express Gender Identities," Maria-Antonieta Avila examines how middle school students negotiated their emerging indigenous gender identities in their drawings and writings, examining these literacy practices through the theoretical lens of indigenous feminist theory.

Part III: Gender, Sexualities, and Adolescent Literacies

These chapters focus on the literacies of youth who are considered adolescents by the chapter authors for not only their chronological ages, but by their dispositions, inclinations, and behaviors in their transition from childhood to adulthood, including older middle school students. In Chapter 7, "'Holy Gendered Resource, Batman!': Examining the Broader Application of Comics and Superhero Fiction Beyond Their Restrictive Relationship with Boys," Jacob Cassidy and Michael Kehler explore the rich multimodal and critical literacy opportunities that comics can provide for a wide spectrum of readers, not just boys alone. In Chapter 8, "'This Is Why We Talk About Race and Sexuality Too': Challenging White Feminism in and Through Literacy," Stephanie Anne Shelton and Shelly Melchior use intersectional feminist theory to explore how adolescents in a summer English/Language Arts program engaged in journaling and art-based projects to consider gender. In Chapter 9, "How Gender and Intersectionality Inform Adolescent Literacy," Kathleen A. Hinchman and Donna E. Alvermann use intersectionality theory to explore four studies to show how gender intersects with other aspects of adolescents' identities. In Chapter 10, "'Outside Voices': Justice-System Involved Adolescent Males Writing Their Identities," Thomas Bean, Judith Dunkerly-Bean, Barbara J. Guzzetti, and Julia Morris use masculine theory to explore how two incarcerated youth portray their masculinities through multimodal literacy practices, including creating zines and writing hip-hop lyrics. In Chapter 11, "Embedding the Complexities of Gender Identity Through a Pedagogy of Refusal: Learning the Body as Literacy Alongside Youth," sj Miller shares interviews from adolescents, their teachers, and their parents to suggest how to recognize, affirm, and teach myriad gender identities. In Chapter 12, "Breaking Gender Expectations: Adolescents' Critical Rewriting of a Trans Young Adult Novel," Rob Simon and the Addressing Injustices Collective explore the development of a music video by eighth- grade youth in response to the young adult novel, *Beautiful Music for Ugly Children*, which prompted teens' inquiry into and desire to trouble stereotypical gender representation through a queering space perspective. In Chapter 13, "Defining Gender and Sexuality in LGBTQ Memoirs," Kate E. Kedley and Jenna Spiering examine three LGBTQ memoirs through queer theory and the potential to disrupt discourses that may create and limit possibilities for understanding and discussing gender and sexualities.

Part IV: Gender, Sexualities, and Adult Literacies

These chapters focus on adults beyond their schooling years who participate in online or offline literacies in informal settings. In Chapter 14, "Performing and Resisting Toxic Masculinities on Sports News Comment Boards," Erik Jacobson uses Bakhtinian analysis to consider the literacy practices and positioning in sports-related online discussion boards where posts range across politics and gender roles and represent toxic masculinities. In Chapter 15, "Transnational Women's Online Literacies: Writing as Social Action," Jin Kyeong Jung explores how Korean American women learned from one another and positioned themselves as social actors, defying gender and racial stereotypes. In Chapter 16, "Diverse Men Making Media: Creating Cultural (Re)constructions of Gender and Race," Barbara J. Guzzetti explores the experiences of two racially diverse men (Native American and African American) to detail how they represent their gender, race, and culture through zines. In Chapter 17, "Reading Fatherhood: The Importance of Fathers in Children's Literacy Development," Theodore S. Ransaw uses masculine theory to explore the influential roles fathers can play in their children's literacy development by using alternative materials, including magazines, newspapers, maps, and computer- generated writing activities.

We hope you will find these chapters helpful in considering current events and issues related to representations and performances of gender and sexualities through literacy practices. Much of these chapters were written from the standpoint of education as we are all teachers and learners in our interactions with others whether we are inside or outside of classroom settings. We anticipate that these chapter authors will raise our readers' awareness and consideration of alternative ideas about contemporary social issues that permeate everyone's daily life and influence individuals' worldviews. It is our hope that these research reports and research reviews will offer alternative viewpoints that will resonate with you and inform your future beliefs and behaviors.

Barbara J. Guzzetti
Thomas W. Bean
Judith Dunkerly-Bean

References

Davies, C. (2017, October 23). Female politicians speak out about sexual assault experiences. *Guardian*. Retrieved from www.theguardian.com/world/2017/oct 23/female-politicians-sexual-assault-experiences-jess-phillips-mary-creagh-theresa-villiers-anne-jenkin-me-too.

Hayn, J.A., Klemmons, K., & Langley, L. (2015, November 24). Putting books to work: Beyond Magenta: Transgender teens speak out. *Literacy Daily*. Retrieved from www.putting-books-to-work-em-beyond-magenta-transgender-teens-speak-out-em.

Phillips, D. (2017, November 21). Second judge blocks Trump's transgender ban in the military. *New York Times*, A20.

What are human rights? Retrieved from YouthforHumanRights.org.

PART I

Gender, Sexualities, and Early Childhood Literacies

1

NAVIGATING GENDER AND SOCIAL INFLUENCES ON EARLY LITERACY DEVELOPMENT

Jacqueline Lynch

Children look for guidance on the activities they engage in, in relation to literacy. Children's environment can direct them to appropriate or inappropriate behaviors. Influential adults in a child's life, such as their parents and teachers, can demonstrate the importance of a literacy practice by their modeling of and interactions with literacy. Researchers suggest that parents' and teachers' literacy practices can shape whether a child values or engages in a literacy activity based on his or her gender (e.g., Davis, 2007). That is, a child might think that certain literacy activities are only appropriate for boys or only for girls based on if and how influential others in their lives engage in literacy practices. Adults can influence a child's willingness to read, time spent reading, interest in different genres of texts, and self-confidence with literacy (Moss & Washbrook, 2016). Given the importance of early literacy development for school success, including high school graduation and related educational choices (Hernandez, 2012), it is critical that children are not limited in their engagement in literacy activities based on their gender. Therefore, this research review examines the role of parents, teachers, and children's peers in interacting with children and shaping their views about gender in their early literacy development.

Perspective

Socioecological systems theory is routed in Bronfenbrenner's (1989) ecology of human development. Socioecological theory can assist in understanding the relationships among various personal and environmental conditions. "Socio-ecological systems theory demonstrates the nested and interdependent nature of human development and interactions at the personal, relational, and collective levels" (Henderson & Baffour, 2015, p. 1962). Parents, teachers, adults interacting with children, and their peers can have direct or indirect influence on a child's beliefs or engagement, and these social influences can play a role in children's understanding of gender in early literacy. These influences are not unidimensional. For example, children's behaviors can affect parents' behaviors, which can reinforce a child's behavior. "Individuals influence their social ecology by controlling the cycling of resources and constructing norms, beliefs, and culture across multiple systems" (Henderson & Baffour, 2015, p. 1962). Social ecology pays explicit attention to the social, institutional, and cultural contexts of people–environment relations, and how individual knowledge emerges from these social systems (Smith & Osborn, 2007).

Children are exposed to countless influences and activities in their daily living. Literacy is a social act from the beginning (Street, 2001). For example, the way that teachers interact with students is a social practice that affects children's learned views of literacy. "Sociocultural production of discourse about reading relate[s] first to neighbourhood and family practices, with gendered positionings within these" (Davis, 2007, p. 238). Discourse about reading may place reading as more marginal or central in children's lives, and this may be related to gender stereo-typical positions within families. As children navigate social influences, the ways in which they engage in literacy in their everyday lives can affect their literacy learning and development (Barton & Hamilton, 1998). The values and attitudes children observe among those engaging in literacy practices can affect whether they choose to engage in similar literacy practices, and similarities between the home and school environment can create a context that reinforces children's beliefs about whether literacy activities are valued (Purcell-Gates, Jacobson, & Degener, 2004). Interactions, such as writing a grocery list with children, can provide knowledge on how, why, and who engages in a literacy event. For example, is it always the mother in the family who writes the grocery list? What attitude does the adult portray when engaging in a literacy event? Social interac-tions and models that shape a child's own actions and behaviors may be related to gender. A child who only sees one parent engaging in a literacy practice may associate that practice as being feminine or masculine. Children's motivation and participation in reading and writing are often related to the literacy actions of those around them.

Social Influences: Parents

Parents or caregivers have a critical influence on what children learn about early literacy and gender. Resources given to children from birth can affect their gen-der identity. Being provided with books, especially those provided by positive role models in a child's life, may influence a child's decision to engage in reading (Weinberger, 1996), causing the child to value reading and engage in reading in the future. Who reads to children can reinforce notions of reading as a mascu-line or feminine activity. Furthermore, parents, particularly those with children who are too young to choose books or read on their own, play a critical role in how children learn about gender through books. One way that parents shape children's gender identity is through the books they choose for their children. Anderson, Anderson, Shapiro, and Lynch (2001) found that the most common reason parents chose books for their 4-year-olds was the subject matter – whether the content would appeal to the child, as well as what parents considered to be appropriate or inappropriate reading material for the child's gender. The second most popular reason parents chose books was by considering their children's interests, which parents also connected with the child's gender. For example, some parents considered a book on building machines to be less interesting to their daughters. Parents also chose books for their children based on their own values about gender. One father commented that he would not choose "old style princess books" for his daughter to contest gendered (or gender stereotypical) characters and topics.

The content of a text can support or reinforce children's career goals (Nhundu, 2007). Nhundu's research suggested that girls' exposure to gender-*atypical* books or those that had non-stereotypical gender representations resulted in girls' forming career goals that were more non-traditional, indicating the impact of text exposure on girls' choices and practices. Children's changes in their gender beliefs were, however, limited to changing their ideas about their career possibilities given the alternative careers for males and females that were presented in books.

How gender is portrayed in books may be less important than how parents and teachers use books with children (Wharton, 2005). Adults' communication with children about ideas in texts that represent stereotypical practices can support children's awareness of gender stereotypical behavior (Nhundu, 2007). Furthermore, how parents engage with children in sharing books is related to children's gender. Some research suggests that parents interact with boys and girls differently based on the type of book they are reading. For example, Anderson, Anderson, Lynch, and Shapiro (2004) found that parents of preschoolers, particularly fathers, elaborated more when interacting with boys versus girls in reading a non-narrative text. In contrast, fathers interacted slightly more with girls than with boys when reading narrative books. Although non-narrative texts are known to foster more discussion than narrative texts, it is noteworthy that parents interacted more with boys than girls in extended discussions of non-narrative texts. More than one-quarter of these parents reported they read differently to their child based on the child's gender. Some parents (mainly mothers) considered their sons to be less patient, and others (mainly fathers) felt their daughters required more emotional interactions. Others found that parents consider girls to be more interested than boys in reading storybooks (Baroody & Diamond, 2013).

Parental expectations and beliefs can influence children's beliefs about literacy. Some researchers have shown that families have lower expectations for their sons' interest in reading and consider girls to be more interested in reading (Baroody

& Diamond, 2013; Entwisle, Alexander, & Olson, 2007). Lower expectations for boys appear to be related to differences in reading achievement test scores favoring females (Entwisle et al., 2007). Ozturk, Hill, and Yates (2016) found that parental gender-biased beliefs related to literacy can influence children's attitudes toward reading in a negative way. It was suggested that these parents may view literacy ability as a fixed trait unaltered by effort. Parental beliefs about their ability to support children's reading achievement may also be related to their children's academic outcomes (Bandura, 1986). Lynch (2002) found that mothers had stronger beliefs than fathers about their self-efficacy in supporting children's reading achievement, particularly their sons' reading achievement. This may be related to their greater involvement in their children's reading development in comparison to fathers, given that self-efficacy is associated with effort and engagement.

Fathers' involvement in their children's literacy development and practice affects their children's success in school, particularly for boys (Malin, Cabrera, & Rowe, 2014; Nutbrown, Clough, Stammers, Emblin, & Alston-Smith, 2017). It is known, however, that fathers of girls in their early childhood are more likely to participate with their children in literacy activities than they are with boys, which may promote later differences in reading performance (Leavell Smith, Tamis-LeMonda, Ruble, Zosuls, & Cabrera, 2012). Fathers or father figures who model reading by reading themselves and reading to their children can signal that reading is valued among men. Fathers can be involved in other ways to promote their children's literacy learning, such as through talk or play (Tamis-LeMonda, Baumwell, & Cabrera, 2013), by which parents and teachers can provide explicit links to literacy learning.

Children often model their parents' behavior and use information from parental definitions to interpret gender roles (Antill, Cunningham, & Cotton, 2000). Davis' (2007) research revealed that 7- and 8-year-old students perceived that women read fiction, magazines, and sometimes newspapers whereas men read newspapers. Her study revealed that students believed that reading was "for girls" and "for women" and that women sometimes read for pleasure. Comments from students revealed differences in reading interests based on the parent's gender, making comments like, "lots of women like reading – I see them when delivering Avon magazines," and "Mum reads a lot more than Dad does" (p. 232). Davis' interviews revealed that children perceived men to be too busy to read anything but newspapers. Her findings suggest children's perceptions and observations of their parents' literacy practices, and those of others in society, are influenced by how literacy is valued by those of each gender and sets gender boundaries surrounding literacy practices.

Teachers

Teachers also have an important influence on children's early literacy development and play a significant role in children's early literacy choices and activities based on their gender, thereby impacting children's gender identities. Teachers provide opportunities for early literacy development that can combat or support gender stereotypes. Later literacy learning builds on early literacy skills, including those cultivated at home (Whitehurst & Lonigan, 1998), so supporting early literacy learning is critical to ensure later literacy success.

One of the early literacy practices important for later literacy development is writing. In research with kindergarten and first-grade children, Gericke and Salmon (2014) found that spelling was the most difficult aspect of writing for boys. After an intervention involving more books with male main characters and topics intended to improve boys' motivation for writing (e.g., family, animals, and sports), along with associated mini-lessons, they observed improvements in boys' writing overall. Boys tended to write more and to use a variety of words. They concluded that the students had made personal connections with the texts, and that selecting texts based on students' interests can support learning. It might be argued that teachers reinforce a gender stereotype by promoting books that are typically associated with boys' interests. Nevertheless, providing books that boys are interested in can encourage boys to read and write more often and to write longer texts, particularly when writing strategies were presented in connection to the texts. Free writing encouraged boys to express their thoughts and their creativity, which seemed more important than focusing on spelling. Children who read well also tended to read more, and thereby improve even more (Stanovich, 1986). De Smedt, Van Keer, and Merchie (2016) found that students who write for personal satisfaction perform better than those subjected to external motivations, such as guilt.

Teachers' technology integration may also support boys' writing engagement, including the vocabulary they use in their writing. Sun, Zhang, and Scardamalia's (2010) research at the third- and fourth-grade level found that teachers' knowledge-building activity with technology had benefits for both girls and boys and was specifically beneficial for boys' productive written vocabulary. Technology engagement, along with out-of-school inquiry questions and discussion resulted in more writing engagement among all students, including their use of distinctive vocabulary.

Teachers, as well as parents, can reinforce or refute children's notions of gender through the use of appropriate practices and materials. Edwards and Jones' (2018) interviews with teachers of children ranging in age from 8 to 11 years old revealed that some teachers viewed children through the lens of their own gender, believing that girls are more inclined to read fiction, which can lead to practices that reinforce gender stereotypes, such as exclusively exposing girls to this one literary genre. Other researchers demonstrated that teachers can be more critical of boys' writing than that of girls' writing when they believed the author was a male (Elwood, 2006), which may impact children's perceptions of their writing ability based on their gender. Girls, for example, may believe they are better writers than boys in cases where they are not and may demonstrate more effort for writing. The opposite may be true for boys.

Awareness of supposed gender appropriateness begins in the preschool years and peaks between ages 5 and 7 (Trautner et al., 2007). Even kindergarten- ers categorize activities and objects as more boy- or girl-centered (Martin & Ruble, 2010). Wolter, Glüer, and Hannover (2014) found that boys who had a close relationship with their kindergarten teacher were better at spelling by the end of first grade if the teacher reported that she had offered activities that boys considered appropriate to their gender – either equally often, or more often, than activities typically boys categorize as "for girls only." Similarly, girls with a close relationship with the teacher benefited only when the teacher provided more activities that girls deemed as more appropriate for girls than for boys. As suggested by Wolter et al. (2014), these findings challenge the belief that there should be more male teachers in the early school years and suggest that teacher adaptations to students' interests are more important than the teacher's gender. Zambo and Brozo (2009) recommended that teachers be more knowledgeable about young boys' interests and consider building on children's reading interests outside of school.

Young children should have opportunities to critically reflect on material they have read or that has been shared with them, including media that they may enjoy reading or viewing. Giroux (2000) proposed that this critical decon- struction should be applied to Disney films and stories because they penetrate children's social lives. Typically, families are presented in stereotypical prototypes and stereotypical portrayals of gender roles are perpetuated in Disney films. For example, in *Beauty and the Beast*, Belle is seen as odd for "having her nose in the book" and her role is often to support men's problems (Giroux, 2000). In *The Little Mermaid*, Ariel is informed by Ursula that losing her voice is not a problem because men do not like women who talk (Giroux, 2000). Many of the story lines in Disney films perpetuate female characters in defined gender roles, which can further distinguish female and male gendered or stereotypical practices. The dependence of female characters on male characters may result in girls who persist less in specific literacy practices to achieve individual goals or females who speak up less in mixed gender literacy groupings. As indicated by Giroux (2000), at the very least, Disney movies and texts should be approached with a serious focus on critical analysis. Helping children to identify and reflect on the stereotypical messages in a text in the print and illustrations encourages them to develop their own awareness of stereotypical constructions of gender in texts and to challenge dominant discourses (Levy, 2016). When children are not taught to read visual elements, they assume the elements presented to them are truths and they repro- duce them in their own texts (Albers, 2008).

Children should be made aware of how the media can shape their views of gender roles and representations. These efforts may begin with a teacher or other adult questioning statements or behaviors evidenced in films or books and discussing why certain gender-stereotypical practices may not be generalizable to everyone. With older children, adults might initiate discussions about the persuasive nature of gender roles or the author's intent. This discussion can occur even in the early years. The goal is to discuss beliefs and facilitate discussions where children's voices are heard and knowledge is shared so that they may reconsider their thoughts and ideas. As Albers, Frederick, and Cowan (2009) found, discussion may not be enough to change children's assumptions about gender, however. The provision of non-traditional texts, although effective on some scale for changing students' practices, may also not be sufficient for eradiating gender-role limitations (Nhundu, 2007). Albers et al. (2009) proposed that discussions of identity should occur across texts, particularly since girls easily move into boys' activities, but boys perceive it is less appropriate for them to engage in girls' interests. From a socioecological perspective, adults can provide important support for children's understanding of gender representation.

Peers

Although parents strongly influence a young child's gender identity and self-concept, over time peers become more important in shaping children's self-concept. Gender roles evolve and peers affect a child's early literacy beliefs, as well as their notions of gender-appropriate beliefs and behaviors. Even in the early primary school years, evaluative feedback from peers influence children's perceptions of their competency, which becomes more pronounced as children age. Altermatt, Pomerantz, Ruble, Frey, and Greulich (2002) noted that "the relation between evaluative discourse and competence perceptions may be stronger for older than for younger children" (p. 905).

Researchers have found that girls generally have more positive attitudes than boys about reading (Logan & Johnston, 2009). As with older students, young children have beliefs about their skill in reading compared to those of other children. Viljaranta et al.'s (2017) study in Finland found that all children who had a negative self-concept in terms of reading ability were boys. The researchers concluded that boys' negative self-concept about their reading ability resulted in their low interest in reading. Boys' perceptions of their poor reading ability in comparison with their peers was associated with their lower self-concepts, which can have implications for their reading success. Lynch (2002) found that girls perceived feedback from peers on their reading ability to be more positive than did boys on their reading.

These findings may raise questions regarding the types of literacy activities that have value in school, including the activities that influence boys' perceptions of their reading and writing abilities. Considering some of the marked differences in children's early reading perceptions based on their gender, asking children about activities that might influence their perceptions of their peers' literacy abilities may be informative for widening literacy practices in the classroom. Some children may believe they are more competent in reading and/or writing when they are using technology, which may affect other children's perceptions of their ability, and eventually their own views of literacy. Societal presentations of men as experts in technology (Mims-Word, 2012) may impact peers' expectations for and feedback on children's integration of reading with technology. Boys and girls may perceive that technology literacies are appropriate only for boys. This may support boy's self-perceptions of reading ability, however it is important that girls also see digital literacies as girls' literacies and notice female role models in the technology field given the increasing use of reading and writing with and through technology.

Edwards and Jones' (2018) interviews with boys revealed that children held beliefs about writing related to gender. Rather than taking responsibility for their learning, Edwards and Jones claimed that boys attributed their underperformance in writing to perceptions of injustice on behalf of the teacher or to beliefs that girls had innate superiority in literacy and writing. Boys' perceptions of their ability, including their beliefs about their ability in relation to their peers affected the effort boys exercised in writing tasks and their engagement in writing. Unfortunately, attributions to ability can affect literacy outcomes when children see learning ability as a fixed trait (Bandura, 1986) and should be addressed by educators and others.

Chapman, Filipenko, McTavish, and Shapiro (2007) found that in first grade boys liked storybooks as much as girls did, but perceived boys to like information books more than storybooks. This finding could be related to the increased emphasis on incorporating information books to suit the interests of male learners (Zambo & Brozo, 2009), and that such texts are socially appropriate for boys. Therefore, it is important to ensure that recommendations based on research related to gender differences do not promote inequitable literacy practices (Nichols, 2002). Not all boys prefer non-fiction, as observed by Chapman et al. (2007), and many girls enjoy non-fiction. Peers can put pressure on other children when it comes to reading specific topics in texts, as they can with book genres. Dutro's (2001/2002) research found that boys who publicly reported rejecting reading a book about girls would privately confess to gladly reading such a book in private. Telford's (1999) research with 10- to 11 year-old boys revealed that they were uninterested in belonging to a group of girl readers. Telford stated that, "boys are constantly pushed towards a particular model of masculine behaviour which, although valuing academic achievement, does not value reading for its own sake, partly because reading is essentially a private activity which falls into the feminine zone" (p. 95). Safe spaces to discuss crossing these gender boundaries would open new learning opportunities for boys and girls. It is important to note that not all boys who view reading as a feminine practice dislike reading, and that not all boys who dislike reading view it as feminine (Katz & Sokal, 2003). Furthermore, many girls struggle with their self-perceptions and achievements in reading and integrating popular culture and non-fiction texts can support their learning as much as it can for boys (Wohlwend, 2009).

Implications for Literacy Education and Cross-Disciplinary Fields

Parents, teachers, and peers play a role in shaping children's perception of gender and their gender identity. From this review of the research, implications are shared and further research is warranted. Providing children with opportunities to combat gender stereotypes through discussion across contexts is critical to advancing children's literacy development and practice. By discussing ideas about gender roles and representations depicted in print, digital, and media texts, teachers, parents, and other adults may challenge stereotypical generalizations about gender and question their appropriateness. Such discussions can alert children to the reasons for their beliefs about gender representations, performances, and relations and assist them in considering alternative views. A critical analysis of texts can enlighten children to their own beliefs and perceptions, not just about gender, but other influences that shape their identity (Albers et al., 2009). When several social entities are working together to shape gendered practices, success in widening children's views of literacy and gender appears more imminent. This effort involves partnerships between homes and schools.

The adults and peers in children's lives can impact children's beliefs about their competency in and choices of literacy practices. If literacy activities are deemed to be feminine or masculine, young children may choose not to participate in them or attribute any lack of success they may experience to their imagined innate abilities based on their gender. Adults can help to change these attitudes by placing value on a child's efforts and by challenging notions of intrinsic abilities related to gender. Furthermore, parents' and other adults' engagement in reading or other literacy activities, particularly ones that are enjoyable (Sonnenschein, Baker, Serpell, & Schmidt, 2000), can serve as a model for children's take up of literacy practices and demonstrate the value of literacy. Fathers or father figures may particularly serve as role models for boys' literacy engagement and influence boys' view of literacy as a masculine practice (Ransaw, 2014). Less research has focused on the role of fathers in children's reading development, although some findings have been published on the role of fathers in supporting children's emergent literacy learning, beyond that of mothers (e.g., Malin et al., 2014). Further insight into these roles may enhance children's school success and participation in society.

Shared book reading can be important to children's early reading development. Levy (2016) noted that "while there is value in selecting texts for children that offer positive role models, this is more about encouraging children to respond to all texts with criticality and resistance" (p. 290). Learning begins with discussion of ideas presented in texts, fostering an awareness of representations, and ideas about how these may or may not be accurate for all circumstances or characters. As Francis and Skelton (2005) argue, children need to reflect and critique what they read, how they are engaged in learning, and then be assessed based on it. Bausch (2007) claims that teachers (or other adults) should observe gender patterns and "lean in and listen to *what* is being said rather than *how* it is being said" (p. 216). Educators, parents, and other adults should ensure that girls are involved in activities that have been considered to be masculine and boys should engage in activities considered to be feminine. These practices can reinforce the importance of defining children's gender knowledge and enhancing their early literacy success.

References

Albers, P. (2008). Theorizing visual representation in children's literature. *Journal of Literacy Research, 40*(2), 163–200.

Albers, P., Frederick, T., & Cowan, K. (2009). Features of gender: A study of the visual texts of third-grade students. *Journal of Early Childhood Literacy, 9*(2), 243–269.

Altermatt, E., Pomerantz, E., Ruble, D., Frey, K., & Greulich, F. (2002). Predicting changes in children's self-perceptions of academic competence: A naturalistic examination of evaluative discourse among classmates. *Developmental Psychology, 38*(6), 903–917.

Anderson, J., Anderson, A., Lynch, J., & Shapiro, J. (2004). Examining the effects of gender and genre on interactions in shared book reading. *Reading Research and Instruction, 43*(4), 1–20.

Anderson, J., Anderson, A., Shapiro, J., & Lynch, J. (2001). Fathers' and mothers' book selection preferences for their four-year-old children. *Reading Horizons, 41*, 189–210.

Antill, J., Cunningham, J., & Cotton, S. (2000). Gender-role attitudes in middle childhood: In what ways do parents influence children? *Australian Journal of Psychology, 45*, 25–33.

Bandura, A. (1986). *Social foundations of thought and action: A social cognitive theory*. Englewood Cliffs, NJ: Prentice-Hall.

Barton, D., & Hamilton, M. (1998). *Local literacies: Reading and writing in one community*. London, UK: Routledge.

Bausch, L. (2007). Boy-talk around texts: Considering how a third-grade boy transforms the shape of literacy in book talk discussions. *Journal of Early Literacy, 7*(2), 199–218.

Bronfenbrenner, U. (1989). Ecological systems theory. *Annals of Child Development, 6*, 187–249.

Baroody, A., & Diamond, K. (2013). Measures of preschool children's interest and engagement in literacy activities: Examining gender differences and construct dimensions. *Early Childhood Research Quarterly, 28*, 291–301.

Chapman, M., Filipenko, M., McTavish, M., & Shapiro, J. (2007). First graders' preferences for narrative and/or information books and perceptions of other boys' and girls' book preferences. *Canadian Journal of Education, 30*, 531–553.

Davis, P. (2007). Discourses about reading among seven- and eight-year-old children in classroom pedagogic cultures. *Journal of Early Childhood Literacy, 7*(2), 219–252.

De Smedt, F., Van Keer, H., & Merchie, E. (2016). Student, teacher, and class-level correlates of Flemish late elementary school children's writing performance. *Reading and Writing, 29*(5), 833–868.

Dutro, E. (2001/2002). "But that's a girls' book!": Exploring gender boundaries in children's reading practices. *The Reading Teacher, 55*, 376–384.

Edwards, G., & Jones, J. (2018). Boys as writers: Perspectives on the learning and teaching of writing in three primary schools. *Literacy, 52*(1), 3–10.

Elwood, J. (2006). Formative assessment: Possibilities, boundaries and limitations. *Assessment in Education, 13*(2), 315–232.

Entwisle, D., Alexander, K., & Olson, L. (2007). Early schooling: The handicap of being poor and male. *Sociology of Education, 80*(2), 114–138.

Francis, B., & Skelton, C. (2005). *Reassessing gender and achievement: Questioning contemporary key debates*. Abingdon, UK: Routledge.

Gericke, N., & Salmon, L. (2014). Digging deeper into the culture of writing: Do mentor texts inspire male students to write? *Networks: An Online Journal for Teacher Research, 15*(2), 1–11.

Giroux, H. (2000). Are Disney movies good for your kids. In L. Diaz Soto (Ed.), *The politics of early childhood education* (pp. 99–114). New York, NY: Peter Lang.

Henderson, D., & Baffour, T. (2015). Applying a socio-ecological framework to thematic analysis using a statewide assessment of disproportionate minority contact in the United States. *The Qualitative Report, 20*(12), 1960–1973.

Hernandez, D. (2012). *Double jeopardy: How third-grade reading skills and poverty influence graduation rates*. Retrieved from the Annie C. Casey Foundation: http://gradelevelreading.net/wp-content/uploads/2012/01/ Double-Jeopardy-Report- 030812-for-web1.pdf.

Katz, H., & Sokal, L. (2003). Masculine literacy: One size does not fit all. *Reading Manitoba, 24*(1), 4–8.

Leavell, A., Tamis-LeMonda, C., Ruble, D., Zosuls, K., & Cabrera, N. (2012). African American, White and Latino fathers' activities with their sons and daughters in early childhood. *Sex Roles, 66*(1–2), 53–65.

Levy, R. (2016). A historical reflection on literacy, gender and opportunity: Implications for the teaching of literacy in early childhood education. *International Journal of Early Years Education, 24*(3), 279–293.

Logan, S., & Johnston, R. (2009). Gender differences in reading ability and attitudes: Examining where these differences lie. *Journal of Research in Reading, 32*(2), 199–214.

Lynch, J. (2002). Parents' self-efficacy beliefs, parents' gender, children's reader self-perceptions, reading achievement and gender. *Journal of Research in Reading, 25*(1), 54–67.

Malin, J., Cabrera, N., & Rowe, M. (2014). Low-income minority mothers' and fathers' reading and children's interest: Longitudinal contributions to children's receptive vocabulary skills. *Early Childhood Research Quarterly, 29*, 425–432.

Martin, C., & Ruble, D. (2010). Patterns of gender development. *Annual Review of Psychology, 61*, 353–381.

Mims-Word, M. (2012). The importance of technology usage in the classroom, do gender gaps exist? *Contemporary Issues in Education Research, 5*(4), 271–278.

Moss, G., & Washbrook, L. (2016). *Understanding the gender gap in literacy and language development*. Bristol, UK: University of Bristol Graduate School of Education.

Nhundu T. (2007). Mitigating gender-typed occupational preferences of Zimbabwean primary school children: The use of biographical sketches and portrayals of female role models. *Sex Roles, 56*, 639–649.

Nichols, S. (2002). Parents' construction of their children as gendered, literate subjects: A critical discourse analysis. *Journal of Early Childhood Literacy, 2*(2), 123–144.

Nutbrown, C., Clough, P., Stammers, L., Emblin, N., & Alston-Smith, S. (2017). Family literacy in prisons: Fathers' engagement with their young children. *Research Papers in Education*, 1–23.

Ozturk, G., Hill, S., & Yates, G. (2016). Girls, boys and early reading: Parents' gendered views about literacy and children's attitudes towards reading. *Early Child Development and Care, 186*(5), 703–715.

Purcell-Gates, V., Jacobson, E., & DeGener, S. (2004). *Print literacy development: Uniting the cognitive and social practice theories*. Cambridge, MA: Harvard University Press.

Ransaw, T. (2014). The good father: African American fathers who positively influence the educational outcomes of their children. *Spectrum: A Journal on Black Men, 2,* 1–25.

Smith, J., & Osborn, M. (2007). Interpretative phenomenological analysis. In J. Smith (Ed.), *Qualitative psychology: A practical guide to research methods* (pp. 51–80). Thousand Oaks, CA: Sage.

Sonnenschein, S., Baker, L., Serpell, R., & Schmidt, D. (2000). Reading is a source of entertainment: The importance of the home perspective for children's literacy development. In K. Roskos & J. Christie (Eds.), *Play and literacy in early childhood: Research from multiple perspectives* (pp. 125–137). Mahwah, NJ: Erlbaum.

Stanovich, K. (1986). Matthew effects in reading: Some consequences of individual differences in the acquisition of literacy. *Reading Research Quarterly, 22,* 360–407.

Street, B. (2001). *Literacy and development: Ethnographic perspectives.* London, UK: Routledge.

Sun, Y., Zhang, J., & Scardamalia, M. (2010). Developing deep understanding and literacy while addressing a gender-based literacy gap. *Canadian Journal of Learning and Technology, 36*(1). Retrieved from www.learntechlib.org/p/43125.

Tamis-LeMonda, C., Baumwell, L., & Cabrera, N. (2013). Fathers' role in children's language development. In N. Cabrera & C. Tamis-LeMonda (Eds.), *Handbook of father involvement: Multidisciplinary perspectives* (2nd ed., pp. 135–150). New York, NY: Routledge.

Telford, L. (1999). A study of boys' reading. *Early Child Development and Care, 149,* 87–124.

Trautner, H., Ruble, D., Cyphers, L., Kirsten, B., Behrendt, R., & Hartmann, P. (2007). Rigidity and flexibility of gender stereotypes in childhood: Developmental or differential. *Infant and Child Development, 14,* 365–381.

Viljaranta, J., Kiuru, N., Lerkkanen, M., Silinskas, G., Poikkeus, A., & Nurmi, J. (2017). Patterns of word reading skill, interest and self-concept of ability. *Educational Psychology, 37*(6), 712–732.

Weinberger, J. (1996). *Literacy goes to school.* London, UK: Paul Chapman.

Wharton, S. (2005). Invisible females, incapable males: Gender construction in a children's reading scheme. *Language and Education, 19*(3), 238–251.

Whitehurst, G., & Lonigan, C. (1998). Child development and emergent literacy. *Child Development, 69,* 848–872.

Wohlwend, K. (2009). Damsels in discourse: Girls consuming and producing gendered identity texts through Disney princess play. *Reading Research Quarterly, 44*(1), 57–83.

Wolter, I., Glüer, M., & Hannover, B. (2014). Gender-typicality of activity offerings and child–teacher relationship closeness in German "Kindergarten": Influences on the development of spelling competence as an indicator of early basic literacy in boys and girls. *Learning and Individual Differences, 31,* 59–65.

Zambo, D., & Brozo, W. (2009). *Bright beginnings for boys: Engaging young boys in active literacy.* Newark, DE: International Reading Association.

2

PRESCHOOL-AGED CHILDREN'S GENDER IDENTITY DEVELOPMENT

Exploring Gender Through Multicultural Literature

Rebekah Piper

Over the past ten years, identity development and equal rights based on gender have been topics of much discussion within social and political movements. For example, topics of bathroom availability for those who identify as a gender different than their biological sex, transgender individuals in the military, and same-sex marriage continue to receive attention in the news. Discussions about these topics are vital. Unfortunately, there is resistance to conversations about gay and lesbian families (Jozwiak, Cahill, & Theilheimer, 2016) and gender identity within early childhood settings. The most critical voices, children's voices, have been silenced in the construction of early childhood education and topics around early learning (Cannella, 1997). Discussions around early education policy do not include topics of gender identity. This is concerning because as children get older, they confront topics of gender issues and they are forced to make sense of social issues. Individuals are required to consider how these ideas about gender roles and representations are powerful as they relate to children's social development. Therefore, it would be wise to follow the guidance of Delpit (2006) who suggests that there must be an unwillingness to remain silent so that the voices of younger beings can be heard by everybody's children.

There are multiple characteristics or subjectivities that influence identity development, including race, ethnicity, social class, language, sexual orientation, religion, ability, and gender (Nieto & Bode, 2012). It is important to consider that every child maneuvers through different stages of development and learning in his or her own time. This is, in part, because of the complex way that personal subjectivities intersect with and shape a child's growth. As the United States continues to grow more and more diverse, parents, caregivers, educators, and others who interact with young children must recognize the authenticity that each child has by recognizing that there is a combination of social and cultural conditions that influence a child's ability to learn and develop and ultimately influence his or her identity.

Individual Learning Processes and Development

There are various elements that influence a child's learning and social development. From a young age, children's home life and experiences shape and inform their identities within their own cultural context. Once a child enters the educational setting, however, this cultural development that has taken place at home undergoes modification as the "imagination" becomes familiar with different personalities, behaviors, and intellects. Ladson-Billings (1995) argues that the *culture* of a classroom has the potential to challenge, oppose, or align with the child's home culture. The outcome that this cultural continuity or discontinuity has on the child's development is less dependent on the degree of continuity or discontinuity that exists but is highly dependent on the relationship that emerges between individuals (Jozwiak et al., 2016). Therfore, the development of a child's imagination or worldview lies in the child's cultural development. It is in the cultural settings of family rooms, childcare centers, and classrooms that children begin to develop their own thinking, personalities, and identities. Knowing this, it is important to consider a theory of child development in exploring young people's learning.

Sociocultural Theory

Sociocultural theory is derived from the notion that an individual's development is based on both cognitive and social experiences (Vygotsky, 1978). This view is rooted in the idea that social development is dependent on the social influence of others. Moreover, because individuals learn and develop in both social and cultural settings, it is evident that the circumstances in which they learn will evolve and provide different opportunities for learning.

Sociocultural Theory and Child Development

Much of what children learn is influenced by caregivers, parents, and peers. Various social settings provide opportunities for children to develop in their own way. Vygotsky (1978) suggests that as children develop, there is a process that takes place on a social level first and later an individual level. This perspective suggests that children acquire concepts by cooperative group learning and by jointly constructing knowledge within a social setting, emphasizing the important relationship between children and families. The foundation of sociocultural theory supports child development in that this view recognizes that different knowledge emerges for each child based on the child's experiences and that sociocultural contexts of new experiences coalesce with his or her prior experiences. This theoretical structure supports the way children work cooperatively, how they develop their critical thinking skills, and how they progress in their cognitive and social development.

Sociocultural Theory and Identity Development

With the globalization of economies and cultures, there has been a shift in the ways that children are being raised in a range of family structures (e.g., extended families, single-parent families, step-families, and same-sex parents) (Dau, 2001; Ryan & Grieshaber, 2005). Gee (2000) suggests that identity is about "being recognized as a certain kind of person in a given context" (p. 99). Therefore, it is important to consider how the contexts of diverse families can shape identity. Identity development is influenced by multiple factors, including the experiences of an individual, inclusive of family dynamics. For example, family makeup and interactions have the potential to influence the ways in which children interact with one another and with parents as a direct result of the family's comfort or discomfort with issues of gender identity. The construction of gender identity is often influenced by adults who stereotypically assume that boys are inherently masculine and girls are feminine (Martin, 1990). Complex gender representations have other components, which include activity choices, interests, and dress. Casper, Cuffaro, Schultz, Silin, and Wickens (1996) described a common parent-to-teacher discussion around identity development through the "is my child gay?" question. For example, parents may suggest that their son only likes to play with girls.

While this question about their child's gender identity is often one that families consider as they see their children develop, it is important to approach this conversation from a stance that does not impose traditional gender designations on children (Sprung, 1975). The ways in which parents, caregivers, teachers, peers, and others interact with children and the messages they give about gender identity do matter to the ways in which children perceive themselves. This is particularly important as children's development changes and they begin to compare themselves to others. A critical consciousness is necessary so that children are supported as they develop an understanding of *who* they are becoming as opposed to accepting an identity that reflects societal gender norms that have been imposed on them.

Critical Literacy

Critical literacy can be understood as an approach that emphasizes teaching children to "read the word and the world" (Freire, 1970; Freire & Macedo, 1987, p. 4). Reading the word is the technical part of learning to read – the mechanics of reading – whereas reading the world might be understood as learning to read between the lines or the ability to infer or to deconstruct subtle or underlying messages in a text. Freire (1970) describes critical literacy as the process of coming to consciousness about issues of power, privilege, and oppression in the world, and then using that consciousness to push back against societal injustices. Freire's work suggests teaching reading and writing while also teaching self-efficacy and agency. Children learn to read and write while also learning to recognize that no text is neutral (Janks, 2000; Luke, 2000).

Because critical literacy is rooted in the struggle or a problem of historically marginalized people becoming educated, this perspective calls for teachers and others interacting with children to foster and teach reading and writing through "problem-posing" processes (Freire, 1990, p. 27). Accepting the premise that social experiences are educational, everyone who interacts with children takes on the role of teacher. Key elements of teaching through a critical literacy lens for parents, caregivers, teachers, or others interacting with children include socio-political analysis, cultural critique as it relates to dominant cultures, and action to bring about social change or justice when reading and thinking about a text. These elements are critical to consider when transitioning from literacy instruction to critical literacy instruction, which requires rethinking traditional and often biased assumptions that are made about learners, curriculum, power, and equity (Rogers, 2014). It is also equally important for children, particularly young children, as they learn through critical literacy instruction to recognize and question power structures in classrooms and in society at large.

Critical Literacy and Child Development

Supportive early education is vital to young children's success. No matter what the setting, children should be provided with instruction that focuses on their understandings, interests, and cultural backgrounds to give them meaningful learning experiences. Understanding the relationship between what a child knows and can do and how to move that development forward is essential for anyone who works with children. The debate around what children can do at certain ages is problematic as children develop at different rates. While it is possible for teachers and caregivers to provide appropriate practices and curriculum by being "nurturing, caring, supportive, and responsive to the needs and interests of individual children" (Grieshaber, 2001, p. 60), simultaneously drawing on understandings of gender and class can be problematic. The differences in discourse could theoretically provide different meanings of what it means to truly educate a child and *effective* teaching.

Children benefit educationally from rich learning opportunities – especially those that use a critical literacy framework – for gaining knowledge about diverse cultures in the context of exploring ideas of power and agency that provide opportunities for questioning and acting to reconcile injustices (Fisher & Serns, 1998; Stevens & Bean, 2007). A critical literacy framework should not be considered a strategy or skill that children are taught. Rather, being critically literate should be something children become that empowers them to exhibit their agency and better their own world.

Critical Literacy and Identity Development

A strong critical literacy foundation gives children opportunities to question social constructs and explore topics that are often silenced. Adults' first inclination may be to ignore questions raised by a child that are uncomfortable. This response will have a negative impact on a child's curiosity. Furthermore, when children are taught to read critically they are enabled to create their own meaning about a topic or situation. This idea is important when it comes to identity development as many families have beliefs that could negatively impact their children's gender identity development, leaving them to have a sense of discomfort about their own emerging gender identities.

Exploring children's curiosities is essential to identity development and is exactly what critically conscious people do. For example, a student in a kindergarten classroom, being raised by her two mothers, may experience peers questioning her family makeup, suggesting that it is impossible to have two mothers and that she must in fact have a father who lives at home. While some teachers or childcare providers may be equipped to facilitate a discussion around this topic of same-sex marriage, others may in fact shy away from the conversation in fear that their own perspective and beliefs will be revealed. Early childhood educators' opposing beliefs about gender identity and same-sex marriage was illustrated in a study conducted by Jozwiak et al. (2016), who shared the story of a heated discussion between childcare directors, some of whom argued that it was not developmentally appropriate to include stories of gay and lesbian families in classroom literature. Others defended the importance and appropriateness of representing all families.

A prime example of how teachers and others interacting with children can encourage the representation of all families is to open conversations about how many "moms" a child can have and provide different views that could benefit all children in understanding diversity in gender roles and relations. If the topic is ignored, the message is sent to children that their negative comments are valued, leaving the un-represented children feeling devalued. Cahill and Theilheimer (1999) suggested that adults make no assumptions about who children are and instead focus on identifying their cultural understandings. Children should have opportunities to build a community that is respectful of all. This can be accomplished by creating a space that is inclusive and allows for the open-ended conversations that are relevant to children's identity development.

Critical Pedagogy

Children of all ages benefit from a critical pedagogy approach where the relationship between teaching and culture is coupled with human difference, thereby enriching knowledge building and cultural understandings (Nieto & Bode, 2012). Many children are taught not to ask questions or even consider their own "funds of knowledge" that relate to their learning (Moll, Amanti, Neff, & Gonzalez, 1992). Kincheloe (2005) suggests that, "all descriptions of critical pedagogy – like knowledge in general – are shaped by those who devise them and the values they hold" (p. 7). Therefore, it is vital that when engaging with children or teaching (intentionally or unintentionally) about gender roles, power, oppression, or societal issues that can be uncomfortable to confront, that new ways of thinking about gender are welcomed and addressed. Moreover, critical pedagogy is more of an *action* that takes place in supporting critical literacy. It is vital to consider and address the fact that children begin forming gender stereotypes in their early years.

To look closer at the notion of gender stereotypes, consider the themes often presented in children's literature. There has been an emphasis on princesses, ballerinas, glitter, and glamour in books for young girls; typical storylines include girls' feelings of sensitivity and sometimes helplessness. In books marketed toward young boys, there has been an emphasis on trucks, monsters, and superheroes, conveying a sense of strength and heroism. These story elements leave children with ideas about the types of behaviors they should exhibit and how they are expected to relate to others in society.

To resist the notion of gender stereotypes, parents, caregivers, and teachers can introduce literature through a critical pedagogical approach where questions and dialogue occur to encourage children to view gender roles from various perspectives. For example, consider the story, *The Paper Bag Princess* (Munsch, 1980). *The Paper Bag Princess* addresses gender stereotypes that are often placed on children from young ages. In this story, Elizabeth, the princess, is emotionally distraught when a dragon destroys the castle, burns her fabulous clothes, and carries off her love, Prince Ronald. Elizabeth who is in complete shock works tirelessly to find something to wear as she leaves to save her prince. Because the castle was destroyed, Elizabeth sets out on the search for Prince Ronald in a paper bag, as it was the only item she could locate that was not destroyed. As she approached a cave, she encountered the dragon. The dragon loved the princesses but was exhausted from destroying the castle earlier in the day. She repeatedly bothered the dragon by asking him all he can do with his fiery breath and powers. The dragon demonstrated strength by burning items with his fire and flying around the world in just seconds. By distracting and tiring the dragon out, Elizabeth eventually saved Prince Ronald. Once she reunited with Prince Ronald, however, she was stunned that he was furious that she is wearing a dirty, old paper bag. He chastised her by informing her that she looked filthy and smelled like ashes, and she was not dressed as a *real princess*. Elizabeth fired back as she told Ronald his clothes and hair were nice and that he looked like a real prince but that he was a bum. Elizabeth decides she does not want to marry the prince and leaves. Upon reading this story to a child, some critical questions that could be discussed include: *In your opinion, what does a real prince or princess look like? Why do you believe the princess tried to save her prince? What do we learn about the power of girls from this story? Can you think of a time when someone told you that you couldn't do something because you were a girl or a boy? How does this story compare to another fairytale where a prince rescued a princess? Do you think the princess can be happy without a prince?* Questions like these may result in conversations that cause children to become uncomfortable. Critical pedagogy pushes individuals to confront topics and issues that are not generally discussed in typical responses to reading. A critical pedagogic approach suggests responding to children's reactions to a story with critical questions to help them develop critical thinking skills and abilities. Through this process, children begin to question relationships of hegemony and power while they are engaged in literacy (Freire, 1970).

Critical pedagogy does not apply to only read-aloud experiences with children. The types of critical conversations described above can also apply to viewing images; interacting with others; reading environmental print, such as food labels and billboards; watching movies; and listening to music vocals. Engaging in critical conversations with children in their "reading" of these everyday texts is another way to address children's thinking about gender roles and representations. While it may seem intimidating, the most crucial point to remember for adults is that children should be asked questions that invite them to offer their own ideas. Children should be supported in their literacy development and practice by efforts to develop their thinking skills that enable them to see different perspectives. Adults will need to keep an open mind and avoid suggesting a child is *wrong* in his or her thinking while helping to find ways to think about ideas representing various viewpoints. This practice of making ideas more complex and developed is a key approach to advancing young children's cognitive and social development.

Other Children's Literature that Introduces Gender Issues

There are various and broad definitions used to describe *multicultural literature*. Yokota (2001) defines multicultural literature as stories about groups of individuals outside of mainstream society and who are, in some way, marginalized. For example, people of color, working class and/or working poor, people who speak English as a second language, as well as people with disabilities, lesbian and gay people, people who identify as trans*, and women. While there are multiple categories situated under the umbrella of multicultural children's literature, providing opportunities for children to expand their knowledge and understanding about topics related to race, ethnicity, and gender is imperative to their development. Children's early literacy development can be enhanced by the types of literature that they engage with and ultimately motivate them to increase their awareness of social topics, such as gender identity. Increased motivation and connections to literature will likely impact children's attitudes toward social issues, as well as their attitudes toward reading.

Multicultural children's literature is an essential resource to use not only to engage a robust selection of texts for children, but through which to teach about topics such as racism, religious belief, gender equity and identity, and socioeconomic class divisions, topics that are often not introduced in early childhood settings. Multicultural children's literature provides opportunities for all children to build background knowledge in various content areas while also building on varied literacy skills (e.g., character recognition, plot familiarity, setting) concomitant with literacy skills (e.g., reading comprehension and read-aloud fluency). Although multicultural children's literature can facilitate the introduction of topics related to racial and gender diversity, adults must facilitate meaningful dialogue around these topics to enable children to realize cultural responsiveness and improve children's social awareness and development. When adults engage in sharing multicultural children's literature with children, they can foster critical discussion of a broad range of topics related to diversity. Multicultural literature helps children to learn to broaden their perspectives on and understandings of society and their important places in it. When this happens, parents, caregivers, and teachers have become culturally responsive to the needs of children who can and do affirm their being.

Since the dawn of the twenty-first century, there has been an increase in the number of books that feature lesbian, gay, bisexual, transgender, and queer (LGBTQ) topics. Many of these texts only feature LGBTQ parents, however (Epstein, 2014). Currently, there are numerous lesbian and gay characters in children's literature, but few transgender and bisexual characters (Bittner, Ingrey, & Stamper, 2016; Epstein, 2014). Within the last 15 years, there has been an increase in the number of books that focused on gender-nonconforming biologically male children, such as boys wearing dresses (Bittner et al., 2016). These books include, *10,000 Dresses* (Ewert, 2008), *My Princess Boy* (Kilodavis, 2011) and *Jacob's New Dress* (Hoffman & Hoffman, 2014). Many parents, teachers, and caregivers may be hesitant to share books that address such topics (Flores, 2014, 2016).

Gender Roles

The story of three small mice, *Horace and Morris But Mostly Delores* (Howe, 2003) is a story about friendship. Horace, Morris, and Delores are best friends and they do everything together, including going on adventures and planning grand schemes, until one day, Horace and Morris join the Mega-Mice club, where no girls are allowed, and Delores joins the Cheese Puffs club, where no boys are allowed. From the illustrations, it is implied that the Mega-Mice club for boys promotes boys playing cops and robbers while the Cheese Puffs have the young girl mice having tea parties, playing with dolls, and doing art projects. Delores realizes that she is not happy to be separated from her friends, Horace and Morris, and takes a hike with her new friend, Chloris. During the hike, which has been identified by the author as a traditional activity for boys, Delores and Chloris meet up with Horace and Morris and their new friend Boris and create their own club where everyone is allowed.

Howe approaches the topic of gender roles in a unique format. He describes activities that both boys and girls can participate in, like building forts, going on hikes, and playing with the opposite gender. His style of writing allows the reader and young children who are listening to see how the various characters in the book resist society's pressure to conform to gender stereotypes and instead follow their own path. Incorporating a text that addresses the idea of gender roles and gender stereotypes with early learners can lend to critical conversations about how young children view their gender in society. Therefore, it is vital to consider how children engage in conversations around both the story and the images in a text. Supportive adults and peers can provide opportunities for children to make connections by asking open-ended question, such as, *How would you feel if you were Delores? What characteristics did Delores have that made her take a stand to get back to her friends? If you were in a club that was only for boys/girls, what kinds of activities would you like to do?* These questions are brief but powerful conversation starters for children and adults alike to begin to gain a wider understanding of gender roles through a critical pedagogical framework.

Same-Sex Marriage

Told through the eyes of a young boy, *Donovan's Big Day* (Newman, 2011) is a heartwarming story about marriage. The story builds on the various tasks that Donovan must complete in the day, like feeding his dog, brushing his teeth, and getting dressed in preparation for being a ring bearer for a special wedding. In this story, Donovan's two mothers, Mommy and Mama are getting married and he is ecstatic to be sharing in their day. As Donovan hands the rings over to his two mothers, he stands in awe of his wonderful family, hugging his mothers, and kissing the brides! This story provides an exclusive view of one child's experience, as a controversial topic is uncovered. Donovan has a major role in the celebrations, conveying justice to the topic of same-sex marriage by portraying the day's events as joyful and memorable for family members and friends alike.

It is not uncommon to hear individuals suggest that it is not necessary to discuss topics such as same-sex marriage if they do not apply to an individual's own family structure. A critical pedagogical approach, however, advances confronting topics that are relevant to society and visible to children through media outlets, interactions with peers, and societal understandings. Furthermore, applying a critical literacy framework would suggest that topics such as power, oppression, and hegemony be addressed through discussion and experiences with other media texts, including movies, television shows, billboards, or discussions with others. Applying this critical literacy framework will influence the ways in which children develop their own gender identity while also impacting their early literacy development.

Gender Identity

Based on the real-life story of a transgender child, *I am Jazz* (Herthel, 2014) recounts a young child's gender transition. From 2 years old, Jazz Jennings knew that she had a girl's brain in a boy's body. She liked the color of pink, dancing, makeup, and dressing up. Initially, her family was confused as they had always thought of her as a boy. Then one day, Jazz's parents took her to a physician who said that Jazz was transgender and that she was born that way. From that moment on, Jazz's parents supported her and reminded her that being different but the same is possible. Jazz described the sad feelings that she experienced as other children would tease or ignore her. In the end, however, she recognized that she was different, special, and happy.

While this story uses the narrative of being born in the wrong body, it also uses traditional gender stereotypes when describing how the character knows that she is a girl through her gender-stereotypical preferences. Recognizing that promoting gender stereotypes can be problematic, the storyline can help young children identify and make connections to the ways that people feel. By sharing the story of Jazz, children can begin to understand and have compassion for the experiences of transgender youth. This story helps children to recognize Jazz's courage while also noting that being different is acceptable. Jazz's parents remind her that she is both the same and different. This story affords the opportunity to help preschool-age children move beyond their singular ideas and advance their thinking about gender identity. In addition, introducing a story such as this that presents a transgender person allows children to develop understanding and respect for others.

Implications for Literacy Education and Cross-Disciplinary Fields

Multiple conditions influence gender identity, including home-based cultural understandings and societal norms. Erikson (1968) noted that students' healthy identity development from childhood to adolescence is vital to their immediate and future educational success and success in society. Introducing a variety of multicultural literature allows for the consideration of the experiences of all children and offers a diverse perspective for readers. Simply introducing this literature is not enough, however. Dialogue about and interaction with a text allows readers to recognize how society impacts the ways that individuals develop their own gender identities. Children deserve a space to openly dialogue about topics and express their feelings toward societal issues. Adults can be empowering by providing a safe space for discussion and by facilitating children's dialogue. Through this process, children can apply a critical lens to any situation. For example, in a text that addresses traditional gender roles, children can apply a feminist lens by questioning gender stereotypical ideas in a story or informational text. Using a critical literacy framework while reading aloud allows for children to make text-to-self connections with characters in the story and possibly influence their own understandings of identity and identity development.

Adults have an influential role when interacting with children. The importance of deconstructing complex concepts and images for young children is critical to ensuring their success in understanding topics of diversity. The question "Is this developmentally appropriate for early childhood?" will remain when attempting to advance this understanding and possibly cause hesitation for some. Teaching children about stereotypes and bias is necessary, however, and should be started early. Simply correcting a child for making a biased statement or for promoting a gender stereotype will not necessarily change the way a child thinks about gender. For that reason, adults must be willing to trust their own understandings and apply them to different contexts of learning. Formulating questions and discussions that build on the work of Freire in prioritizing critical literacy and emphasizing the use of critical pedagogy will not place limitations on the types of conversations or materials that are or are not appropriate for children.

References

Bittner, R., Ingrey, J., & Stamper, C. (2016). Queer and trans-themed books for young readers: A critical review. *Discourse: Studies in the Cultural Politics of Education, 37*(6), 948–964.

Cahill, B.J., & Theilheimer, R. (1999). "Can Tommy and Sam get married?" Questions about gender, sexuality, and young children. *Young Children, 54*(1), 27–31.

Cannella, G.S. (1997). *Deconstructing early childhood education: Social justice and revolution. Rethinking childhood, volume 2*. New York, NY: Peter Lang.

Casper, V., Cuffaro, H., Schultz, S., Silin, J., & Wickens, E. (1996). Toward a most thorough understanding of the world: Sexual orientation and early childhood education. *Harvard Educational Review, 66*(2), 271–294.

Dau, E. (2001). *Exploring families: The diversity and the issues*. In E. Dau (Ed.), *The anti-bias approach in early childhood* (2nd ed, pp. 115–133). Frenchs Forest, Australia: Pearson Education.

Delpit, L. (2006). *Other people's children: Cultural conflict in the classroom*. New York, NY: The New Press.

Epstein, B.J. (2014). The case of the missing bisexuals: Bisexuality in books for young readers. *Journal of Bisexuality, 14*(1), 110–125.

Erikson, E.H. (1968). *Identity: Youth and crisis (No. 7)*. New York, NY: W.W. Norton & Company.

Ewert, M. (2008). *10,000 dresses*. New York, NY: Seven Stories Press.

Fisher, P., & Serns, S. (1998). *Multicultural education with pre-service teachers: Literature discussion as a window of thought*. Paper presented at the annual meeting of the National Reading Conference, Austin, TX.

Flores, G. (2014). Teachers working cooperatively with parents and caregivers when implementing LGBT themes in the elementary classroom. *American Journal of Sexuality Education, 9*(1), 114–120.

Flores, G. (2016). Best not forget lesbian, gay, bisexual, and transgender themed children's literature: A teacher's reflections of a more inclusive multicultural education and literature program. *American Journal of Sexuality Education, 1*, 1–17.

Freire, P. (1970). *Pedagogy of the oppressed*. New York, NY: Continuum.

Freire, P. (1990). *Education for critical consciousness*. South Hadley, MA: Bergin & Garvey.

Freire, P., & Macedo, D. (1987). *Literacy: Reading the word and the world.* South Hadley, MA: Bergin & Garvey.

Gee, J.P. (2000). Identity as an analytic lens for research in education. *Review of Research in Education, 25,* 99–125.

Grieshaber, S. (2001). Advocacy and early childhood educators: Identity and cultural conflicts. In S. Grieshaber & G.S. Canella (Eds.), *Embracing identities in early childhood education: Diversity and possibilities* (pp. 60–72). New York, NY: Teachers College Press.

Herthel, J., & Jennings, J. (2014). *I am Jazz.* New York, NY: Penguin.

Hoffman, S., & Hoffman, I. (2014). *Jacob's new dress.* Park Ridge, IL: Albert Whitman Co.

Howe, J. (2003). *Horace and Morris but mostly Dolores.* New York, NY: Simon & Schuster.

Janks, H. (2000). Domination, access, diversity, and design: A synthesis for critical literacy education. *Educational Review, 52,* 175–186.

Jozwiak, M.M., Cahill, B.J., & Theilheimer, R. (2016). *Continuity in children's worlds: Choices and consequences for early childhood settings.* New York, NY: Teachers College Press.

Kilodavis, C. (2011). *My princess boy.* New York, NY: Simon & Schuster.

Kincheloe, J.L. (2005). *Critical pedagogy.* New York, NY: Peter Lang.

Ladson-Billings, G. (1995). Toward a theory of culturally relevant pedagogy. *American Educational Research Journal, 32*(3), 456–491.

Luke, A. (2000). Critical literacy in Australia. *Journal of Adolescent and Adult Literacy, 43,* 448–461.

Martin, C.L. (1990). Attitudes and expectations about children with nontraditional and traditional gender roles. *Sex Roles, 22,* 151–165.

Moll, L.C., Amanti, C., Neff, D., & Gonzalez, N. (1992). Funds of knowledge for teaching: Using a qualitative approach to connect homes and classrooms. *Theory into Practice, 31*(2), 132–141.

Munsch, R. (1980). *The paper bag princess.* Buffalo, NY: Annick Press.

Newman, L. (2011). *Donovan's big day.* New York, NY. Random House Digital.

Nieto, S., & Bode, P. (2012). *Affirming diversity: The sociopolitical context of multicultural education* (6th ed.). Boston, MA: Pearson.

Rogers, R. (2014). Coaching literacy teachers as they design critical literacy practices. *Reading and Writing Quarterly, 30*(3), 241–261.

Ryan, S., & Grieshaber, S. (2005). Shifting from developmental to postmodern practices in early childhood teacher education. *Journal of Teacher Education, 56*(1), 34–45.

Sprung, B. (1975). *Nonsexist education for young children: A practical guide.* New York, NY: Women's Action Alliance.

Stevens, L.P., & Bean, T.W. (2007). *Critical literacy: Context, research, and practice in the K-12 classroom.* Thousand Oaks, CA: Sage.

Vygotsky, L.S. (1978). *Mind in society: The development of higher psychological processes.* Cambridge, MA: Harvard University Press.

Yokota, J. (2001). *Kaleidoscope: A multicultural booklist for grades K–8. National Council of Teachers of English (NCTE) bibliography Series.* Urbana, IL: NCTE.

3

CHILD'S PLAY

Reading and Remaking Gendered Action Texts with Toys

Karen E. Wohlwend

The term *child's play* calls forth images of young children pretending with dolls, blocks, stuffed animals, miniature cars, games, and other toys in playrooms or playgrounds. Play suggests an aimless innocence that belies the rigorous work children do as they try on cultural scripts about who they should be and become. During play, children explore the many roles they have observed as participants in everyday events in their worlds. Children's playthings are designed to communicate cultural expectations and anticipated futures to players (Brougère, 2006). For example, toy ads in the 1925 Sears catalog focused on the value of toys as preparation for gender-specific vocations: kitchen playsets and baby dolls forecast roles for girls as "little homemakers" and mothers while mechanical cars and construction sets positioned boys as budding industrialists and entrepreneurs (Daly, 2017). A century later, gender division remains a key strategy by the toy industry for marketing toys, evident in toy manufacturer annual reports that measure earnings by consumer gender and are readily apparent in color-coded toy aisles: pastel colors mark toys for girls, neon and metallic for boys. Thus, cultural messages about gender expectations are expressed in multiple ways: through the roles and practices a toy inspires, through advertising that entices consumers to buy it, and through its design and sensory messages molded into its color, texture, and shape. In this way, toys communicate identity expectations about who children should become and how they should play.

Toys are big business, distributing their gendered messages on a global scale. In 2016, worldwide retail sales of toys totaled over 88 billion dollars (Toy Association, 2018). Today, extensive media franchises merge toys with a line of everyday consumer products, licensed and decorated with popular media characters. Children can live in their favorite character's merchandise, dressed head to toe from breakfast to bedtime in licensed apparel, fortified by branded vitamins, fueled by branded snacks, and tucked snugly into cartoon-festooned bedding at night. Popular media franchises touch every aspect of daily living, making toys intensely personal for children. As many parents know too well, children can develop passionate attachments to favorite characters, so that a special doll or toy becomes essential to family routines and bedtime rituals (Marsh, 2005). The pervasive reach and immersive nature of commercial franchises in children's play has prompted ongoing debate over the identity-shaping impact of gender messages in children's media (e.g., Buckingham, 2007; Hains & Forman-Brunell, 2015).

We still know too little about the ways very young children take up gendered texts in toys and play. What happens when children bring the toys they love to preschool? What kinds of pretense do the toys inspire as children play together? What do children make of the emphatic gender divisions in popular media? How do they navigate the tangle of identity expectations that comes with their toys? This chapter focuses on data excerpted from six years of research on early childhood literacies, focusing here on a year-long study of play literacies in one preschool classroom. A close look at one playgroup's interactions with media toys reveals that while six young girls took up normative expectations for highly feminized performances as they pretended to be fairies and ponies, they also drew on the transformative power of pretense and wielded toys strategically to carry out their own social purposes: to get their hands on a coveted toy, to enact a powerful character, to create an exciting story, to take the lead in a popular playgroup, and to find a place to belong in the preschool peer culture.

Play, Gender, Literacies, and Toys

Play and Expected Gender Practices

Through play, children re-enact everyday practices, performing their understandings of the naturalized ways of belonging expected within a particular culture (Bourdieu, 1977). Mediated discourse focuses on mediated action (Vygotsky, 1935/1978; Wertsch, 1991), in this case, the ways players wield toys and rework their meanings to create a play scene and participate in a playgroup. Mediated actions are the embodied ways of using things, acquired and engrained through participation in routine practices shared by a cultural group (Scollon, 2001).

In preschool, 3–5-year-old children are just learning how to play together and how to belong in peer and school cultures. Early childhood curriculum explicitly develops social abilities by teaching children how to take turns and share scarce classroom materials, how to cooperate rather than playing alone, or how to negotiate who plays which roles (DeVries & Zan, 2012). As young children learn how to cooperate by sharing toys and pretending together, they also learn unspoken rules for gender performances: who can play a fairy or a superhero, who decides which ideas for stories are followed, who distributes the toys, and which characters can be revised. Play invites performances of femininities and masculinities beyond media content. As children play, they are also learning how to do gender in everyday practices and to enact becoming girls and women in a gendered community of practice (Paechter, 2006). A community of practice suggests a peopled set of identities, positions, and roles but here the focus is on social practices – the doings rather than the beings.

Butler's (1990) feminist conceptualization of gender performativity theorizes gender as a thing (fluidly) done through performances of available identities. In this perspective, gender is accomplished through action and participation, rather than internalized as an innate, universal, or unified subjectivity. Particular combinations of practices are performed, justified, and expected by overlapping, and often contradictory, global discourses that circulate within a given place, such as a preschool classroom. In early childhood, young children's emergent performances emulate and approximate the gendered sets of practices they observe as they participate as novices within a *nexus of practice* (Scollon, 2001), a set of naturalized expectations and engrained actions for participating and making sense with materials in a culture. Play enables children to intentionally try on otherwise inaccessible identities in their performances and to pretend they are more powerful and more adept at enacting the core practices in a nexus of practice (Vygotsky, 1935/1978).

Gender performances are not predetermined, however, even by the well-worn ways of doing things within a nexus of practice. When children pick up toys, they pick up a set of expected social practices and gender performances for playing with each toy. But there is agency in the ways players navigate among these practices, shifting among a toy's repertoire of anticipated identities and practices and slipping past the limitations of media stereotypes through each player's enacted pretense and intentional performance. In play, meanings are imagined, agreed upon, and reimagined for toys in the moment. These improvisations are invented spontaneously and always provisional. Play produces a collective representation of agreed-upon meanings in an imaginary context that suspends the conventional meanings of people and things in a physical location and replaces these meanings with pretend ones.

Play Literacies, Action Texts, and Toys

What does all this have to do with literacy? Definitions of literacy are in transition and expanding to include messages of all sorts in diverse forms of communication. At a fundamental level, literacy uses bodies, tools, and materials to make sense of and participate in the world. From this wider perspective, toys are texts and play is a literacy that produces a live-action story full of meanings composed by its players. Research on early childhood literacy in New Literacy Studies (Gee, 1996) has established that learning that builds upon young children's popular media passions deeply engages them in storytelling. Play can develop literary skills by tapping into children's media knowledge of story structures such as dramatic action and characterization (Dyson, 2003; Marsh, 2014; Paley, 2004). More importantly, this research establishes that children at play also wield literacies to enact more empowered identities, to express their cultural knowledge, and to shape their social worlds.

Play is a powerful and accessible literacy that enables children to independently express ideas through storytelling with bodies and imaginary worlds, rather than with pencil and paper. Through pretense, children craft *action texts* with bodies and toys as they enact scenarios made up on the spot that are meaningful and transformative in the moment to the players, whether or not they are captured in a photo or video (Wohlwend, 2011). The pretend stories produced during play are situated in complex and dynamic relations among children, friendships, and childhood cultures. Action texts engage a toy's dense set of possible practices suggested by its embedded messages: emotional attachments to characters, corporate marketing strategies, community gender performances, character roles in film narratives, and peer friendships and social relationships at school. The notion of toys as texts draws from research on artifactual literacies (Rowsell & Pahl, 2007) that unpacks the histories of prior meanings, identities, and uses in household artifacts and family keepsakes. Elsewhere, I have argued that anticipated identities for gendered players and consumers are designed into media toys such as Disney Princess dolls or Star Wars light sabers and circulated through media storylines and marketing processes (Wohlwend, 2009, 2012).

Methods: Tracking Gendered Action Texts in a Preschool Classroom

To understand how children played with the identity texts in media toys and negotiated player and adult expectations for gender performances and play-group participation, I used mediated discourse analysis (Scollon, 2001; Scollon and Scollon, 2004) that began with mapping popular classroom locations where children frequently played to identify preferred play practices, themes, toys, and playgroups. Video data captured play activity during 16 two-hour morning sessions across an academic year. Participants were 21 (12 boys and 9 girls) 3–5-year-old children, two teachers, and one paraprofessional in a preschool in a Midwestern university community in the United States.

Analysis of video data located instances where children used a set of media toys to see how they negotiated (1) their shared storytelling and (2) their social relationships in the playgroup. Children's negotiations with toys were examined within play events when a group of children shared a common set of toys and played together to produce an agreed-upon pretend scenario. To look closely at children's interaction with popular media, I compared play events to examine gender performances as children negotiated issues of toy possession, spoken references to media content (e.g., character names or actions, lyrics from media songs, scripts for character actions), player roles such as who could direct/follow play themes, and class histories of shared agreements about how a toy should be used, what it could mean, and whether its meaning could be changed. Multimodal analysis of video data made visible the unspoken ways players also negotiated the unfolding story. Modes signaled changes in participation when players shifted bodies and objects in their toy handling, their body posture, or proximity to one another, or movement across classroom locations that indicated possession, insider/outsider status, agreement or leadership in the playgroup, or authorship in initiating a new story direction.

Playing Fairies and Ponies in Preschool

Children in the 3–5-year-old preschool class stayed together for up to three years, but the class changed each fall as a new group of 3-year-olds arrived and a group of 5-year-olds moved on to kindergartens in other schools. In addition, some children arrived throughout the year as families moved in and out. Nevertheless, the membership of the playgroups remained remarkably stable throughout the year of the study. Most playgroups consisted of the same two or three players; a few children played alone or moved among the groups. The 3-year-old children often wandered or watched, playing briefly with a group but largely played alone or near the periphery of playgroups. Analysis of video data recorded in weekly visits over the course of the year showed that the playgroups in this classroom were typically divided by gender: girls played with girls and boys played with boys.

Each playgroup developed their own favorite themes for pretend play and many of the preferred themes that spanned the entire year were media-based. For example, two 5-year-old boys often pretended they were Marvel and DC superheroes; two 4-year-old girls played scenes from Disney's *Frozen*, and three 4-year-old boys pretended that the miniature cars and wooden train sets were Transformers, based on Hasbro's franchise of toy cars that twist and turn into robots. The largest playgroup consisted of six 4-year-old and 5-year-old girls who shared a passionate interest in princess and fairy media themes, and their play reflected this in fantasy scenes intertwined with family events such as mealtimes, baby care, and pet care.

Each day, the teachers set out new materials for children to explore. For example, literacy activities included paging through new picture books on the small sofa and tracing letters with glitter glue. Sensory activities included blowing bubbles and playdough sculpture, math activities included block construction and stretching measuring tapes around classroom objects. Science activities included sorting stones and shells and filling containers at the water table and other activities often found in progressive play-based preschool education. These daily activities inspired the children to play across same-sex playgroups for as long as their interest in the materials held, but when their interest faded, the children usually returned to play with their same-gender playgroups and preferred media themes.

Negotiating Passion, Possession, and My Little Pony Toys

The following excerpt from the video data shows the complexity that children faced when negotiating a role to play and a chance to hold a treasured toy when My Little Ponies came to preschool.

> It's early morning in preschool but play is already in full swing. Three girls – Ella, Leah, and Maya – are running back and forth between the blocks center and the house corner, waving xylophone drumsticks repurposed as fairy wands. Each girl is wearing a set of pastel fairy wings made of a glittery gauzy fabric stretched over plastic frames. The fairies stop to inspect the satin and lace princess gowns on the dress-up clothing rack. Pulling a pink gown off the dress-up clothing rack, Maya asks, "Where's my magic wand? I'm Ariel the Queen."
>
> At this moment, Riley and Morgan arrive with their mother. They've brought four My Little Pony toys to school today and Julia immediately walks over to see if she can hold one of the toys. She carries the toy back to the house corner and sits down at a small table. Without removing her parka, Riley follows Julia who is now cuddling the plush "Twilight Sparkle," stroking the pony's pink and purple yarn mane and its silky iridescent wings.
>
> Riley: "That's my Twilight," pointing to the stuffed pony. Julia places the toy on the table but keeps a firm grip on one of the pony's hind legs as the playgroup begins a complex negotiation over how six girls will play with four toys.

The fairy imaginary had been going on for weeks and sharing patterns were already established for the fairy wings. The ponies were new on this day, and that novelty alone produced intense interest in toys among preschoolers. This desire mixed the attraction of a favorite media character with the sensory experience of handling the toy itself: children spent a great deal of time gazing at the colorful sparkly accessories on the ponies and fingering their soft manes.

The color of each pony mattered as well. In the My Little Pony franchise, each pony has a distinct character, marked by a unique color scheme that provides the means of differentiating the toys, which otherwise have identical hard plastic molded bodies and nylon manes. The overall pastel palette of pink, violet, blue, and yellow for the bodies and manes aligns with color schemes that market toys to a demographic of girls under 5 years old. Twilight Sparkle, a pink and purple pony princess, was represented by two of the four toys in the previous vignette. This character is the lead in the *Friendship Is Magic* animated television series, a 2011 update to the three-decade-long My Little Pony franchise. In the cartoon episodes, Twilight Sparkle is a winged unicorn princess with magical superpowers. The Twilight Sparkle character was desirable to the young girls in this classroom on multiple levels – as a new toy at school, as the main character in one of their favorite franchises, and as a princess/superhero character that opened a repertoire of royal leadership actions and super-powered abilities within any pretense in relation to other possible player roles.

Research demonstrates that popular media knowledge and possession of desired toys can confer status within peer culture (Pugh, 2009). Simply holding a toy can suggest a role and open a spot in a playgroup so that a child can join in the pretense. Over days of play, toys can become anchors that ensure a place in the story and a history of participation in a playgroup. Scarcity of highly valued toys or "entry vehicles" within a preschool classroom gives these treasured objects added allure (Elgas, Klein, Kantor, & Fernie, 1988, p. 149). The desire that the ponies evoked required several rounds of adult mediation in this session, mostly in the form of verbal reminders to Morgan and Riley (and indirectly to the whole playgroup) to share or the ponies would be put away. As a result, Riley and Ella worked to distribute the ponies among the other players peaceably to keep precious toys from being confiscated by monitoring adults. But children also had their own purposes for sharing as distributing toys also assigned a role and included a friend in the story under construction by this established playgroup.

As the next section shows, children's collaborative storytelling required more than amicable turn-taking. Children not only had to reconcile their independent ideas about characters and story actions while managing their friendships, they also had difficulty getting their negotiations over content recognized as valid storytelling by vigilant adults who were intent on keeping the girls from fighting over the My Little Pony toys.

A Harmony Imperative: No Fighting

The *Friendship Is Magic My Little Pony* television series focuses on themes of kindness and friendship among the six main characters: five of the ponies enact "Elements of Harmony" – honesty, kindness, laughter, generosity, and loyalty – each represented by a jewel on the "Tree of Harmony." When combined, the jewels create a super-powered sixth pony: the magical unicorn princess Twilight Sparkle. Harmony – or playing nicely and getting along with friends – is the overarching theme of all the episodes: heroes foster harmony among the pony friends and villains sow discord. A key antagonist, "Discord, the Spirit of Disharmony," is a super-powered chimera whose capricious antics are modeled after the trickster Q in Star Trek's *The Next Generation*. The children's preferred villain was Nightmare Moon, the evil alter ego of Princess Luna, who eventually reverts to her princess form after rescue by the other ponies. A recurring trope in the My Little Pony episodes is the power of friendship to redeem villains and turn them into (somewhat flawed) friends.

The My Little Pony narratives circulate an ethos of friendship and cooperation above all things: friends before self, sharing rather than getting, and cooperation over competition. These might seem innocuous lessons and well-intentioned promotion of pro-social behavior. But this becomes problematic when emphatic gender division in marketing targets girls for a droning insistence on getting along instead of getting ahead, deferring and helping rather than claiming credit, and of putting others before self in episode after episode. So, what happened to this feminized obligation to maintain harmony during young girls' play with the pony toys? The following excerpt from the video data of the same morning of preschool play illustrates how the girls negotiated around gendered media narratives.

The playgroup clusters around Ella and Maya, debating who should play which character.

Morgan:	[arguing for a role] A tree of harmony. A tree of harmony. A tree of harmony.
Riley:	A tree of harmony.
Ella:	I'm the Queen of Melody.
Maya:	[agreeing] I mean, I'm not the Queen of Melody anymore.
Ella:	No, I am.
Maya:	[attempting to make clear that she agrees] I am too. Just because you said it, you are.
Teacher:	[misinterpreting this negotiation of roles as a dispute over possession of the pony toys] If you guys all fight, then it needs to go in your cubby.

Holding the pony aloft, Ella announces, "The Queen of Melody is the queen!" and runs out of the library and away from the adults. All the ponies follow, running, skipping, and galloping in a looping line around the classroom, ending in the far corner of the play kitchen and well away from the teacher's monitoring gaze.

In this moment, Ella established herself as leader and rescued the ponies from removal by the adults. Ella's shift to pretense foreclosed the confused negotiations about who was playing the queen. Suddenly, turn-taking around Nightmare Moon interrupts Ella's nascent story and re-alerts the adults to the potential for discord.

Morgan:	[rushing into the playgroup, grabs the Nightmare Moon out of Maya's hands] Noooooo, nooooo. I want to play with this blue [Nightmare Moon].
Morgan's mother to Morgan:	[taking Nightmare Moon away from Morgan] Hey! Hey! I think we need to take the pony home.
Morgan to her mother:	Ok, you win. Morgan walks up to Julia and takes the small Twilight pink pony away from Julia and hands her the large Twilight plush pony in exchange. Riley

watches the exchange, hands clasped tightly as if in silent prayer. Morgan returns to her mother and hands over the small pink Twilight pony while Julia watches.

Mother to Morgan:	I don't think you're ready to bring toys to school.
Morgan:	I want my pony.
Mother, handing Nightmare Moon back to Morgan:	*Ok, but I don't want any fighting.*
Riley:	[repeating her mother's point, Riley returns to Ella and Maya, shaking her finger for emphasis] Guys, no fighting. No fighting, guys.
Maya to Riley:	We're NOT fighting.
Mother to Morgan:	I was talking to YOU.
Maya:	[shouting at Riley angrily about losing Nightmare Moon to Morgan] I don't have any more powers and that's because of my ponies!
Ella:	[quickly halts Maya's scolding of Riley by offering her own toys to Maya and shifting back into pretense] Don't worry. You can use my wand and my pony and take care of it.
Maya:	[objecting] But the queen has a lot of power.
Ella:	Don't worry. We can do this together. Let's go! But we don't have much time! [Ella runs away to the block center.]
Maya:	[following Ella] I have ten power. I have a hundred. I have ten hundred.

The girls are off to wage war against the imaginary Queen of Melody, using their magic wands and toy ponies to battle an army of "wizards with ten millions of powers."

Pastel ponies and fairy wands are examples of toys with hyper-feminine texts that target preschool girls. The repeated expectations across such toys create resonances that seem to close off alternative performance options. Media franchises such as My Little Pony or Disney Fairies circulate similar expectations for "girly girls'" identities in an emphasized femininity discourse (Blaise, 2005). Yet in this episode, prohibitions against fighting in the toys' narratives about harmony were easily set aside during girls' negotiations for turns, or in their storying that focused on magical powers to battle enemies. Adult monitoring constructed these negotiations as fighting and threatened to shut down play at the first sign of conflict among the girls. Still, the children were also able to use the accessibility of play to escape confining adult rules and to gallop away into pretense.

Embracing and Slipping Past Media Stereotypes

Child's play produces fluid performances that are subject to continual negotiation among players. In preschool peer cultures, issues around sharing materials and ideas rise to the forefront as children work through the problems of working together, managing desirable toys, and becoming friends while producing space distinct from adults. The notion of toys as texts enables a look beyond surface gender stereotypes in verbal scripts in film narratives, advertising messages, and corporate marketing strategies. Contradictions among the toys' designed texts and the meanings children give to them create slippages that open the range of action texts that children play. In this play instance, deferential gendered roles associated with pony toys were twisted or remade through pretend meanings that children created, overlooking multimodal messages designed into toy materials' shapes, textures, and colors, and slipping past school rules that governed how players were to behave and how toys were to be shared.

Implications for Literacy Education and Cross-Disciplinary Fields

This short analysis of a morning spent with girls, fairies, and ponies in preschool suggests several implications for thinking about gender performances in children's play, not just in early childhood education but in a range of fields. The realization that children are actively co-producing and remaking action texts with toys as they play should give rise to more creative approaches for engaging children as participants and learners in math, science, arts, and other fields. Children can negotiate roles and even highly gendered materials in quite sophisticated ways when they are given meaning-making tools that are appropriate for them, such as play that enables negotiation and collaboration. The degree of collaboration in pretend play is influenced by children's developing abilities to communicate their intentions through language and literacy. One of the strengths of play is that it is a natural literacy that enables children to communicate and negotiate their individual ideas for storytelling as they work to maintain a shared imaginary context (Wohlwend, in press).

Despite an excess of pastels, glitter, and directives for harmony and peace, girls were able to take up satisfying roles and invent powerful characters, even while playing fairies and ponies. At the same time, the longstanding and incorrigible gender division in the toy industry with its insistence on pink identifiers and passive storylines for girls should concern parents, educators, and producers of children's media and toys. Heightened awareness of the gender-emphatic messages children encounter through popular media and toys is only a tiny step toward expanding the range of play exploration for children. Educators and caregivers of young children also need to examine how children's play is interpreted, which kinds of play are sanctioned and for whom, and how to restructure play opportunities to invite a wider range of gender performances and representations.

Finally, children need places to play together to make sense of their worlds. The fluidity in children's action texts suggest the potential of play as a key site for understanding new practices for cultural participation for children and youth. It is just as important to recognize the significance of play as a space for identity exploration for older youth and to understand the value of play in spaces beyond early childhood and beyond classrooms. The disappearance of play spaces from neighborhoods, playgrounds, and even from early childhood classrooms means that children have fewer opportunities to open up pretend worlds and to negotiate together as they work out possible meanings and re-makings of gendered identities.

References

Blaise, M. (2005). *Playing it straight: Uncovering gender discourses in the early childhood classroom.* New York, NY: Routledge.

Bourdieu, P. (1977). *Outline of a theory of practice.* Cambridge, UK: Cambridge University Press.

Brougère, G. (2006). Toy houses: A socio-anthropological approach to analyzing objects. *Visual Communication, 5*(1), 5–24.

Buckingham, D. (2007). Childhood in the age of global media. *Children's Geographies, 5*(1), 43–54.

Butler, J. 1990. *Gender trouble: Feminism and the subversion of identity.* New York, NY: Routledge.

Daly, N. (2017). How today's toys may be harming your daughter. *National Geographic.* Retrieved from www.nationalgeographic.com/magazine/2017/01/gender-toys-departments-piece.

DeVries, R., & Zan, B. (2012). *Moral classrooms, moral children: Creating a constructivist atmosphere in early education* (2nd ed.). New York, NY: Teachers College Press.

Dyson, A.H. (2003). *The brothers and sisters learn to write: Popular literacies in childhood and school cultures.* New York, NY: Teachers College Press.

Elgas, P.M., Klein, E., Kantor, R., & Fernie, D. (1988). Play and the peer culture: Play styles and object use. *Journal of Research in Childhood Education, 3*(2), 142–153.

Gee, J.P. (1996). *Social linguistics and literacies: Ideology in discourses.* London, UK: Routledge.

Hains, R., & Forman-Brunell, M. (Eds.). (2015). *Princess cultures: Mediating girls' imaginations and identities.* New York, NY: Peter Lang.

Marsh, J. (2005). Ritual, performance, and identity construction: Young children's engagement with popular cultural and media texts. In J. Marsh (Ed.), *Popular culture, new media and digital literacy in early childhood* (pp. 28–50). New York, NY: Routledge.

Marsh, J. (2014). Media, popular culture and play. In L. Brooker & M. Blaise (Eds.), *Sage handbook of play and learning in early childhood* (pp. 403–414). London, UK: Sage.

Paechter, C. (2006). Constructing femininity, constructing femininities. In C. Skelton, B. Francis, & L. Smulyan (Eds.), *The Sage handbook of gender and education* (pp. 365–377). London, UK: Sage.

Paley, V.G. (2004). *A child's work: The importance of fantasy play.* Chicago, IL: University of Chicago Press.

Pugh, A.J. (2009). *Longing and belonging: Parents, children, and consumer culture.* Berkeley, CA: University of California Press.

Rowsell, J., & Pahl, K. (2007). Sedimented identities in texts: Instances of practice. *Reading Research Quarterly, 42*(3), 388–404.

Scollon, R. (2001). *Mediated discourse: The nexus of practice.* London, UK: Routledge.

Scollon, R., & Scollon, S.W. (2004). *Nexus analysis: Discourse and the emerging Internet.* New York, NY: Routledge.

Toy Association. (2018). Global sales data. Retrieved from www.toyassociation.org/ ta/ research/data/population/toys/research-and-data/data/global-sales-data.aspx.

Vygotsky, L. (1935/1978). *Mind in society: The development of higher psychological processes* (A. Luria, M. Lopez-Morillas, & M. Cole, Trans.). Cambridge, MA: Harvard University Press.

Wertsch, J.V. (1991). *Voices of the mind: A sociocultural approach to mediated action.* Cambridge, MA: Harvard University Press.

Wohlwend, K.E. (2009). Damsels in discourse: Girls consuming and producing identity texts through Disney Princess play. *Reading Research Quarterly, 44*(1), 57–83. doi: 10.1598/rrq.44.1.3

Wohlwend, K.E. (2011). *Playing their way into literacies: Reading, writing, and belonging in the early childhood classroom.* New York, NY: Teachers College Press

Wohlwend, K.E. (2012). The boys who would be princesses: Playing with gender identity intertexts in Disney Princess transmedia. *Gender and Education, 24*(6), 593–610. doi: 10.1080/09540253.2012.674495

Wohlwend, K.E. (in press). Play as the literacy of children: Imagining otherwise in contemporary early childhood education. In D.E. Alvermann, N.J. Unrau, & M. Sailors (Eds.), *Theoretical models and processes of literacy* (7th ed.). New York, NY: Routledge.

PART II

Gender, Sexualities, and Childhood Literacies

4

A LITERACY OF RESISTANCE

Girlhood and Domestic Violence

Tracey Pyscher

An intense interaction I observed in a middle school classroom was written on the bodies of Jen, a bi-racial eighth-grade girl with a history of childhood domestic violence, and her two teachers. Jen, who proudly identified as a survivor of childhood domestic violence, stared forward and used her body to resist her teachers' demands. She purposefully positioned her body away from the attention of her math teacher and a special education teacher in her classroom. Both teachers hovered near Jen positioning their bodies near her to insist that she engage in her math assignment. The reasons for her teachers' intense stance never became clear to me. Jen was not acting out or talking back. She was attempting, in spurts, to engage in her math assignment. Continuing to stare forward, she refused to acknowledge the teachers for several minutes before abruptly standing up and storming out of the room.

This social interaction illustrates a troubling and well-worn reality in the everyday classroom and is well documented in the educational literature that addresses the needs of marginalized youth who resist "schooling" or being "schooled." Sadly, this reality is easily used to justify the punishment of youth deemed to be emotionally and behaviorally "troubled" in schools and other institutional spaces. In my previous work, I have attempted to counter the deficit logic that girls and youth who grow up in trauma and domestic violence need to be socially and emotionally "fixed "by offering a counter narrative grounded in critical sociocultural theory (Pyscher, 2015). What this means in my research is that I tackle the challenge made by Lewis and Moje (2003) that researchers pay close attention to "how identities are shaped within and shaping social and cultural contexts" (p. 1981). Toward this goal, I have spent numerous hours studying girls with whom I share similar standpoints (Hill Collins, 2000) as victims of domestic violence and whose young lives are dramatically shaped by childhood experiences of domestic violence; I attempt to convey and re-represent their perspectives on navigating social spaces like schools.

In my larger study (Pyscher, 2016), I followed a girl name Jen through her middle school classrooms where she performed embodied literacies of resistance, and I also observed numerous other girls who shared similar standpoints of being victims of domestic violence, and/or being raced, queered, and classed. I have suggested that growing up in traumatic experiences of familial violence is not so different from the experiences of growing up raced in a white world, gendered in the realities of misogyny, or traversing wealth while living in poverty (Pyscher, 2017b). Although often theorized as an individualized and behavioral experience, domestic violence is a social experience. Knowing how to navigate such intimate relationships to violence(s) from birth throughout childhood culturally resides in the body, mind, and psyche, not so unlike other socially marginalizing experiences. These cultural knowledges constantly push the marginalized self, especially the younger self, toward access to and a desire for agency.

This cultural and psychic desire for a more agentic life shapes Jen's complicated "readings" of teachers and adults, especially in moments of intense interaction. Jen's resistive performances, or what I refer to in this chapter as an embodied literacy of resistance, mostly transcended language and tended to hinge on a repertoire of intricate movements of her body and a variety of affective responses when she felt socially violated by adults in positions of authority. For girls like Jen, the "problem girl" narrative is especially dangerous because it often sets life trajectories toward the school-to-prison or prostitution pipeline (Psycher, 2017a; Pyscher & Lozenski, 2014). This reality is especially true with the onslaught of deficit-based trauma-informed approaches finding popular residence in schools and social service agencies today.

In this chapter, I am interested in flipping the popular script of the "troubled girl" by rethinking what literacy means in the context of social interactions with special attention to literacies in and of the body (Jones, 2013). I believe an analysis of embodied resistance *as* literacy (a literacy of resistance) shapes how girls like Jen, whose lives have been culturally built out of an intimacy to trauma and domestic violence, engage and often resist deficit institutional practices "written" and performed from the bodies of adults in positions of authority. Using this one social situation set in a classroom, I investigated how Jen negotiated power while also advocating for her own agency through embodied resistive literacies in response to adults' disproportionate expectations.

I attempt to challenge three popular scripts to re-represent Jen and her embodied resistance by (1) reframing trauma *as* sociocultural experience, (2) reframing literacy *as embodied practice* rather than a practice only of traditional literacy performance, and (3) theorizing that resistance and adult authorative practices (hegemony) are written on the bodies of youth like Jen and the adults in positions of power, and that these literacies or performances of the body considerably shape social interactions. It is my hope that by analyzing embodied resistance *as* literacy an alternative story will emerge compelling any adult, including parents and others who inhabit roles of authority and interact with girls like Jen to rethink how they are both read by and how they read the resistive bodies of girls with histories of trauma and domestic violence.

How to Read and Represent within Embodied Literacies

The literacy practices of children and youth like Jen are not well understood. Researchers who theorize about the lives of girls and youth know little to nothing about how girls like Jen whose childhoods have been culturally shaped by experiences of domestic violence embody resistance and engage with and resist violating social experiences. While marginalized childhood and youth resistance have been documented in the professional literature (Tuck & Yang, 2014), performances of resistance built from marginalized experience are not traditionally theorized as embodied literacy practices. Moreover, my analysis also reconceptualizes trauma as a sociocultural phenomenon. This reconceptualization collides with currently popular trauma-informed pedagogies, which are built upon deficit behavioral and medical models and are rapidly being advocated for in all kinds of social spaces, including schools and other youth spaces, as well as in research (Carello & Butler, 2015). This deficit logic is difficult to break. It is easier to believe girls like Jen, girls who have survived childhood and teenage domestic violence and who often experience other intersectional marginalizations (Hill Collins & Bilge, 2016) need to rid themselves of their traumatic experience. In the zeal to "save" such girls, such efforts erase the important fact that experiences of trauma and domestic violence are deeply cultural and shape who these girls are and how these girls navigate their social worlds.

A Literacy of/as Embodied Resistance

The literature of both traditional and critical literacy perspectives tends to frame literacy practices as actions in response to teaching and learning expectations (e.g., cognitive, ideological). Tuck and Yang (2014) challenge researchers to unearth complicated performances of youth resistance in educational contexts that highlight agency. In similar ways, Jones (2013) pushes literacy scholars to move beyond traditional notions of literacy engagements to focus on literacies of the body. I take up this challenge and suggest that close attention be paid to the literacies of the bodies, especially those that express resistance, like Jen's. Complicating Jen's embodied acts of resistance as a literacy of the body opens a more agentic perspective on how girls like Jen encompass the keen ability to read social violation and rewrite social experience. This view affords an analysis to make sense of how violation is written intricately on the bodies of adults who serve in positions of authority and offer these same adults alternatives to disrupt their often-problematic responses to girls like Jen in a variety of social situations.

For girls like Jen who have learned to "read" social violation in its most intimate form as domestic violence, their experiences shape their habitus, or what Bourdieu (1997) refers to as deeply ingrained habits, skills, and dispositions that everyone possesses due to their early life experiences. Embodied resistance becomes an ability to keenly read all kinds of social violation, such as an elongated glance by an adult in an authorative position meant to discipline in a social situation. Jen reads adults' behavior as social violation at times when adults choose to demonstrate their authority and power in their efforts to get Jen and other girls like Jen to comply with their wishes.

I have written extensively about being born into and socially navigating childhood experiences of trauma and domestic violence and how such experiences shape an individual's cultural identities in fundamental ways (Pyscher & Lozenski, 2014). If these profound social experiences shape the life of a girl as a part of her marginalized standpoint (Hill Collins, 2000), then an embodied literacy of resistance as a part of her standpoint of growing up in domestic violence will influence how she reads violating experiences in all social situations. In this chapter, a multitude of resistances as embodied literacies will be examined that directly connect to the authorative practices from two teachers that range from the use of affective responses that are read as violating, such as prolonged gazing, touch, or bodily proximity. The goal of theorizing resistance as literacy is an effort to challenge adults in authority roles to reconsider how their authorative responses are read as violating literacies of the body by marginalized youth like Jen. Adults in roles of authority underestimate how these common affective literacy acts shape the culture of social spaces and young people's engagement in them.

Resistance as a Literacy of the Body: Methodological Approaches

From a literacy perspective, Jones (2013) offers a two-pronged approach to thinking about literacies that both "engage and cultivate for making sense *of* bodies" and are "performed through and experienced *as* bodies" (p. 525). Although Jones is a proponent for seeking understanding of their co-use, she also challenges literacy scholars to "glean insights for transformative thought and action" by theorizing literacy as body.

Jones' (2013) perspective is complemented by Scollon and Scollon's (2003) methodology of mediated discourse analysis (MDA). MDA helps to document and name how common actions, like tones of voice or gazing, shape relationships between girls like Jen and adults' embodied literacies. Using MDA offered the advantage of disrupting "the scientific canons of objectivity and distance" (p. 612), which is needed in troubling deficit beliefs and practices of adults in schools related to trauma and domestic violence. MDA has become a notable method for researchers who share standpoints of marginalization (like domestic violence) to "report out to other academic communities" (p. 615).

A Case of Literacy as Resistance: Jen's Counter Narrative

In the following analysis, I describe Jen's literacies of resistance through one moment of time in an eighth-grade math class. This one social interaction can be easily reimagined in a variety of other social situations between Jen and other adults positioned in authoritative roles, including parents, caregivers, social workers, youth service providers, etc. Jen's relationship between her home life and her school life was fraught with violating experiences. As a young child, she navigated her father's daily violence while living under protective services; as she navigated school, she was often labeled an emotionally and behaviorally troubled girl (or EBD) as early as third grade. In my larger study (Pyscher, 2016), Jen's mother described attempts by elementary school officials, including school psychologists, to label her daughter as EBD. Although Jen and her mother described Jen's middle school as a more agentic school space compared to the culture of her elementary school, similar expressions of Jen's resistance flowed into her experiences in middle school, especially when she "read" a range of adults' actions as violating.

The following case revisits Jen's 57-second interaction with the two middle school teachers who carried EBD-like deficit beliefs about Jen and practiced more violating practices to get Jen to comply to their desire for order. The interaction described is set in the context of a Midwestern public charter middle school serving the needs of urban girls and is also shaped by a school culture that promotes a learning model committed to social justice. Jen's embodied literacies of resistance are personified through actions that range between contradiction and struggle, including bodily gestures like grumbling, staring forward, and refusing to look at or engage with the two teachers standing near her. Also analyzed is the resistive performance of her friends who share similar standpoints of childhood domestic violence and who also responded to both adults with resistive literacies similar to and different than Jen's responses.

The Fluidity of Shared Resistive Literacies

In this eighth-grade classroom, students were gathered in groups of three and four at tables for math instruction and assignments. Jen was engaged in a tense interaction with Ms. Citra, the math teacher, and Ms. Kathy (all names are pseudonyms), a special education teacher who stood watching, about five feet away from where Jen was seated. Standing directly above her was Ms. Citra, who spoke softly to Jen, attempting to persuade her to do her math assignment. Ms. Kathy gazed on from afar, never turning her eyes away from the interaction. It was not clear why Jen garnered so much adult attention. Perhaps she had not turned in homework for a while, or perhaps she was on "the list" of academic problem students, or simply viewed as a "troubled kid." Jen and her tablemates (three teen girls who self-identified as having histories of domestic violence) seemed to be behaving like many of the other students in the room. They were talking, joking, doing some assignments, and at points, standing up, their bodies "off topic."

Jen continued to stare forward, her body statue-like, ignoring Ms. Citra's presence and calm directives. Ms. Citra continued to hover over Jen and quietly ask her to work on her math problems. Jen remained staring forward, shrugging her shoulders and staring in the opposite direction, refusing to explicitly acknowledge this adult's presence. Two of Jen's friends rose and circled both her and Ms. Citra. Ms. Kathy, the special education teacher, held her closed palm to her chin, arms crossed. She intensely watched the interaction from a few feet away. Jen was performing low forms of resistance, like refusing to engage, refusing to acknowledge either teacher, and shrugging her shoulders in response to inaudible words by Ms. Citra. Both teachers seemed inflexible in their social responses to Jen's resistance in changing her behavior (e.g., continual redirectives, hovering, gazing from afar), to get Jen to comply differently than other students in the classroom. Again, Jen's behavior was not disrupting the general classroom environment and it was unclear what the adults desired from Jen.

As the teachers continued to try to get Jen to comply, she became more resistant. As a researcher with a shared standpoint of domestic violence, I was interested in what was shaping the chemistry between Jen's resistance and the responses by these two adults positioned in roles of authority. Although Ms. Citra had a quiet and kind demeanor, Ms. Kathy's presence and intense gaze seemed to be penetrating. For Jen and her friends, their shared standpoints seemed to fuel the resistive literacies at play – not only in this moment of time, but in hundreds of interactions throughout my year-long study. Throughout the longer study, intense and farcical resistive social responses were common themes when adults demanded compliance with this group of girls in ways that appeared at times unwarranted and/or even slightly controlling. These girls' well-honed readings of violating experience positioned them to not only respond with resistive stances, but collectively, they seemed to strategically counteract the power being exercised in the moment by adults who used their authoritative positions in problematic ways. Such an affiliation was a topic that Jen's mother, Jess, described in detail as she suggested that Jen shared an identity of histories of trauma and domestic violence with this friend group as a badge of honor (Pyscher, 2016, p. 198).

A Shared Resistive Reading of Authority

Jen's uncanny ability to read experiences of social violation continued to shape not only the teachers' responses, but also her friends' responses who shared standpoints of domestic violence with her. In this less than 30-second moment of time, Jen used no words in the resistive literacies she was performing although her body demanded something very different than Ms. Citra and Ms. Kathy expected. Ms. Citra attempted to engage Jen in dialogue while her body continued to stand above, hovering as Jen sat; Ms. Kathy remained far off relative to Ms. Citra's body, watching their interaction. Within 50 seconds, Jen abruptly stood, faced the opposite direction of the teachers, and intensely, yet quietly, walked out of the classroom. Ms. Citra attempted to get Jen's attention; she called after her in a tenuous tone, attempting to remind Jen that she would need a pass to leave. Jen outright ignored her and walked out. It seemed Jen had decided to break the intense surveillance she felt. Perhaps she read this situation as violating and felt compelled to leave – a necessary rupture or *a literacy of resistive ambivalence* (Pyscher, 2015). Neither teacher went after her. Ms. Kathy only looked toward the open door and then strategically moved close to Ms. Citra, leaning in and whispering something inaudible. Both of their eyes then fixed on the open door where Jen had just stormed out. It seemed both teachers felt more relieved than worried about the rough interaction.

No more than 30 seconds after Jen exited, another friend of Jen's, who I'll refer to as "Kendra," one of the two friends who circled Ms. Citra and Jen while Jen refused Ms. Citra's attention, stood and shouted loudly with fixed eyes on Ms. Kathy: "She's nosy!" Ms. Kathy continued to stare back at Kendra watching the scene with quiet intensity. Within moments of Kendra shouting this statement in response to Ms. Cathy's gaze and Ms. Citra's presence, she stormed out in a similar fashion as Jen while both teachers stood still in response. If Jen and Kendra's bodies were ideologically "read" through a deficit behavioral perspective, the analysis might be one that claims that Jen and Kendra were disruptive – both socially and emotionally – and in need of special services to fix their pathological responses. When read through a lens of cultural resistive literacies predicated upon shared standpoints of domestic violence (and perhaps other shared marginalizations like race and class), a different interpretation emerges, however. When these kinds of power-laden social interactions are interpreted through the cultural resistive literacies of Jen and Kendra's bodily responses, it becomes clear why both girls felt a need to resist and eventually rupture the social situation with the two adults who held and continued to exert their authority in oppressive ways. The viewer can move beyond believing these kinds of "troubled" girls are in need of being fixed and better understand their desire for agency.

These collaborative kinds of resistive literacies begged for a different understanding in unpacking the potential importance of Jen's shared standpoint (identities) of domestic violence with her friends. Jen and her friends' ability to read violating actions is also a literacy performance – a keen reading that is a socially shared cultural practice. This was a heavy burden for Jen to bear in social situations and it shaped her relationships with friends in important ways. These affiliations also seemed to serve as a powerful connector for Jen and her friends. The girls who shared this standpoint affiliation seemed proud of their shared histories and standpoints of domestic violence. Often worn like a badge, their communal literacies of resistance created an environment of resistant rebelliousness that often positioned the girls in perpetual trouble with adults who seemed determined to have the girls solely change their behaviors in response to inflexible expectations of compliance.

These girls' shared resistive readings also appeared in anonymous spaces, such as hallways, the lunchroom, and on Facebook, and for most of the middle school staff, they unknowingly shaped interactions. For instance, in the moment of Jen resisting both adults in this social space, Kendra and another friend of Jen's, who I'll refer to as "Brianna," circled Ms. Citra and Jen with laughter and farcical-like resistive literacies as Ms. Kathy watched quietly and intensely from the side. Scott (1990) suggests that homogenous groups of the marginalized do not require physical distance from the authority figure to perform low forms of resistance, or what he refers to as hidden transcripts, "so long as the linguistic codes, dialects, and gestures – opaque to the masters . . . were deployed" (p. 121). These hidden expressions of resistance are reflected in Scott's assertion that distinctive marginalized subcultures share similar cultural practices of marginalization, often producing a shared social mantra of "a strong 'us vs. them' social imagery" developed much like a dialect that unifies and is "bound by powerful mutual sanctions that hold competing discourses at arm's length" (p. 135). This unified subculture can become "a powerful force for unity as all subsequent experiences are mediated by a shared way of looking at the world" (p. 135).

I would argue that the "looking" and subsequent "dialect" Scott refers to for Jen and her friends is a nuanced reading of social violation and serves as a unique collective literacy performance dramatically misread by adults when social interactions are ripe with dynamics of power and resistance. Girls like Jen, Kendra, and Brianna can keenly read the social contours of violation. Therefore, it is safe to assume that that ability to "read" is written *on and of* the body and is predicated on navigating similar contours as part of an individual's childhood experience of domestic violence, developing cultural habits (habitus) that affect other social experiences that feel violating.

Neither adult in this interaction seemed to comprehend that their actions negatively intensified and/or incited Jen and her friends' embodied acts of defiance shaped by their cultural reading of a socially intense situation. It seemed that Jen's friends, Brianna and Kendra, colluded with Jen through literacies of resistance by standing and moving their bodies in circling motions around Jen and Ms. Citra as Ms. Citra struggled to get Jen's attention and hold the attention of her friends who shared the same table. Later, as Jen fiercely walked away from the interaction, Kendra followed suit, as both adults seem paralyzed and eventually relieved when the girls walked out of the classroom without permission. The adults' reactions can be explained as a lack of consciousness related to how these youth read and thus navigated this intense experience.

Jen's movements between these tension-filled negotiations were complicated. It seemed this social situation and the adults' cultural reading were especially difficult for Ms. Citra and Ms. Kathy. Although this situation illustrates Jen and Kendra's ability to take agentic steps toward a desire for agency, collectively these kinds of interactions tend to add up over time and to carry weighty social implications that often position marginalized girls' lives and their trajectories in problematic ways.

Some Key Implications: Agency Set in Larger Problematic Life Trajectories

Sharing a similar standpoint as a participatory researcher, I too found myself reading the actions of these adults as socially violating while holding the harsh reality that Jen was exhibiting agency while missing her traditional math literacy. Her shared performance of resistive literacies with her friend Kendra can be both admired and feared. Such interactions sit at the heart of inequity in our schools and institutional spaces. Jen and Kendra's experiences of reading, navigating and rupturing the perplexing intensity with their teachers is culturally necessary as their bodies literally refused to participate. Yet, they also missed learning math.

From one perspective, Jen and her friend's resistive literacies of the body, especially those written on their bodies and performed as resistive readings of adults' actions, were shaped by a larger learning culture committed to engaging youth in learning about social justice. Jen and her friends often expressed how this middle school was "their school." They felt pride and felt like it was a space they took ownership in. This is important in being truly dedicated to creating more equitable institutional spaces where marginalized girls with standpoints of domestic violence especially feel agency in the social spaces they reside in outside of the home, especially if that home has remained violent.

Yet, once those resistive literacies of the body were performed, Jen often found herself on the outside of traditional access to academic literacies and learning. For instance, in the moment featured in this chapter, Jen missed at least 20 minutes of math instruction. When she returned to the classroom 11 minutes after storming out, Jen sat next to me and stated brazenly, "Ms. Kathy is getting on my nerves." She was still unable to re-engage in learning. While surprised by the fact that Jen's heated resistance was directed at Ms. Kathy and not Ms. Citra, I responded: "You don't want to negotiate it?" This was my attempt to convince Jen to return to her math and try to move beyond the oppressive experience. Jen responded just as intensely: "Nay, I'm not about to negotiate right now." Jen's visceral resistance could be felt as she continued to stare forward at the two teachers. It surprised me that Jen had read Ms. Kathy as the teacher who she felt was oppressive, because it was (or what I assumed was) Ms. Citra who was directly attempting to engage Jen in a special performance of compliance, both in language and the use of her body's close distance to Jen's body. During the whole interaction, Ms. Kathy stood at least five feet away, watching intensely, before Jen walked out.

My camera continued to capture our conversation and images of both teachers walking to and from other students. The kind of compliance Ms. Kathy was seeking from Jen is most difficult to understand by watching her although it was clear that she was intending to send such a message with her body from five feet away. Kendra, Jen's friend who walked out minutes after Jen walked out, expressed a similar explicit resistance to Ms. Kathy's gaze, yelling loudly toward Ms. Kathy's direction: "She's irritating and nosy!" Kendra never returned to the classroom that day. Jen's responses swung between performances of resistance, affiliation, re-reading, negotiation, and advocacy – perhaps necessary moves when working between the literacies of resistance to navigate experiences of social violation. Perhaps this is an example of *a critical literacy of the body* – where an individual both deconstructs and reconstructs resistive identities in new ways toward agentic aspirations (Janks, 2009). Yet, the question that constantly surfaces is: To what extent do these resistive literacies serve both as agentic cultural ways of navigating violating experience and as hindrances to a longer trajectory of success in life and school for girls like Jen?

Jen's statement, "Ms. Kathy's getting on my nerves," exposes how the pernicious grip of inequity takes hold in the everyday power plays between a youth's resistance and an adult's desire for compliance. Such words by girls like Jen offer an important cultural lesson in understanding why Jen and Kendra feel compelled to rupture by reaching for liberation from an oppressive experience regardless of the result. Although Jen's resistive literacies in relation to bodily actions (re) shaped opportunities for different agentic opportunities to arise in this moment, girls like her will overwhelmingly fail in institutional situations when the adults in authority roles choose to practice control over the bodies of girls like Jen. The brutal fact that the adults in charge seemed unaware that Jen and Kendra felt violated by their temporal actions is especially daunting. This is a piece of the complicated inequity puzzle that begs for attention. Ms. Kathy, positioned as an authority figure, refused to read what was written on and expressed through Jen's body. Although Jen and Kendra would be continually positioned to becoming less and less literate in academic mathematics, it seemed Ms. Kathy was also *illiterate* in reading their resistive bodies.

The Illiteracy of an Adult Gaze

Literacy researchers have described the impact of lost opportunities for learning for marginalized youth like Jen who either leave classrooms (via truancy) or are removed because of punishment from their classes (Alvermann, 2001). Compensatory learning opportunities will never make up for the learning loss in the math class that Jen and Kendra experienced during my year-long study. Alternative ways to move forward must be discovered to address the powerful realities shaping inequitable learning experiences for girls like Jen. Adults in positions of authority must grapple with their own illiteracy in reading the literacies of the body that girls like Jen and Kendra perform. Adults need to become more literate in not only reading girls like Jen, but also learning to read and rewrite the kinds of dominant ideologies they hold that fester and create problematic situations like the ones featured in this chapter. If adults in all kinds of important social roles refuse to acknowledge this literacy practice of the body, they should expect literacies of resistance from girls like Jen as a consistent experience in their social interactions with them. Resistive literacies of the body are not overstated when a child learns to read the contours of social violation at the hands of their parents/ caregivers. Why would anyone expect Jen to not read the nuances of social violation as a cultural literacy when she learned at a tender age to read and navigate the violence of her own father? Would any adult positioned as an authority figure be surprised that in her refusal, Jen performed literacies of resistance as a way of rejecting other violating experiences outside of the violence experienced in her own home?

Reading and Negotiating Embodied Literacies of Resistance

Girls like Jen, whose young lives are built on childhood experiences of domestic violence, often tend to experience other intersecting standpoints of racialization and poverty that make them deeply misunderstood and further marginalized. Jen's readings of the body signify a different, more pronounced reading of the world, perhaps naming a pedagogy of the oppressed (Freire, 1996) for children and youth with histories of trauma and domestic violence. Adults could learn how to respond more humanely if they paid a different kind of attention to the resistive expressions that girls like Jen and Kendra respond with as their own pedagogy of navigating deficit ideologies and practices that feel oppressive. This navigation is a literacy of resistance, and one of cultural survival built upon an individual's earliest history shaped by an intimate relationship to physical, emotional, and psychic familial violence. Jen's resistive reading and critique of the social worlds she traverses is a necessity built upon her will to survive and resist violating social experiences that should not be underestimated.

As a survivor of domestic violence and a former urban teacher for over 15 years, I believe it is imperative to learn from such brilliant literacies of the body – an artful vigilance. When Jen stares forward in a resistant stance under the weight of two adults wielding power over her, why should she change her behavior under the pressure of such an oppressive social experience? What do these adults want and need from this girl?

Implications for Literacy Education and Cross-Disciplinary Fields

Adults, such as parents, teachers, youth service providers, and others working with girls like Jen can potentially change trajectories for themselves by reading bodies more humanely even when it is emotionally painful to do so. This counter-reality is difficult for adults, especially for those positioned as authority figures who do not share similar standpoints of domestic violence. It will always be easier to subscribe to the popular and deficit beliefs doled out by medical and psychological experts that frame Jen's cultural resistance as something to fix, if not erase altogether. Social situations like the one examined in this chapter will almost always turn out to be a no-win situation. For youth like Jen, more unbending authoritative force will create more embodied resistance. Such conditions demand a different kind of engagement for adults positioned in roles of authority when working with children and youth with histories of trauma and domestic violence. Adults must also engage in rethinking what a critical literacy of the body means for the children and youth who resist them.

My hope is that discussions about and narratives of these kinds of "problem girls" (and boys) might change while also setting conditions for different life trajectories beyond prison and/or prostitution. This alternative perspective affords a different view of girls like Jen offering insight into how their agency, power, and subjectivity are tied to the embodied resistive literacies they perform. To understand these kinds of subjectivities of children and youth with histories of trauma and domestic violence, adults will need to practice a much more sensitive and humane way of interacting with youth. They will need to remember to revisit their beliefs that inform their responses and consider the ways that girls like Jen and Kendra are reading their authoritative will and violating desire for compliance. Equally important, this kind of theorization in coalition with and for girls like Jen helps adults in authority roles to better understand how literacies of the body shape possibilities toward more equitable social experiences for girls with childhood histories of trauma and domestic violence.

This chapter aimed to go beyond solely challenging the traditional beliefs that permeate practices in schools or in other educational or social settings with youth and promote further theorization within critical literacy scholarship. Jen's story also serves as a place of retelling across disciplinary fields, including gender, women and sexuality studies, psychology, and dis/abilities studies. This story adds to the existing literature by stressing how girls with standpoints of trauma and domestic violence agentically reshape social situations through resistive cultural literacies or performances. The implications of Jen's counter narrative are vast and wide. An alternative analysis of resistive literacies can influence many fields and support scholars in their efforts to reframe popular educational, psychological, and medical literature mostly grounded in psychological deficit perspectives. Scholars from each of these fields operating from critical and differing perspectives are always attempting to uncover what agency feels and looks like for marginalized girls like Jen.

References

Alvermann, D.E. (2001). Reading adolescents' reading identities: Looking back to see ahead. *Journal of Adolescent & Adult Literacy*, 44(8), 676–690.

Bourdieu, P. (1997). *Pascalian meditations*. Stanford, CA: Stanford University Press.

Carello, J., & Butler, L.D. (2015). Practicing what we teach: Trauma-informed educational practice. *Journal of Teaching in Social Work*, 35(3), 262–278.

Freire, P. (1996). *Pedagogy of the oppressed (revised)*. New York, NY: Continuum.

Hill Collins, P. (2000). *Black feminist thought*. New York, NY: Routledge.

Hill Collins, P., & Bilge, S. (2016). *Intersectionality*. Hoboken, NJ: John Wiley & Sons.

Janks, H. (2009). *Literacy and power*. London: Routledge.

Jones, S. (2013). Literacies in the body. *Journal of Adolescent & Adult Literacy, 56*(7), 525–529.

Lewis, C., & Moje, E.B. (2003). Sociocultural perspectives meet critical theories. *International Journal of Learning, 10*, 1979–1995.

Pyscher, T. (2015). Against rubbish collecting: Educators and resistively ambivalent youth. *Journal of Educational Controversy, 9*(1), 6.

Pyscher, T. (2016). *Contradictions and opportunities: Learning from the cultural knowledges of youth with histories of domestic violence*. Dissertation, University of Minnesota.

Pyscher, T. (2017a). Domestic violence and girlhood: The making and breaking of a dis-ordered subjectivity. *Cultural Studies↔Critical Methodologies, 17*(5), 399–405.

Pyscher, T. (2017b). *TEDtalkXWWU presenter, rethinking trauma: What youth from domestic violence have to teach us*. Bellingham, WA: Western Washington University.

Pyscher, T., & Lozenski, B.D. (2014). Throwaway youth: The sociocultural location of resistance to schooling. *Equity & Excellence in Education, 47*, 531–545.

Scollon, R., & Scollon, S.W. (2003). *Discourses in place: Language in the material world*. New York, NY: Routledge.

Scott, J.C. (1990). *Domination and the arts of resistance: Hidden transcripts*. New Haven, CT: Yale University Press.

Tuck, E., & Yang, K.W. (2014). *Youth resistance research and theories of change*. New York, NY: Routledge.

5

GENDER IN THE MAKING

Literacies and Identities in Girls' Self-Initiated Making Activities

Elisabeth Gee and Priyanka Parekh

Making has become a popular way to engage children and youth in active, hands-on learning experiences in school as well as in informal learning settings, such as libraries, museums, and after school programs. A plethora of products, such as kits that introduce children to basic electronics or allow them to program a simple robot, are aimed at encouraging parents to support their children's making at home. Making has roots in problem-based and project-based learning, reflected in its emphasis on "learning by doing," collaborative problem-solving, and actively constructing knowledge. While making and maker education encompass a wide range of potential educational goals and practices, a common assumption is that designing, creating, and modifying physical or virtual objects can be a powerful means of enhancing conceptual understandings, technical skills, and problem-solving practices (Blikstein, 2013; Martin, 2015), particularly those associated with science, technology, engineering, and mathematics (STEM). Maker education often emphasizes the use of new tools and technologies, such as 3D printing, robotics, e-textiles, circuit boards, and new programming languages, as well as engagement in design processes similar to those in engineering and related fields.

Making has frequently been characterized as a way to engage learners who might otherwise be disinterested in traditional STEM learning activities through first-hand engagement with materials, an emphasis on interest-driven projects, and the potential to encourage broader conceptions of STEM (Vossoughi, Hooper, & Escudé, 2016). Critics of maker education have argued, however, that dominant approaches to Making may reinforce, rather than redress, social and educational inequities. For example, popular maker kits for use at home are typically expensive and thus unaffordable for lower-income families; the kinds of making promoted in these kits (robotics, computer programming) may be unfamiliar and intimidating to parents who do not already have relevant skills.

Inequities associated with gender and race have also been a focus for scrutiny. In a 2013 keynote at the FabLearn Conference at Stanford, Dr. Leah Buechley (2013), now a prominent advocate for making, pointed out that *Make Magazine* tended to feature a narrow range of makers on its covers – mostly white men and boys – and a similarly narrow selection of making activities, such as electronics and robotics. Other scholars and educators have pointed out that the kinds of making valued in formal and informal maker education, with its emphasis on technical skills and digital tools, has marginalized forms of making such as crafting, which tend to attract higher proportions of women. In recent years, there have been numerous efforts to engage more girls and women in maker education, through strategies ranging from all-girl maker clubs (Sheffield, Koul, Blackley, & Maynard, 2017) to offering forms of making that promote technical skill development through projects that are less stereotypically masculine, such as working with e-textiles (Buchholz, Shively, Peppler, & Wohlwend, 2014) or that emphasize the use of low-cost materials and tools (Vossoughi, Escudé, Kong, & Hooper, 2013). Such efforts have been successful in broadening participation in formal maker education, though they seem to have had more limited success in challenging the priority given to technical making (Vossoughi et al., 2013).

Involving girls in high-tech making activities as a way to encourage their participation in STEM areas where they have been traditionally underrepresented is certainly valuable. This approach runs the risk of reinforcing a deficit view of girls and women, however, with its goal of giving them access to types of making associated with males. From this perspective, to be a maker requires participation in a certain kind of making, and implicitly devalues other forms of making.

In this chapter, we use a case study of girls' self-initiated making and tinkering activities to suggest a broader conception of the kinds of making that are valuable for engaging girls in STEM-related learning. Formal maker education activities often emphasize the "construction" aspect of making and STEM, contributing to a somewhat one-dimensional conception of the nature and value of making. Making involves a wide repertoire of STEM literacy practices, yet these practices have been given limited attention by educators and scholars (Tucker-Raymond, Gravel, Kohberger, & Browne, 2017). In our case study, we give particular attention to the role of STEM literacies in the girls' projects and in their learning. We also hope to offer a more nuanced, complex view of the gendered identities involved in making, one that takes into account how gender is situated and enacted in the context of local communities of practice (Paechter, 2003). These more expansive conceptions of making, along with a better understanding of the role of STEM literacies and of gendered identities in making can suggest new pathways into STEM learning for girls.

Our Perspectives

Our analysis is informed by sociocultural and situated views of literacies, learning, and the construction of identities (Gee, 2012). These perspectives each assume that literacies are forms of meaning-making that are plural, situated in social practices and communities, and involve multiple modes of representation and expression (Gee, 2012). STEM literacies are literacies that are central to the work of scientists and others involved in STEM fields. These will vary across particular professional communities, and we use the term here to indicate the kinds of literacies involved in practices that are relevant to, but not necessarily uniformly applicable to STEM. From this perspective, learning involves the increasing ability to participate in socially and culturally valued practices, including forms of meaning-making, within communities of practice. Communities of practice exist around many topics and interests, ranging from professional occupations to hobbies and informal pastimes; they are defined by a shared domain of interest, a group of people committed to that domain who interact and learn together, and collective forms of knowledge, values, and skills (Wenger, 1998).

Identity is central to both literacies and learning within these frameworks. The forms of meaning-making that people take up, and the social practices in which they seek to participate are associated with their identities within these communities (Wenger, 1998). An individual's identities shape how that person views the world and how that person relates to others within shared communities; furthermore, the identities that people enact, or aspire to enact, are shaped by their positions in these communities and the kinds of identities, or ways of being, that are valued. For example, a child who is taught by a parent how to hold and use a hammer is not simply learning how to use a tool; she or he is also learning to enact an identity in which using a hammer is desirable and acceptable.

Gender is a central aspect of identities, and thus integral to learning and literacies. Individuals learn how to "do gender" through their families, peers, and other social groups. Paechter (2003) has developed the concept of "communities of gendered practice" to describe the local and situated nature of how children learn how to enact masculine and feminine identities. While societal conceptions of masculinity and femininity transcend and influence local conceptions of gendered norms and practices, children and youth are exposed to, adopt, or resist these conceptions within their immediate social groups, "as simultaneous members of child and adult communities of masculinity and femininity practices" (p. 551). As applied to making and maker education, this perspective suggests the need for closer examination of how peers, families, and other relevant communities are actively involved in children's construction of gender in relation to making.

Background

In collaboration with a local library, over the last several years the two of us have been exploring the potential value of tinkering with everyday materials for developing children's understanding of science concepts. While making and tinkering are sometimes used synonymously, in our scholarship we have adopted the term tinkering to characterize our emphasis on playful, open-ended activities that allow children to pursue their own design aspirations, and experiment with different materials and tools. Priyanka has organized workshops for children in which we provide low-cost, "found" materials such as broken toys, paper plates, glue, straws, and so forth, and set a simple goal, such as "make something with wings." Children are free to determine their own specific design objective and are given support by the workshop facilitator and occasionally parents who choose to observe or participate. The facilitator adopts a "just-in-time" approach to teaching and learning, introducing scientific concepts or vocabulary as they become relevant to a child's project, or organizing a workshop around the use of basic circuits.

Through this work, we have become particularly interested in how children develop ideas for projects, the role of peers and family members as sources of inspiration and support, and the connections between what they choose to make in our loosely structured workshops and their interests beyond the program. The case study described here is based on data collected by the second author of this chapter, Priyanka, as a participant observer and mentor in a series of loosely structured making activities involving her daughter and two sisters who are her neighbors. Priyanka and the sisters' father (he was separated from their mother) often shared responsibility for supervising the girls and they often played together, forming a natural friendship group. Priyanka's involvement was an extension of her routine interactions with the girls. She met weekly with the three girls to support their tinkering activities over eight weeks, with the goal of documenting the evolution of their interests and practices over time. Priyanka provided materials and tools, occasionally helping them work through challenges in their projects and suggesting next steps. The girls set the direction for their projects, however, and pursued ideas that they found appealing and meaningful.

Making: From Printing Tattoos to Creating Business Plans

Priyanka's daughter, Mayra, was 9 years old at the time of the study, and the sisters were 12 and 7 years old. Their summer making project was inspired when the sisters' father, Mike, gave the girls some stick-on, temporary tattoos and explained that, like stickers, the tattoos could be peeled off their backings and transferred to another surface, i.e., their skin. He also mentioned that these temporary tattoos could be printed, which sparked the girls' interest. The girls conducted their own research by searching the Internet for information on how tattoos could be printed. These sessions were led by Kate, the 12-year-old, who did searches on a laptop, while Mayra sat beside her and double-checked facts on her iPad. Susie, the 7-year-old, offered opinions about the feasibility of the tattoo printing procedures they discovered. Their online research was entirely carried out by the girls, with no adult involvement.

Through their research, the girls learned about transfer paper, a special kind of paper on which tattoos could be printed and then transferred. They asked Priyanka if she could supply them with transfer paper, which she purchased.

Mike had a very old inkjet printer that he refilled occasionally, after trying to make as many prints as possible. He let the girls use the printer but cautioned them to be careful about the amount of ink and paper they used since these were expensive resources. He taught the girls how to fit multiple images on one Word document for more efficient printing. The girls located images of games and game characters through a Google image search, downloaded them, and prepared the Word document. Mike helped them print the document onto the transfer paper and then apply the tattoos to their arms.

Despite the girls' careful research, their tattoos did not turn out well. Mayra noticed information on the pack of transfer paper and realized that this brand of paper needed heat to transfer images. In fact, the paper was meant for transferring images to fabric, like t-shirts. The girls asked Priyanka to make another purchase as soon as possible. This time, however, they did an Internet search and identified special transfer papers meant specifically for no-heat transfer of tattoos onto skin. They sent Priyanka a link to the product page via a text message. The following week, with the use of the appropriate transfer paper, the tattoos turned out perfectly.

The girls then decided to make use of the original set of transfer paper to print images onto t-shirts. They first experimented with old t-shirts that they bought on sale from Goodwill, and once their technique was perfected, they used new t-shirts. Through experimentation, the girls discovered that t-shirts varied in quality and suitability for printing, and again used the Internet to determine the most appropriate quality of fabric. The 12-year-old girl in the group felt that their usual loose-fitting, boxy t-shirts were not very "form flattering" and the girls requested more stylish Faded Glory t-shirts from Walmart.

Ultimately, Priyanka bought the girls a cast-off HP deskjet inkjet color printer from Goodwill. The printer did not function well at first so Priyanka helped the girls identify and fix the problem, which was that the ink had dried up in the printer cartridges. The girls experimented with printing on t-shirts with light and dark colored fabrics, and then moved on to use other heat-transfer technologies to make iron-on patches and badges. The girls were very pleased with the quality of their products and thought that they might be able to sell them online. They were inspired by popular creators of Minecraft videos on YouTube, including StampyCat and StaceyPlays, who have online stores and sell a variety of custom items. With encouragement from both adults, the girls made a basic business plan for a for-profit mini venture to sell badges, art supply cases, iron-on patches, and similar products that they could customize. While their regular meeting schedule ended with the start of the school year, the girls have continued to pursue projects together with the support of both parents.

STEM Literacy Practices

Tucker-Raymond et al. (2017) developed five broad categories of STEM literacies applicable to making, including using texts to pose and solve problems, identifying, organizing, and integrating information, creating representations and traversing representational systems and materials, communicating information, and documenting making processes. The girls' tinkering activities involved a wide range of these STEM literacy practices. These practices were integral to and distributed across the girls' projects just as Tucker-Raymond and his colleagues found in their study. Several themes described below characterized the girls' literacy practices.

Literacies as Integral to Making

One aspect of the girls' engagement in making that characterized their efforts was how they moved among identifying goals, seeking information relevant to those goals, experimenting with physical objects and tools, and then seeking further information when problems arose. While making is often portrayed as a somewhat linear process, with identifiable stages such as ideation or fabrication, it was clear in the girls' projects that the process was much more fluid and emergent. The girls' processes of seeking and evaluating information from various types of texts (e.g., websites, product descriptions, images, instructions) was interwoven throughout their projects. These literacies were integral to making. The girls' ability to locate relevant information shaped the direction of their projects.

Differentiating Knowledge Domains

While their adult mentors could provide some assistance, they were not experts in printing with varied materials, so the girls had to rely on the Internet for much information. As Tucker-Raymond and his colleagues noted, since making tends to draw on multiple domains, a crucial component of literacy practices in making involves identifying relevant knowledge domains and communities. As the girls moved from printing temporary tattoos to t-shirts to creating business plans, they were exposed to and drew on different online communities and their associated knowledge domains. This kind of horizontal (moving across) rather than vertical (diving deep) explorations (by horizontal explorations, we refer to how the girls experimented with different kinds of making and related practices, while vertical explorations would consist of developing a deeper knowledge of one particular kind of making, such as learning more about printing tattoos) helped them refine their understanding of how these domains differed as well as related to each other. For example, they discovered that printing self-adhesive tattoos and printing images for t-shirts required quite different materials, tools, and practices.

(STEM) Literacies of the Body

Designing and printing tattoos and selecting images for t-shirts are forms of making that are literacy practices in themselves, involving the creation and display of literacy artifacts that allowed the girls to construct identities that were simultaneously personal and global. All the girls chose words associated with video games for their t-shirts, including Minecraft, BeanBlockz (a Minecraft server), Roblox (an online game creation platform), and Terraria (a sandbox-type online game very similar to Minecraft). While the connection of these practices to STEM might seem less clear, the girls' affiliation with these games reflected their collective interest in games that are typically associated with male gamers and with STEM-related practices (i.e., building and manipulating objects in a 3D environment).

Constructing Capable Identities

Scholarship on gender identities and STEM typically has focused on how scientific practices and identities are associated with masculinity, and the challenges for girls and women in gaining acceptance as female scientists in this masculine culture of science (Barton & Brickhouse, 2006). Recent scholarship has emphasized diversity in how gender is enacted in the local context of classrooms and workplaces; Paechter (2007) suggests that masculinities and femininities are problematic and constraining terms, and that it might be more useful to "think of masculinities in terms of power/knowledge that are traditionally, but not always successfully, claimed by men, and make the case that these are also mobilised by women and girls" (p. 10). Paechter argues that issues of power need to be taken into account in relation to different individuals' possibilities to negotiate meaning within a community of practice.

Below we describe how the girls positioned themselves as makers – both makers of physical artifacts and makers of meaning. We focus in particular on how the context and activities made it possible for girls to claim power and authority in knowledge construction, something that is crucial to girls' developing sense of themselves as capable users of technical tools and practices. We identify several ways in which the girls were able to construct capable identities: directing and setting rules for activities, explaining or demonstrating how to complete a task, providing information, and sharing stories or experiences.

Providing Direction and Setting Rules

In contrast to many teacher-directed or adult-directed settings, Priyanka played a limited role in determining what the girls would do or how they would do it. The girls decided what they wanted to make (tattoos, then t-shirts) and collectively worked toward their goals. Kate, the 12-year-old, most frequently took charge of directing the girls' making activities, likely because she was the oldest child and the older sibling. She did not simply tell the other girls what to do, but suggested alternative ways to approach a task, implicitly or sometimes explicitly clarifying what was "acceptable" for their projects. For example, the girls began by drawing images for their tattoos, but Kate noted:

"So, while we're working on our tattoos, if either of you think that you are not that good at making sketches, you can also think up ways to use printed pictures or something." Mayra tended to be less directive, but often affirmed or elaborated on Kate's instructions in a way that demonstrated her own abilities. Following Kate's statement, Mayra offered: "Yeah, what I did was, I pulled up Google images so if anyone finishes or they want to do that, what they can do is they can look up something and they . . ." While Susie less frequently offered direction for their work, she did feel comfortable in contributing to the conversation. For example, when Priyanka playfully asked, "Hey, what about doodle tattoos?" Susie replied: "You can just use a doodle too. So technically, you can use sketches, doodles, signatures, anything." Thus, the girls collaboratively constructed their activities in a way that allowed them all to assert their opinions and ideas.

Explaining or Demonstrating

Another way that the girls created capable identities was through providing explanations of how to do something or demonstrating a process. When Priyanka stated that they needed to buy printer ink, Susie retorted: "Ask Google, Aunt Know-It-All. Hey Google, where can I buy printer ink for an old printer?" and when the search results appeared, she stated triumphantly: "See? Told you! Here's the map." Kate, who adopted the role of software expert, explained to the group how to transfer a paper drawing to their software application, stating:

> So, you take a snap of a doodle that's on paper and use the image as a base layer on Ibis. Then you just trace it on another blank layer on Ibis. Print it out, blah, blah, blah, meh, meh, meh, and you're done.

Mayra followed up by stating, "You can then print it out on transfer paper and use it as a tattoo."

Providing Information

In some cases, the girls shared relevant information that was not directly aimed at completing a task. Mayra was particularly excited when her mom explained that the computer she bought at Goodwill didn't work, and they would have to fix it: "Yay! I'm good that these kind of things. Every time my daddy refills the toner in our printer, I help him. That's how I know about these things." Priyanka mentioned that they needed to install the printer drivers on her laptop, and when Kate seemed confused, Mayra responded: "The installation software, they speak computer language to the printer. If you buy an old printer, you get the drivers from the internet."

Sharing Stories or Experiences

The girls were comfortable with sharing personal stories and experiences, and they used these experiences to reinforce their capabilities with technologies or skills and knowledge related to their making activities. Kate shared a humorous story about her mom dropping and breaking Kate's phone, observing that if she had kept it, the phone would be ok. When Priyanka demonstrated how to save the QR code stickers and apply them to refilled printer cartridges, Kate asked why that was important. Mayra explained:

> To protect the machines, you know, to prevent them from being broken by us, and also to detect fakes. That's why they keep saying buy original HP supplies and all that. The last time daddy and I refilled the other printer we forgot to reset one small arrow and it kept saying that.

Of course, the girls' interactions were not uniformly positive. In particular, Susie was at times upset by Kate's teasing. For example, in the conversation about doodle tattoos, Susie asked: "What's the difference anyway? Between sketches and doodles and anything on paper?" Kate replied: "You scribble and doodle, mostly, I sketch. Got it?" Susie replied, "No, just use like . . . Kate you're such a Donald Trump, so mean," and stormed off to her father in the apartment next door. After a short interval, she reappeared and re-inserted herself into the group, stating somewhat officiously, "So, are we making tattoos today or not? How long is this going to take? Just do it already!" The other girls quickly tried to pull her back into the activity.

Recent scholarship on STEM education emphasizes diversity in how girls and boys enact STEM identities (Parsons, 1995). In the context of this friendship and family group, the girls were able to take on differing and complementary "identities of expertise" (O'Connor, 2003) in relation to the use of tools, materials, and design. Their engagement in various literacy practices was central to the construction of these identities, as they set goals, solved problems, and created artifacts that were concrete instantiations of their expertise. Parents played important roles in supporting their projects by providing information and supplies when needed and by modelling proactive stances toward troubleshooting and learning from failures.

Notably, the girls did not enact stereotypically feminine forms of gender identity in these sessions. While their interest in tattoos and clothing might be interpreted as particularly feminine interests, their choice of images (the names of video games) was not obviously "girlie" and in fact connected them to communities typically associated with boys and masculinity. One of their YouTube role models was a young woman, but the other was a young man. Instead, their interactions were notable for how they positioned themselves as knowledgeable and proactive creators and users of technological tools.

Implications for Literacy Education and Cross-Disciplinary Fields

A frequently stated goal of maker education is to help all students develop identities as "makers," and by extension, as potential engineers or scientists (Sheffield et al., 2017). Research on making and identities has focused primarily on the contexts of classroom and informal learning environments, such as libraries and science museums. However, children's experiences at home and among their peer groups are also influential contexts for STEM learning and for acquiring STEM literacies, as well as for experimenting with STEM identities. Many scientists, both male and female, describe informal childhood experiences with science as sparking their initial interests and identities as scientists (Root-Bernstein, 2014).

One implication for educators and science and technology providers in informal settings is to determine how to better identify experiences at home and with peers that can be a basis for science education and for connecting students to scientific communities of practice. Barton and Brickhouse (2006) call for educators to "offer girls opportunities to engage in science in ways that foster the development of scientific identities, teach them about the content and practice of science, and give them credibility (power) within local communities" (p. 231). Such calls might be interpreted as implying that girls do not already have scientific identities; our findings suggest that while girls may not formally identify themselves as engineers or computer scientists, their out-of-school identities may be associated with skills and knowledge that can be aligned with and recruited in more formal STEM learning. For example, Mayra took pride in demonstrating her knowledge of how printers function; in school, teachers might help her see how her interest in "making things work" could be further extended to the study of engineering.

The findings from this study illuminate how informal making activities can be a context for STEM literacy learning for both girls and boys. There have been many calls for more deliberate and explicit attention to literacy learning in the context of STEM education (English, 2016). Teaching disciplinary literacy is one approach to STEM literacy that has become predominant in recent years. Disciplinary literacy refers to "the knowledge and abilities possessed by those who create, communicate, and use knowledge within the disciplines" (Shanahan & Shanahan, 2012, p. 7). This kind of literacy instruction focuses on the specific forms of reading, writing, reasoning, and tools used by experts in a particular field. For example, engineers often rely on diagrams and models to communicate design plans. Disciplinary literacy instruction tied to engineering would help students learn to interpret and create such visual representations in the context of "real-world" engineering problems, such as designing a bridge. This approach presumes, however, that students already have some degree of interest in and affiliation with disciplinary content, such as science or technology. In contrast, a focus on "everyday" STEM literacies, identities, and practices may be a better means of engaging a wider range of children, and allow them to build on their existing strengths and interests. Literacy educators' role should be to recognize and capitalize on young people's existing strengths and interests and to help them regardless of their gender to broaden their skills to engage with scientific literacies and practices that transcend their local and classroom contexts.

Parents, other family members, and community organizations have important roles to play in the use of making and tinkering to foster STEM literacies, identities, and abilities among all children. Our work reinforces the idea that making and tinkering do not need to involve expensive, high-tech tools to engage girls in non-stereotypical STEM practices. Instead, parents can start by encouraging girls to tinker with everyday technologies to build their confidence and interest. As in our example, parents can take on different roles, as mentors, resource providers, and facilitators, among others. What's important is that making and tinkering become family activities, regardless of gender, age, or expertise. Families are significant influences on children's early attitudes towards STEM and their STEM identities; to adopt Paechter's terms, families as communities of gendered practice can serve as initial contexts for girls to construct identities that challenge stereotypes of females as less capable STEM learners. For girls to do so, making activities at home should give them opportunities both to develop STEM knowledge and to display their growing expertise, in the ways suggested by our findings.

Lastly, we suggest that parents and informal educators give more attention to the importance of peer groups and affinity spaces in the learning outcomes of making and tinkering activities. In our example, the girls supported each other's development of capable STEM identities as they engaged in making activities around shared interests. Gee (2000) suggests that affinity identities, those associated with shared interests, experiences, and related practices, can be powerful counterpoints to stereotypes associated with gender, race, socioeconomic class, or other social categories. All too often, particularly as girls reach adolescence, the gender norms and expectations of their peer groups conflict with (school-based) identities and practices associated with many STEM fields. In our example, the girls were forming an affinity group that could offer an alternative to these potentially restrictive peer group norms. Rather than trying to attract more girls to makerspaces or engineering clubs, an alternative approach can be to work with existing peer and friendship groups, introduce making activities related to their current interests, and gradually make connections to STEM as they emerge. Such an approach can also offer girls more agency in constructing their own communities of STEM practices that transcend current gender stereotypes.

References

Barton, A., & Brickhouse, N. (2006). Engaging girls in science. In C. Skelton, B. Francis, & L. Smulyan (Eds.), *The sage handbook of gender and education* (pp. 221–235). London, UK: Sage.
Blikstein, P. (2013). Digital fabrication and "making" in education: The democratization of invention. In J. Walter-Herrmann & C. Büching (Eds.), *FabLabs: Of machines, makers and inventors* (pp. 203–222). Bielefeld, Germany: Transcript Publishers.

Buchholz, B., Shively, K., Peppler, K., & Wohlwend, K. (2014). Hands on, hands off: Gendered access in crafting and electronics practices. *Mind, culture, and activity*, *21*(4), 278–297.

Buechley, L. (2013, October 28). *A critical look at MAKE-ing [FabLearn keynote video recording]*. Retrieved from http://edstream.stanford.edu/video/Play/883b61dd951d3f90abe ec65eead2911d.

English, L.D. (2016). STEM education K-12: Perspectives on integration. *International Journal of STEM Education*, *3*(3), 1–8.

Gee, J.P. (2000). Identity as an analytic lens for research in education. *Review of Research in Education*, *25*, 99–125.

Gee, J.P. (2012). *Situated language and learning: A critique of traditional schooling*. New York, NY: Routledge.

Martin, L. (2015). The promise of the maker movement for education. *Journal of Pre-College Engineering Education Research (J-PEER)*, *5*(1), 30–39.

O'Connor, K. (2003). Communicative practice, cultural production, and situated learning: Constructing and contesting identities of expertise in a heterogeneous learning context. In S. Wortham & B. Rymes (Eds.), *Linguistic anthropology of education* (pp. 61–91). Westport, CT: Praeger.

Paechter, C. (2003). Learning masculinities and femininities: Power/knowledge and legitimate peripheral participation. *Women's Studies International Forum*, *26*, 541–552.

Paechter, C. (2007). *Being boys, being girls: Learning masculinities and femininities*. Maidenhead, UK: Open University Press.

Parsons, S. (1995). Making sense of students' science: The construction of a model of tinkering. *Research in Science Education*, *25*(2), 203–219.

Root-Bernstein, M. (2014). *Inventing imaginary worlds: From childhood play to adult creativity across the arts and sciences*. Lanham, MD: Rowman & Littlefield.

Shanahan, T., & Shanahan, C. (2012). What is disciplinary literacy and why does it matter? *Topics in Language Disorders*, *32*(1), 7–18.

Sheffield, R., Koul, R., Blackley, S., & Maynard, N. (2017). Makerspace in STEM for girls: A physical space to develop twenty-first-century skills. *Educational Media International*, *54*(2), 148–164

Tucker-Raymond, E., Gravel, B.E., Kohberger, K., & Browne, K. (2017). Source code and a screwdriver: STEM literacy practices in fabricating activities among experienced adult makers. *Journal of Adolescent & Adult Literacy*, *60*(6), 617–627.

Vossoughi, S., Escudé, M., Kong, F., & Hooper, P. (2013, October). *Tinkering, learning and equity in the after-school setting*. Paper presented at the FabLearn conference, Stanford University, Palo Alto, CA. Retrieved from www.sesp.northwestern.edu/docs/publica tions/49224626354098196e0b03.pdf.

Vossoughi, S., Hooper, P.K., & Escudé, M. (2016). Making through the lens of culture and power: Toward transformative visions for educational equity. *Harvard Educational Review*, *86*(2), 206–232.

Wenger, E. (1998). *Communities of practice: Learning, meaning, and identity*. New York, NY: Cambridge University Press.

6

UNDERSTANDING HOW INDIGENOUS LATINX CHILDREN EXPRESS GENDER IDENTITIES

Maria-Antonieta Avila

Little has been written about children who identify as indigenous although indigenous youth compose about 1% of the student population. About 23% of the indigenous student population in the United States is Latinx (U.S. Census Bureau, 2017). Throughout this chapter, I use the term Latinx to intentionally respect gender diversity of people who identify as being from Latin American descent (Love Ramirez & Blay, 2016). In this chapter, I follow the United Nations' (2006, p. 1) understanding of indigenous identification, which includes

> self-identification of indigenous people at the individual level and accept-
> ance by the community as a member; historical continuity with precolonial
> and/or pre-settler societies; strong links to territories and surrounding
> natural resources; distinct social economic or political systems; distinct lan-
> guage, culture and beliefs; origin from nondominant groups of society;
> resolve to maintain resources in the ancestral environments and systems;
> and recognition as distinctive peoples and communities.

This chapter focuses on Latinx students who identify as indigenous although they may or may not identify or affiliate with any particular nation or language group in Mesoamerica (Northern Mexico to Central America), but who are nevertheless interested in learning about Mexica (Central Mexico) culture and language (Nahuatl). In present-day Mexico (and much of Latin America) identifying as indigenous is stigmatized due to a history of the racial caste system introduced by the Spanish (Menchaca, 1993). Similarly, many indigenous Latinx in the United States deny their indigenous roots and identify as mestizo, a term used by the Spanish caste system to identify people of mixed European and indigenous descent, to appeal for acceptance and fight prejudice against indigenous peoples.

Mexica or Aztec culture and language had a resurgence with the Chicano Civil Rights movement in the 1960s and 1970s. As Mexican Americans "rediscovered pride in their racial and class status," Aztec culture and language practices were adopted by the new generations (Garcia, 1997, p. 10), allowing for a reclamation of indigenous identities and spiritual practices. In present-day Los Angeles, California, interest in Mexica cultural practices and language is present in various communities throughout the city. For example, a full moon circle organized by a group called *Mujeres de Maíz* or Corn Women, meets once a month in East Los Angeles. This is a group that fosters and shares indigenous teachings and invites "all womxn, grrrls, trans and gender non-conforming folx" (Mujeres de Maíz, 2018) to attend their ceremonies. In addition, the Nahuatl language is being learned, studied, and taught at the University of California at Los Angeles (McInerny, 2017), which legitimizes the culture and language with a modern presence not only in Mexico, but in California specifically, and in the United States. There are similar programs in Austin, Texas, and Ann Arbor, Michigan.

Much of the literature related to gender in education is informed by a binary view of gender (girls and boys). Advocates seek to promote gender equity in education to improve educational outcomes for girls (Connell, 2010; Fennell and Arnot, 2008). As Connell writes, advances in gender theories help to understand that "gender patterns are not fixed, that identities are negotiated in individual lives and categories emerge historically, that masculinities and femininities are multiple, and that gender relations vary in different class, ethnic and national contexts" (p. 605). Therefore, the purpose of this chapter is to highlight the ways that indigenous Latinx students create identity texts and how these texts are related to their gender performance. As young people learn more about gender, it is important for the adults that care for them to be informed of how gender identity and expression has evolved and how indigenous youth can be supported by adults. It is necessary to learn how to support young Latinx's indigenous literacies, which are increasingly more complex and reflect their emerging understandings of gender identities and performance.

Gender as Balance in Mexica Culture

In Mexica culture, gender identity and expression are understood as binary or as male and female. This understanding, however, is nuanced as male and female and always in relation to each other, one cannot exist without the other. For example, the concept of *Ometeotl* is one of the most important in Mexica culture. The term refers to the highest creator, who is neither female nor male, but rather both and many at the same time. Equally important is *balance* in all aspects of culture. For instance, during spiritual ceremonies, both female and male energies are represented in some way to achieve balance. As part of their immersion experience in Mexica language and culture, young Latinx youth learn about *Ometeotl*, and express their understandings through their practices during spiritual ceremonies. For example, one customary spiritual ceremony, the Four Directions Ceremony, is used for asking for permission, giving thanks, and honoring ancestors. During this ceremony the Four Directions (East, West, North, and South) are greeted. Each direction represents one half of a duality: East is male, West is female, North is death, and South is life. Essential in this ceremony is acknowledging the need for both halves of the duality to achieve balance.

Nepantla as a Framework

Nepantla is a Nahuatl word that means in the middle or in between. Defined by Gloria Anzaldúa (2002) as an in-between space that is neither here nor there, *nepantla* is a space that offers more than one perspective. *Nepantla* is a "zone of possibility" (p. 544), a "site for transformation" (p. 548), and a fluid and holistic space. Anzaldúa uses this definition to explain a space where a person can move away from binaries and live in a space that contains multiplicities that can bring about personal transformation. *Nepantla* is a useful concept as it provides a framework that enables researchers, teachers, parents, and others working with children to analyze the texts produced by bicultural children from various points of view without privileging one above another. For example, Fránquiz, Avila, and Lewis (2013) showed how in two bilingual classrooms students produced work that was in English, Spanish, and a mix of the two, and how students worked in an in-between place intertwining knowledge from home, school, community, and the Internet. All of the students' languages and knowledge were validated as important, while students became more comfortable blurring traditional linguistic and disciplinary knowledge boundaries, thus, working in and through *nepantla*.

Nepantla also provides a lens to understand how traditional curricular and language borders constrain knowledge and learning. This holistic space of *nepantla* has much potential to influence literacy learning and literacy education by collapsing the binaries conventionally used to compartmentalize learning. For example, it is common in dual-language programs to plan for the separation of languages and disciplinary boundaries in the classroom, program, or school. Some schools separate the language of instruction (teaching content through the target language) by day or by subject (Dual Language Training Institute, 2018), while academic subjects become more compartmentalized as children move through their school years. It is through *nepantla* that "binary thought is challenged; instead different perspectives are invited and may come into conflict, [and] individuals or groups may question the basic ideas, tenets, and identities inherited from family, schooling or cultural affiliations" (Fránquiz, et al., p. 143).

Indigenous Feminism

Indigenous feminist theory helps to make sense of how children perform gender by understanding the intersectionality of gender, ethnicity, and class.

Intersectionality as coined by Crenshaw (1989) is a description of the ways that people experience oppression and inequality. For example, Crenshaw argues that intersectionality recognizes that multiple oppressions are not separate from each other (i.e., being Black, female, poor) but rather they are experienced simultaneously. Furthermore, Tefera, Powers, and Fischman (2018) note that intersectionality explains the "dynamic and complex ways that race/ethnicity, class, gender, sexuality, religion, citizenship, ability, and age shape individual identities and social life" (p. vii). In this manner, native feminist theories (Arvin, Tuck, & Morrill, 2013) focus on issues that are intersectional for indigenous youth: gender, sexuality, race, indigeneity, and nation (p. 11). Ramirez (2007) uses native feminisms to explain how "experiences with racial, gender, sexual, class, and other oppressions" (p. 34) need to be at the center of analysis and practice. Therefore, when working with indigenous youth, I use native feminism to understand how the intersectionality of race, gender, class, and indigenous identities affect how children perform and present their gender through the various texts they produce.

Identity Texts

To understand how Latinx indigenous youth express gender, I assigned middle school children to create several identity texts, particularly texts that illustrated themselves as scientists. Identity texts are "products of students' creative work or performances carried out within the pedagogical space orchestrated by the classroom teacher" (Cummins et al., 2005, p. 5). Identity texts can be written, spoken, created as visual or musical pieces, or a combination of these (Cummins, et al., p. 5) and can be composed both in and out of school. Asking the children to illustrate themselves as scientists helped them to imagine themselves and feel comfortable with seeing themselves from a third-person point of view, and further their authorship of self. Additionally, this was an opportunity to acknowledge and draw forth the students' identities to cultivate their well-being, which is a tenet of culturally responsive science teaching (Aikenhead et al., 2014). For indigenous youth, culturally responsive science teaching is important as it is centered on their cultural identity and the cultural resources they bring into the classroom. Students should not feel they have to leave their identities outside the classroom to succeed in science (Aikenhead et. al., 2014).

Draw Yourself as a Scientist Assignment

At the beginning of the school year, children were asked to illustrate themselves doing the work of scientist. Figure 6.1 demonstrates how one student, Rosa, perceived herself as a scientist, doing the work of a scientist.

FIGURE 6.1 Rosa illustrated herself mixing chemicals.

In this activity, children were provided the opportunity to visualize them-selves as active participants in science. In her drawing, Rosa explained how she mixed chemicals to make different medicines. She drew herself at the center of scientific activity. At the top of her drawing she wrote, "Since [*sic*]," an approxi-mation of the spelling of the word science, which she corrected at a later time. At the bottom of the drawing she wrote, "I am mixing different qimiqals too make different kinds of explosions [*sic*]." She included laboratory equipment in her drawing, such as test tubes, flasks, and a microscope. Rosa drew goggles on herself and illustrated what could happen during a chemical reaction by drawing smoke and labeling it as "Hot." Rosa drew herself with a ponytail, wearing a lab coat, and speaking English. She used her knowledge of English phonetics to spell words such as "qimiqals [*sic*]" and "diffrend [*sic*]."

Although she did not use standard spelling, the meaning of her sentence is not obscured. In her illustration, Rosa is interpreting and doing science, and appro-priating the identity of a scientist. This activity, known as the Draw a Scientist Test (DAST) (Chambers, 1983) is used to investigate children's images of a scien-tist through drawings. When Rosa and her peers took up the activity of drawing themselves as scientists they generally demonstrated a positive relationship with science. Most of the students identified scientific activities they thought they would engage in as scientists. These activities included mixing chemicals, inves-tigating germs, animals and plants, observing insects, and making/constructing robots and trampolines.

Almost all the children drew themselves alone, mirroring stereotypes that are held in popular culture about scientists working in isolation. Traditionally the DAST asks students to draw a scientist, however, this activity was modified to ask the children to draw themselves as scientists. This departure from presenting the students with more traditional illustrations of scientists as White men with wiry white hair may have contributed to the positive self-identifications with science visible in the children's illustrations. Eighteen students described themselves in the first person. For instance, Lalo wrote, "Aqui soy un cientifico investigando un germene" ["Here I am a scientist investigating germs"]. In this sense, the children envisioned themselves as doing the work of scientists. Reveles (2009) found that third-grade students who illustrated a scientist held some stereotypical images of scientists: working alone, handling lab equipment, and picturing a scientist as a male. In contrast, this activity presented the children drawing themselves as scientists participating in scientific activity.

The students' writing evidenced that they identified themselves as scientists, indicating their appropriation of the Discourse of science. Gee (1990/2007) described Discourse (with a capital D) as a "sort of 'identity kit' which comes complete with the appropriate costume and instructions on how to act, talk, and often write, so as to take on particular social role that others will recognize" (p. 142). The illustrations and grammatical choices that placed themselves at the center of the scientific activity grounded most of the students in their identities as scientists. In other words, they were appropriating the Discourse of science as they illustrated themselves in science labs, such as by wearing a lab coat, or placing themselves as active participants in science. One of the girls, Laura, did not identify herself or illustrate herself as doing the work of a scientist, however. Instead, she self-identified as a good student by paying attention to her teacher because the teacher was talking about science. Figure 6.2 demonstrates how Laura drew herself sitting at her desk, listening to her teacher.

Laura wrote, "Estoy poniendo atencion a la maestre porque esta hablado de sciencias" ["I am paying attention to my teacher because she is talking about science"].

FIGURE 6.2 Laura illustrated herself listening attentively.

As may be the case in some classrooms, being a good student constitutes one who pays attention when the teacher is talking and is one of the identities teachers and schools value (Brickhouse, Lowery, & Schultz, 2000). Laura's drawing reflects how she thought of herself as a good science student by listening attentively to the teacher as opposed to actively participating in science inquiry. Brickhouse et al. (2000) described how girls' engagement in science depends largely on how girls view their identities "and whether or not they are the kind of person who engages in science" (p. 441). Although all four focal students in Brickhouse's study expressed they were good at science, the teachers only recognized one student as fitting the "good student identity" – quiet, attentive, and organized – and qualifying for the Honors track. In this same manner, Laura's illustration of herself sitting and paying attention demonstrates that her "good student identity" had perhaps been recognized previously by her teachers as a "scientific" identity.

Gender Expression and Gender Performance

For indigenous peoples, gender identities and performances have been highly influenced by colonizing forces such as those who invaded native lands and imposed their own cultural views and binary gender behaviors on indigenous peoples. For indigenous nations, the imposition of European ideals of gender identities and performance happened under a violent conquest (Connell, 2010). "Almost immediately after the influx of European explorers, Native women came under the gaze of missionaries, men who could not see women as equals, because these men were coming from a place where women were inferior to men" (Wesley-Esquimaux, 2009, p. 16). Thus, rigid binaries of gender identities and roles are part of a colonial heritage that is generally still reflected within schools that are a major site of gender socialization for children.

Perhaps not surprisingly then, the self-illustrations mirror the colonized messages about gender performance internalized by indigenous children. That is, the girls I worked with drew themselves with long hair while the boys drew themselves wearing pants with short hair. Rosa (see Figure 6.1) drew herself wearing a lab coat and goggles and represented herself as a girl with her long hair tied up in a ponytail. Her choice of including the lab coat, goggles, and ponytail convey that Rosa knew about safety procedures in a science lab. From a binary-gendered standpoint, Rosa's ponytail represents her clearly as a girl. Although Laura drew herself with shorter hair (see Figure 6.2), she added colorful barrettes to her hair. Laura also added long lashes and blue makeup to her eyelids to signify her status as a girl. The boys followed a similar pattern in illustrating themselves sometimes with and sometimes without a lab coat. Thus, both girls and boys stayed within ascribed binary-based gender presentations.

Latinx indigenous youth live in a constant state of *nepantla*, constantly moving between the indigenous and the colonizer: from Spanish and English to Nahuatl, from opposing to balanced, and from home to school. When authoring their selves through identity texts, however, the children defaulted to imposed gender identities and performance as demonstrated in their illustrations of their scientist identities. Illustrating themselves as scientists allowed the indigenous children to think of themselves as scientists, however, which has implications for their academic performance in school as developing scientific identities has been shown to bolster students' persistence in science (Carlone & Johnson, 2007; Eagan, Garcia, Gasiewski, & Hurtado, 2012).

Implications for Literacy Education and Cross-Disciplinary Fields

The value of identity texts created by children extends beyond an autonomous view of literacy that frames literacy as a "technical and neutral skill" (Street, 2006, p. 2). That is, identity texts are multifaceted, and multilayered texts can assist children in understanding their various literacies and knowledges. Authoring identity texts allows for indigenous children to explore their understandings of gender and its performance. Asking children, in an age-appropriate manner, to explore gender from an indigenous point of view and how it intersects with imposed European gender performance and expectations is one way to help them think of ways to deconstruct binary gender expectations.

Indigenous advocates support decolonization of gender to move forward in recognizing indigenous youth's agency. Furthermore, guiding indigenous children in their explorations of gender expression and gender identity should be based on knowledge and insights of historical, colonial, and decolonizing understandings of gender. To support indigenous children's agency and growth, efforts must be made to include indigenous gender perspectives into educational practices as much as possible. As Fennell and Arnot (2008) write, "only a new approach to gender and education can take us away from the consequences of an essentializing [or stereotyping] definition of gender" (p. 536).

Finally, indigenous children's knowledges that have been traditionally dismissed from educational settings in favor of Western knowledge systems should be recognized. For example, indigenous youth know there is a needed balance (i.e., male and female, north and south, life and death) in spiritual ceremonies and act accordingly through their participation in such ceremonies. This knowledge, which I identify as being part of indigenous literacies, has been overlooked because as Hornberger (2003) explains, oral and bilingual literacies do not hold the same power as written and monolingual literacies. Yet, indigenous literacies must be recognized and brought to the forefront for educators, scholars, parents, researchers, and others working with children to advance children's literacy development and practice, and to better understand how complex issues such as gender identities and gender expressions are taken up by indigenous Latinx youth. One way this can be done is through the inclusion of culturally responsive texts, which can be in the form of children's literature that represents their identities and cultures. Additionally, integrating indigenous literacies into Western disciplinary learning can assist in guiding indigenous youth to learn how these they can complement each other.

At home, parents working with their children can start age-appropriate conversations that provide opportunities to explore how gender, race, class, and indigenous identities intersect. In addition, parents can provide opportunities for their children to connect with positive role models and with others who share their background. Making positive connections will provide a sense of group identity needed to feel connected to others. Finally, parents can provide the space for children to create a variety of texts (including oral and visual texts) in their various languages to allow the children to explore and imagine their various emerging identities. As Gloria Anzaldúa (1987) writes, "nothing happens in the 'real world' unless it first happens in the images in our heads" (p. 87).

References

Aikenhead, G., Brokofsky, J., Bodnar, T., Clark, C., Foley, C., Hingley, J., . . . Strange, G. (2014). *Enhancing school science with indigenous knowledge: What we know from teachers and research*. Saskatoon, Canada: Saskatoon Public School Division with Amazon.ca.

Anzaldúa, G.E. (1987). *Borderlands/la frontera: The new mestiza*, San Francisco, CA: Spinsters/Aunt Lute.

Anzaldúa, G.E. (2002). "Now let us shift . . . the path of conocimiento . . . inner work, public acts." In G.E. Anzaldúa & A. Keating (Eds.), *This bridge we call home: Radical visions for transformation* (pp. 540–578). New York, NY: Routledge.

Arvin, M., Tuck, E., & Morrill, A. (2013). Decolonizing feminism: Challenging connections between settler colonialism and heteropatriarchy. *Feminist Formations, 25*(1), 8–34.

Brickhouse, N.W., Lowery, P.A., & Schultz, K. (2000). What kind of a girl does science? The construction of school science identities. *Journal of Research in Science Teaching, 37*, 441–458.

Carlone, H.B., & Johnson, A. (2007). Understanding the science experiences of successful women of color: Science identity as an analytic lens. *Journal of Research in Science Teaching, 44*(8), 1187–1218. http://doi.org/10.1002/tea.20237.

Chambers, D.W. (1983). Stereotypic images of the scientist: The draw-a-scientist test. *Science Education, 67*(12), 255–265.

Connell, R.W. (2010). Kartini's children: On the need for thinking gender and education together on a world scale. *Gender and Education, 22*(6), 603–615.

Crenshaw, K. (1989). Demarginalizing the intersection of race and sex: A Black feminist critique of antidiscrimination doctrine, feminist theory and antiracist politics. *University of Chicago Legal Forum, 189*, 139–167.

Cummins, J., Bismilla, V., Chow, P., Cohen, S., Giampapa, F., Leoni, L., . . . Sastri, P. (2005). ELL students speak for themselves: Identity texts and literacy engagement in multilingual classrooms. Retrieved from www.curriculum.org/secretariat/files/ELLidentityTexts.pdf.

Dual Language Training Institute. (2018). Gómez and Gómez dual language model. Retrieved from http://dlti.us/3.html.

Eagan, K., Garcia, G., Gasiewski, J., & Hurtado, S. (April, 2012). *Passing through the gates: Identifying and developing talent in introductory STEM courses.* Paper presented at the Annual Conference of the American Educational Research Association, Vancouver, BC, Canada.

Fennell, S., & Arnot, M. (2008). Decentering hegemonic gender theory: The implications for educational research. *Compare, 38*(5), 525–538.

Fránquiz, M.E., Avila, A., & Lewis, B.A. (2013). Nepantlera teachers: Engaging bilingual students in sustained literature study in central Texas. *Journal of Latino/Latin American Studies, 5*(3), 142–155.

García, Ignacio M. (1997). Constructing the Chicano movement: Synthesis of a militant ethos. *Perspectives in Mexican American Studies, 6*, 1–19.

Gee, J.P. (1990/2007). *Social linguistics and literacies: Ideology in discourses.* London, UK: Taylor & Francis.

Hornberger, N.H. (2003). *Continua of biliteracy: An ecological framework for educational policy, research, and practice in multilingual settings.* Clevedon, UK: Multilingual Matters.

Love Ramirez, T., & Blay, Z. (2016). Why are people using the term "Latinx"? *Huffpost.* Retrieved from www.huffingtonpost.com/entry/why-people-are-using-the-term-latinx_us_57753328e4b0cc0fa136a159.

McInerny, P. (2017, June 5). *UCLA historian brings language of the Aztecs from ancient to contemporary times.* Retrieved from http://newsroom.ucla.edu/stories/ucla-historian-brings-language-of-the-aztecs-from-ancient-to-contemporary-times.

Menchaca, M. (1993). Chicano Indianism: A historical account of racial repression in the United States. *American Ethnologist, 20*(3), 583–603. Retrieved from www.jstor.org/stable/646643.

Mujeres de Maíz. (2018). In FaceBook [Event page]. Retrieved from www.facebook.com/events/100781700786011.

Ramirez, R. (2007). Race, tribal nation, and gender: A native feminist approach to belonging. *Meridians, 7*(2), 22–40. Retrieved from www.jstor.org/stable/40314242.

Reveles, J.M. (2009). Academic identity and scientific literacy. In K. Richardson Bruna & K. Gomez (Eds.), *The work of language in multicultural classrooms: Talking science, writing science* (pp. 193–218). New York, NY: Routledge.

Street, B. (2006). Autonomous and ideological models of literacy: Approaches from New Literacy Studies. *Media Anthropology Network, 17*, 1–15.

Tefera, A.A., Powers, J.M., & Fischman, G.E. (2018). Intersectionality in education: A conceptual aspiration and research imperative. *Review of Research in Education, 42*(1), vii–xvii. http://doi.org/10.3102/0091732X18768504

United Nations. (2006). *Who are indigenous peoples?* Fact sheet. Retrieved from www.un.org/esa/socdev/unpfii/documents/5session_factsheet1.pdf.

United States Census Bureau. (2017). School enrollment of the Hispanic population: Two decades of growth. Retrieved from www.census.gov/newsroom/blogs/random-samplings/2017/08/school_enrollmentof.html.

Wesley-Esquimaux, C. (2009). Trauma to resilience: Notes on decolonization. In *Restoring the balance: First nations women, community, and culture.* Winnipeg, MB: University of Manitoba Press.

PART III

Gender, Sexualities, and Adolescent Literacies

7

"HOLY GENDERED RESOURCE, BATMAN!"

Examining the Broader Application of Comics and Superhero Fiction Beyond Their Restrictive Relationship with Boys

Jacob Cassidy and Michael Kehler

Despite the unavoidable presence of superheroes, little has been done to acknowledge the power of these figures and their stories or to incorporate super-hero fiction into literacy instruction. Superhero fiction has struggled to find a place on the shelves, despite the role it played in the mid-twentieth-century rise of the comic medium and its continued role in sustaining and growing the comic's popularity and readership. Superhero fiction – and graphic novels in general – have gained the most ground as texts to attract struggling and reluctant readers in schools, and specifically reluctant *boy* readers in an ongoing effort to "save the boys."

Provincial (in Canada) and international testing data continue to indicate that boys regularly underperform in literacy achievement as compared to girls. Over the past three decades, sensationalized responses to these findings have fed into a discourse around the education of boys, particularly in literacy, that frames boys as "at risk" or "newly disadvantaged" – a "boy crisis." To close the achievement gap between boys and girls, efforts have been made to reform literacy education to better respond to boys' distinct needs, learning styles, and interests. Emphasis has been placed on the necessity of providing "boy-friendly" resources to engage and motivate boys to read, including comics and superhero fiction.

Literacy Reform and Reaffirming Stereotypical Masculinities

Much of the "boy crisis" discourse in the public sphere has been propelled by stereotypical views arguing that there are, "*essential* and *natural* differences between boys and girls . . . that there is something fundamentally different about the way men and women think, feel and act" (Rowan, Knobel, Bigum, & Lankshear, 2002, p. 29, original emphasis). Within this framework, boys are believed to be innately disadvantaged in schools since literacy education caters to the "natural" interests and skills of girls. Initiatives designed to improve literacy achievement among boys routinely rely on this essentialist or stereotypical mindset, resulting in a boy–girl, us–them binaristic framework that invariably pits boys and girls in opposition to one another. The implication is that *all* boys are underachieving and learn one way. In Canada, Ontario Ministry of Education (2004, 2009) documents are full of matter-of-fact statements that coach teachers into a binary mindset about gender and literacy achievement: boys take longer to learn to read than girls, boys read less than girls, boys value reading as an activity less than girls, and boys have much less interest in leisure reading than girls. This polarization of boys and girls fails to reflect diversity *among* and *within* boys and girls. Moreover, this ideology relies on a unitary and oversimplified, one-size-fits-all solution for literacy teachers, while invoking a bio-determinist, or innately gendered, view of learning styles or preferences.

Rather than simply framing the issue as one that arises out of "natural" differences between boys and girls, competing camps of thought argue that "differences in behavior or interests displayed by some girls and some boys are *produced* in particular social and cultural contexts" (Rowan et al., 2002, 29, original emphasis). This perspective acknowledges a complex relationship between boys, girls, and their navigation of, and success within, literacy spaces – a perspective that we similarly argue better reflects the messier reality of fluid gender identities.

Multiple, performed masculinities

Literacy reform initiatives tend to operationalize matter-of-fact statements about boys' behaviors, skills, and interests in which literacy strategies re-inscribe a "normative" masculinity that is singular and dependent on traditional stereotypes – an undifferentiated, static, and biological identity inherent at birth. In contrast, we argue that masculinity, or more accurately, masculin*ies* are multiple, performed, and messy – not something we *are*, but something we *do*. Drawing on Butler (1990) and Connell (1995, 1996), we acknowledge the active role of the self in constructing and shifting identities, that masculinities, "come into existence as people act . . . as configurations of social practice" (Connell, 1996, p. 210). Thus, the "*who*," "*what*," and "*where*" of each social sphere influences the "*how*" of gender performance as the individual purposefully or subconsciously reveals or conceals certain aspects of their identity in differing social contexts. Connell (1995) and Messner (1997) argue that with the acceptance of a diverse masculinities landscape comes the necessary, "examination of inequalities *among* men, rather than relying on a simplistic and falsely universalized definition of 'men' as an undifferentiated sex class" (Messner, 1997, p. 56, emphasis added). This multi-dimensional understanding of masculinities (and femininities) disrupts the oversimplified dichotomy of gendered achievement in alarmist discourses and challenges simplistic boy strategies proposed in literacy initiatives.

Beyond "Boy" Books

Initiatives intended to address underachieving boys' literacy have consistently included directives suggesting more "boy-friendly" resources be used in schools. According to the Canadian Council for Learning (CCL) (2009), "Boys are more interested in cartoons, comics, news, sports pages, science fiction and fantasy stories, hobby, craft, and special interest books" (p. 4), texts and genres that are less common in traditional literacy classrooms. These or similar "boy" interests have been documented across the literature surrounding boys' literacy achievement (Smith & Wilhelm, 2002). By actively promoting such "boys books" the argument follows that boys will gradually see themselves as readers alongside girls.

Concerns about the perceived "femininity" of reading and literacy learning is shared across essentialist and anti-essentialist camps. Both groups agree that upholding this "feminine" label in literacy has the power to influence how many boys choose to associate or, more appropriately, disassociate with reading and literacy instruction. The "resource model" of change pushed by essentialist thinkers remains steadfast in the belief that introducing more "boy-friendly" resources will create a gender balance in literacy spaces. Kehler (2013) has argued that this strategy, "reflect[s] a limiting approach that narrows and ultimately crystallizes traditional notions of masculinity and femininity through gender reforms" (p. 126). Throwing resources at the problem is a superficial solution, constituting a "quick fix" to a complicated problem.

Instead, anti-essentialists see the "feminization" of literacy spaces as a deeply embedded social construct that is perpetuated by long-standing beliefs about stereotypically normative masculinity and femininity. Upholding these assumptions and generalizations about what it means to be a boy or girl, masculine or feminine, creates rigid identity boundaries that young people are forced to carefully navigate. In other words, if interests, practices, or spaces are identified as "feminine" (like literacy spaces and many literacy resources continue to be), some boys may disassociate with these things to avoid emasculation by their peers. The same can be said of some girls' negotiation of "masculine" spaces and resources. Therefore, as we have previously argued, "Structuring literacy reform around competing 'truths' about the interests and skills of boys and girls potentially (and likely) limits opportunities for some students to access certain texts or benefit from particular pedagogical strategies" (Kehler & Cassidy, 2017, p. 41), specifically, in this case, comics and superhero fiction.

Reimagining Comics Through a Multiliteracies Framework

Comics and superhero fiction are considered "boy-friendly" texts or texts boys like to read because they cater to boys' apparent natural inclination for action and adventure (Moeller, 2011). The connection between boys and the comic medium has been cemented into place, linking comic books and graphic novels as effective tools for engaging struggling or disinterested readers (Carter, 2007) – terms in the current literacy landscape that are synonymous with boys and improved literacy achievement. Nevertheless, while evidence may support the successful use of comic books and graphic novels in these contexts, restricting their use to certain groups of students (boys and struggling or disinterested readers), we argue, limits the possibilities for these multimodal texts to benefit all students in literacy classrooms.

Multimodality and Embracing Student Culture

Extended conversations surrounding the specifics of what "literacy" includes and why a more fluid understanding of the concept is necessary have been ongoing since the late-1990s, but have been, and continue to be, cogently expressed through the work of multiliteracies scholars. Since their revolutionary article in 1996, "A Pedagogy of Multiliteracies: Designing Social Futures," the New London Group and its members have recognized that shifts in the global literacy landscape have been initiated by two fundamental principles: multimodality and social diversity. It is through these two tenets of the multiliteracies framework that comics and superhero fiction have the potential to be reimagined as resources in literacy education.

Comics as Complex Multimodal Resources

Multiliteracies scholars argue that *all* meaning-making is multimodal or involves navigating multiple modes of communication (Kalantzis & Cope 2012). This includes any amalgamation of written, oral, visual, audio, tactile, gestural, and/or spatial representations (Kalantzis & Cope, 2012). As multisensory beings, daily interactions with the world are inherently multimodal (Cope & Kalantzis, 2009; Mills, 2009), thus understanding how these multiple and interconnected modes function is crucial. Furthermore, new media that permeates public and private social spheres (e.g., television, Internet, advertisements, video games, etc.) are increasingly multimodal, where, "Whole worlds of meaning are conjured up in a few moments of image plus music plus gesture plus tone of voice" (Kalantzis & Cope, 2000, p. 145). The concentrated meanings of these multimodal representations aim to excite the senses and seize the ephemeral attention and interests of now more active users and discerning consumers of media.

Comics invite students to engage in multisensory literacy practices that mirror the information gathering and processing that students take on in everyday life (Blanch & Mulvihill, 2013). With multiple entry points (or modes) for accessing meaning, students use their strengths (or familiarity) with certain literacies to support personal weaknesses and aid in the decoding or comprehension of new or unknown meanings. The accessibility that familiar modes offer to students working with comics, alongside lower word counts and a primary focus on visuals, furthers the perception that comics are simple texts for readers (Carter, 2008;

Moeller, 2011). This understanding fails to acknowledge the complex interweaving of written, visual, gestural, spatial, and even audial (through onomatopoeia) literacies at play in comics.

Comics as Lifeworld Artifacts

In a multiliteracies framework, social diversity not only accounts for increased local diversity and global connectedness in work, public, and private spheres, but also acknowledges diverse identities. Students bring to school the knowledge and experiences of their unique *lifeworlds* – their everyday lives and experiences (Cope & Kalantzis, 2000; Gee, 2000), which shape "What they know, who they feel themselves to be, and how they orient themselves to education" (Kalantzis & Cope, 2000, p. 121). Students draw from this repertoire of knowledge, language, skills, and experience to gain understanding in school and "real-world" contexts (Cope & Kalantzis, 2009). Thus, failure to engage with students' lifeworlds limits how many can learn or successfully familiarize themselves with school discourses (Kalantzis & Cope, 2000).

Despite growing acceptance of comics in schools, superhero fiction is still situated outside of what qualifies as legitimate literary material. We argue that this is counterproductive given how popular culture saturates students' lives outside of school (Blanch & Mulvihill, 2013) and how popular culture is saturated with superhero content. With such a pervasive presence in the social world and considering education's role to prepare students for life after or outside of school, comics and superhero fiction are a compelling resource to engage *all* youth.

Our Study

Through 2014–2015, we conducted a case study of students in a rural secondary school in southwestern Ontario, Canada. The goal was to build on a growing body of research that addressed the use of graphic novels in English classrooms. More specifically, the focus of this study was on examining the potential of the superhero fiction genre to engage students in meaningful literacy education – to see how superhero stories held up against the "classics" studied in English Language Arts classrooms. Six students participated in the study – three boys and three girls from different academic levels in Grades 11 and 12 English. Students attended three focus group meetings for 45 minutes each. Students initially completed a brief questionnaire about their reading habits, interests, English classroom experiences, exposure to the comic medium and superhero fiction, and how they defined "literacy." The focus group discussed their experiences in English classrooms and probed several comics. Excerpts from *Batman: The Killing Joke* (Moore, 2008), *Batgirl Vol. 1: The Darkest Reflection* (Simone, 2012), and *All-Star Superman* (Morrison, 2011) were given to each student after the first meeting and excerpts from *Marvels* (Busiek, 2004) and *New X-Men Vol. 1* (Morrison, 2001) were distributed after the second meeting. Adopting a flexible and open approach to these focus groups allowed students to direct the conversation and ultimately kept their thoughts, opinions, and co-constructed knowledge – their voices – at the forefront of the study.

"Up, Up, and Away!": Using Comics and Superhero Fiction for Literacy Education

Comics have often been highlighted as a resource amenable to boys' "particular" literacy needs and preferences (Griffith, 2010; Moeller, 2011). A dominant genre (maybe *the* dominant genre) in the comic medium, superheroes or superhero fiction, have also been specifically referenced as primary texts best suited for boys (Morrison, 2012). Despite these claims, boys and girls in this study had a shared level of interest and engagement when it came to pursuing comics as an out-of-school interest, mirroring findings from Moeller's (2011) study exploring high school students' attitudes toward comics. Given the opportunity to experience comics and superhero content in a student-centered environment rooted in dialogue, students engaged in deep discussions about literacy and applying literacy skills beyond the classroom.

"I Think It's So Much More . . . Dynamic": Comics as a Complex, Multimodal Literacy

Students' comments about literacy overwhelmingly focused on traditional literacy skill development – reading and writing. Considering the experiences they shared about literacy education in English class that were deeply rooted in traditional literacy pedagogy, this was not very surprising. Nevertheless, once we started looking at and discussing comics in our focus groups, students quickly and independently broadened their understandings of literacy and showed an appreciation for comics' complex visual and spatial literacies. Vicki expressed an expanded view of literacy by explaining,

Vicki: I think sometimes when we are talking about analyze – like, being literate, we're talking about, we're talkin' about like major novels. Like, analyzing these deep . . . things . . . I think this idea [points to comics on table] is very good because I think it's so much more, like, dynamic – like, I think there's lessons to learn in comics too, not only in other types of novels. Like, there's other ways of being literate than to just, like, analyzing – you know what I mean – like analyzing these works that are so complex.

JC: Right.

Vicki: That *seem* "complex" [does air quotes with fingers].

Vicki identified a connection between her perceptions of literacy and what she has experienced in literacy classrooms. She also explained that comics offer a more "dynamic" literacy experience that extends beyond the seemingly "complex" work of traditional novels. Selina similarly identified comics as "a different way of communicating" that diverges from the traditional "left to right" reading of novels, the challenges of which Selena and Vicki discuss in a later exchange:

Selina: Another thing with familiar, I think, is that, um, like if you've never read a graphic novel before, like, you won't know, like, what box to go to next [*laughter*].

Vicki: Yeah, I had trouble with that.

Selina: Like, who's speaking at what time . . . Like, I'm more familiar with manga, like, Japanese graphic novels, so they're backwards, like right to left. So I struggled a little bit with that and, like . . . And so, yeah, if you don't know how to read it, it's kind of confusing.

Vicki: But, yeah, I was a bit confused, like, okay so what comes first? And, okay, I kind of figured out the little things in, like, squares are her thoughts . . . But, yeah, like, I don't know, it was a bit confusing at times.

Selina: And it's definitely something that we could learn and, like, it's another form of literacy.

In contrast to a left-to-right orientation for reading texts, the reading path in comics, like other visual representations, is less restrictive and requires careful navigation. Combined with the complex interplay of visual, spatial, gestural, audial, and written meanings, reading comics becomes a rich and intricate multi-modal experience that parallels the multisensory world.

Beyond the "Super": Connecting to Comics Through Relevant Human Experiences

Selina recognized that students could take "a lesson or a moral from a comic book . . . understand that and apply it to daily life," suggesting that comics offered learning opportunities relevant to students' lives. Rachel was quick to point out that, "Just from, like, Grade 12 learning about different theories, I saw a whole bunch of stuff that could be identified as, like, feminist theory," while Jason recognized opportunities for looking at Marxist theory and the use of character archetypes. Rachel also talked about the "cliffhanger" ending of one of the excerpts being "helpful in an English class because if you don't give the ending then that helps with, like, inferring skills." Participants were able to independently draw upon aspects of the comic excerpts and connect the content to their prior knowledge and experiences in English class. Recognizing these connections or relevance to specific content in English classrooms is certainly a positive outcome, but it fails to distinguish comics and superhero fiction from the traditional novels that students expressed a great deal of frustration with in English classes.

Students' reactions to reading *X-Men* (Morrison, 2001), on the other hand, starkly contrasted their attitudes toward the stagnant novels of their English classrooms. In her conversation about *X-Men*, Vicki expressed an enthusiasm shared across her peers:

> [R]eading *X-Men* is by far my favourite! I was reading it and I was like, "I really get this point." And I think it has everything, like . . . It has obvious things, like, okay, at the beginning it talks about how, I don't know, like, he killed this guy who was gay, whatever, you can talk about that. But then it has so many other things . . . Like, there's the prejudice that jumps in at the beginning where like all the press is – like all the people are like complaining about how it's so awful, this school, and they want to shut it down, the mutants. And then again, like, with the parents of this girl that's a mutant and how they try to segregate them from society. And then inside the school there's . . . like, in the relationships. The girls, they don't want this other girl, um, to be in the relationship with this boy because they – like I think that has – that can be analyzed too in so many other ways . . . So I think this, in an English class, would have so much potential . . . I don't know I just thought it was great.

The excitement in Vicki's response was palpable. Vicki enthusiastically dove into the important topics and themes in this excerpt (e.g., homophobia, social prejudice, segregation of the other, relationships) and her response revealed an intrinsic motivation to engage with this text, one that Lapp and Fisher (2009) attribute to working with materials deeply connected to an individual's interests and that have meaningful applications to their life.

Vicki expanded, "it's something that students could identify with because, you know, everybody has a bit of outcast in them." The idea of the "outcast" became a recurring theme throughout the discussion of this text. Jason similarly explains that *X-Men*, "kind of shows you, like, even though these are fictional characters and you can't have superpowers, but even to be an outcast is universal to everyone in the world, right?" Todd drew a parallel between the text and his observations in school:

> [W]ith the whole, like, the *X-Men* thing and Xavier's school, like, I find that high school students can relate to it because in the school, you do have the group of the popular mutants, then you have the ones that, you know, they're like, just your regular people and that and then you have the people that do keep to themselves, like, they're not going out, like, trying to make friends.

Finally, Damian inserted that the superheroes' purpose might be grounded in the "outcast" motif:

> I feel like that's why – that's what the characters and the heroes are made to do. They're created to target and relate to the quote-unquote "outcast" of the social – social network in schools and basically anywhere, because the characters are given that, that style and the flair that gives them the hope that, "I'm not alone, I'm not the only one."

This statement was echoed by Jason as well, "and you're like, 'I'm dealing with this too' and, like, 'oh, Wolverine's doin' it too. It can't just be me.'" The personal connections and closeness the students express with the material is powerful. As Rachel said, "in high school you come into your own a lot" and framing this text around being an outcast drew on this familiar teenage struggle to "fit in" and to have membership among peers and friends.

The "outcast" image was not the only point of entry for participants to relate to comic characters, however. For Rachel and Vicki, simply having a diverse group of characters made it easier to locate themselves within the text. Rachel explained, "Maybe because, like, *X-Men* has a variety of characters, so . . . You have more opportunities for people to relate to what characters are going through." Vicki agreed: "Exactly. You have the different types of characters with different superpowers, different personalities, different struggles that you can relate." Jason focused particularly on characters' struggles, commenting that, "the greatest part about that is, like, they don't know how to use their own powers, right? Just like teenagers don't know how to use their own strengths to their advantage, right?" Jason found comfort in a shared and relatable vulnerability of these characters, an often-overlooked trait of superheroes that shifts their character status from super to human, that make their otherworldly lives become familiar and relevant to the reader.

It is important to understand that amid this excitement, students did not dismiss the value of traditional novels. In fact, they were quite aware of the importance of some of these texts, such as George Orwell's *1984* (1949). The constant recycling of classic novels and the unilateral pedagogy of traditional literacy education, heavily (and negatively) influenced their literacy experiences, however. It is equally important to recognize that simply giving students an interest-based text is not enough although catering to students' interests is a valuable approach to increase their engagement in learning (Brozo, 2013). Without student-driven discussion and freedom to challenge what they are reading, literacy instruction remains stagnant.

"We're Here and We're Actively Discussing": Critical Engagement with Superheroes

Long-standing perceptions about superhero fiction that pervade public opinion are largely reductionist and raise skepticism about the quality of the genre as demonstrated by the title of Weiner's (2002) article, "Beyond Superheroes: Comics Get Serious." Through the interpretive lenses of the students in our study, however, reading superhero fiction quickly became "serious" work. With no prompting whatsoever, students independently and organically began a foray into critical discussion about what they were reading.

In the initial focus group meeting, we looked at excerpts from *Superman* and *Batgirl*, texts chosen for their juxtaposed representations of female characters, and the contrast was unsettling for students. Rachel initiated discussion with a fiery comment, saying, "Like, it actually – part of it actually drove me insane about, like, how are women being treated like this?" referring to the male superheroes trying to "win" Lois Lane as their prized possession. The overtly sexist tone, used to satirize brutish masculinities and fragile femininities often depicted in older superhero content, was obvious and although Rachel's comment does not delve further into the problem, her frustration ignited further discussion. Vicki was particularly intrigued by the tension between Lois Lane's passivity in *Superman* and Batgirls' powerful presence:

> [C]omparing it to Batwoman – Batgirl, um, I thought it was, like, I was sur-prised at the beginning to see how, like, muscular and how powerful Batgirl looks and then looking at Superwoman [pointing at Lois Lane in costume], she's like half naked and . . . yeah, I just thought that was a big contrast.

Selina extended the discussion by highlighting Lois' "superhero-for-a-day" storyline as degrading to her character, "and especially that it's just, like, for one day. It's like they assume [Lois] is only strong when she has this power. Whereas when she doesn't have it she's just regular Lois Lane, like, not as special." With the freedom to follow their own line of thinking, participants' discussion allowed for ideas to progress that led to more critical dialogue. In combination with a new or exciting text of interest, the opportunity to co-create their own meaning from their reading through discussion was also a new and exciting approach to look-ing at literature, as Selina pointed out, "discussion is a big thing that we don't do enough." Students' critical engagement with the comics also stretched beyond the printed page. Eventually, the conversation shifted to address the possible bar-riers to using superhero comics in literacy classrooms. Jason explained,

> My Dad just jokingly said that like he, he personally didn't care right, but on the one *X-Men* one there was a scantily clad woman, right? And, um, like he was just joking but he's like, "Is that allowed in a Catholic school?" or something, right? So like, even though she wasn't fully nude, it's like still the . . . she barely was dressed.

Jason emphasized the sexual content as a potential barrier and could have similarly drawn attention to scenes of violence elsewhere in the excerpts. Sexual and violent content is often cited as a barrier for implementing superhero fiction in schools (Moeller, 2011), but excluding content based on its sexual and violent imagery is a naïve limitation. Youth are inundated with sexual and violent imagery in the media that flood their out-of-school lives (e.g., advertisements and commercials, video games, movies, etc.) and need opportunities to critically engage with and interrogate these texts in school. Interestingly, adolescents in this study felt the same way.

Rachel was quick to defend the sexual content saying,

> I think that sometimes things like the way she's dressed are important, almost because you can't shut that out. It's there in the world, you have to deal with it, you're not going to do yourself, or anybody else, a service by covering it up . . . I don't see the problem with it.

Rachel suggested that including this content has valuable application for learning to confront and navigate similarly constructed representations of people (women in this case) that exist in the world outside of school. As Mills (2009) argued, "ignoring the pervasiveness of popular culture leaves a significant number of gendered representations and stereotypes unopposed and unquestioned" (p. 106). Interestingly, students challenged the sheltered attitude in their small community,

Rachel: It's also 'cause we're in a small town. The type of town we're in . . . it's where everybody's close-minded.

Vicki: Yeah, that's true.

Rachel: Like, not to be, like, offensive to anybody, but it's like, we live around where there's a whole bunch of farmers and, I don't know, we're not very diverse, so you kind of close your eyes to whatever else is around you.

Vicki: The really only way that can change is by education and discussion and hope, like, talkin' and informing people and giving different viewpoints.

Without the opportunity to interact with this content and explore the constructed meanings within, students fail to develop and hone critical literacy skills to interpret these meanings.

Implications for Literacy Education and Cross-Disciplinary Fields

Important social factors, such as socioeconomic status, race, ethnicity, have been identified across a wide swath of literature as being relevant markers for addressing which boys and, conversely, which girls are at-risk in the ongoing literacy debate (Martino & Kehler, 2007; Watson, 2011). Engagement and success in literacy is neither a "boy problem" nor is it purely a resource-based problem. As we have highlighted, relevant, youth-centered resources are important for engaging boys and girls in literacy. Without the right pedagogy supporting these resources, however, youth will continue to disengage. The adolescents in this study were clear about their frustrations with stagnant reading lists, limited opportunities for engaging personally with what they were studying, and the writing-heavy focus of English classrooms. They yearned for discussion and expression of opinion and to connect deeply with the materials they were reading – to feel the worth of their learning outside of their classrooms.

Comics and superhero fiction are an excellent platform to make the jump into youth-centered learning that acknowledges their interests and challenges them to critically examine the social commentary within the stories and in the world around them. Through this multimodal medium, young people also begin to understand how to read their worlds and the multisensory meanings that shape their daily lives. We do not see comics as the answer to issues in literacy achievement, but we hope that with a broader appreciation for texts that come from the lifeworlds of adolescents and with a focus on letting them co-construct meaning, more youth, regardless of gender, will be excited to be readers, writers, and critically engage with the word and world around them.

The implications of this research are far-reaching. It is necessary for parents, as well as educators and youth agency staff, to see how gendered assumptions inform day-to-day practices. The divisions that routinely separate boys and girls rely on dated and often unchallenged male–female binaries that do more to create differences than acknowledge similarities. Common and shared interests in comics are characteristic of youth in general rather than being sex specific. Single-sex classrooms or playgroups are supported not because they reflect evidence-based learning differences but rather because they reflect familiar and long-standing assumptions and beliefs about narrow and limited kinds of boys and girls. Moreover, they maintain and restore antiquated views of boys and girls as particular kinds of learners. Instead of re-inscribing limiting and limited ways of reengaging with boys and girls, we argue that educators, parents, and youth agency staff need to think in complex ways to acknowledge the dynamic and diverse ways that interests, attitudes, and gender expressions are taken up and how they can be supported as fluid and negotiable rather than as static and fixed.

References

Blanch C.L., & Mulvihill, T.M. (2013). The attitudes of some students on the use of comics in higher education. In C.K. Syma & R.G. Weiner (Eds.), *Graphic novels and comics in the classroom: Essays on the educational power of sequential art* (pp. 35–49). Jefferson, NC: McFarland.

Brozo, W. (2013). Outside interests and literate practices as contexts for increasing engagement and critical reading for adolescent boys. In B.J. Guzzetti & T.W. Bean (Eds.), *Adolescent literacies and the gendered self: (Re)constructing identities through multimodal literacy practices* (pp. 3–12). New York, NY: Routledge.

Busiek, K. (2004). *Marvels*. New York, NY: Marvel.

Butler, J. (1990). *Gender trouble: Feminism and the subversion of identity*. New York, NY: Routledge.

Canadian Council for Learning. (2009). *Why boys don't like to read: Gender differences in reading achievement*. Retrieved from www.nald.ca/library/research/ccl/lessons_learning/why_boys/why_boys.pdf.

Carter, J.B. (2007). Transforming English with graphic novels: Moving toward our "optimus prime." *English Journal, 97*(2), 49–53.

Carter, J.B. (2008). Comics, the canon, and the classroom. In N. Frey & D. Fisher (Eds), *Teaching visual literacy: Using comic books, graphic novels, anime, cartoons, and more to develop comprehension and thinking skills* (pp. 47–60). Thousand Oaks, CA: Corwin Press.

Connell, R.W. (1995). *Masculinities*. Berkley, CA: University of California Press.

Connell, R.W. (1996). Teaching the boys: New research on masculinity, and gender strategies for schools. *Teachers College Record, 98*(2), 209–235.

Cope, B., & Kalantzis, M. (2000). Designs for social futures. In B. Cope & M. Kalantzis (Eds.), *Multiliteracies: Literacy learning and the design of social futures* (pp. 203–234). London, UK: Routledge.

Cope, B., & Kalantzis, M. (2009). "Multiliteracies": New literacies, new learning. *Pedagogies: An International Journal, 4*, 164–175.

Gee, J.P. (2000). New people in new worlds: Networks, the new capitalism and schools. In B. Cope & M. Kalantzis (Eds.), *Multiliteracies: Literacy learning and the design of social futures* (pp. 43–68). London, UK: Routledge.

Griffith, P.E. (2010). Graphic novels in the secondary classroom and school libraries. *Journal of Adolescent & Adult Literacy, 54*(3), 181–189.

Kalantzis, M., & Cope, B. (2000). Changing the role of schools. In B. Cope & M. Kalantzis (Eds.), *Multiliteracies: Literacy learning and the design of social futures* (pp. 121–148). London, UK: Routledge.

Kalantzis, M., & Cope, B. (2012). *Literacies*. Port Melbourne, Australia: Cambridge University Press.

Kehler, M.D. (2013). Who will "save the boys"?: (Re)examining a panic for underachieving boys. In B.J. Guzzetti & T.W. Bean (Eds.), *Adolescent literacies and the gendered self: (Re)constructing identities through multimodal literacy practices* (pp. 121–130). New York, NY: Routledge.

Kehler, M., & Cassidy, J. (2017). "A literacy landscape unresolved: Beyond the boy crisis and into superhero fiction. *Boyhood Studies, 10*(2), 37–59.

Lapp, D., & Fisher, D. (2009). It's all about the book: Motivating teens to read. *Journal of Adolescent & Adult Literacy, 52*(7), 556–561.

Martino, W., & Kehler, M.D. (2007). Gender-based literacy reform: A question of challenging or recuperating gender binaries. *Canadian Journal of Education, 30*(2), 406–431.

Messner, M. (1997). *Politics of masculinities: Men in movements*. London, UK: AltaMira Press.

Mills, K.A. (2009). Multiliteracies: Interrogating competing discourses. *Language and Education, 23*(2), 103–116.

Moeller, R.A. (2011). "Aren't these boy books?": High school students' readings of gender in graphic novels. *Journal of Adolescent & Adult Literacy, 54*(7), 476–484.

Moore, A. (2008). *Batman: The killing joke*. New York, NY: DC Comics.

Morrison, G. (2001). *New X-Men* (Vol. 1). New York, NY: Marvel.

Morrison, G. (2011). *All-star Superman*. New York, NY: DC Comics.

Morrison, G. (2012). *Supergods*. New York, NY: Spiegel & Grau.

New London Group. (1996). A pedagogy of multiliteracies: Designing social futures. *Harvard Education Review, 66*(1), 60–92.

Ontario Ministry of Education. (2004). *Me read? No way! A practical guide to improving boys' literacy skills.* Toronto, ON: Queen's Printer for Ontario.

Ontario Ministry of Education. (2009). *Realizing the promise of diversity: Ontario's equity and inclusive education strategy.* Toronto, ON: Queen's Printer for Ontario.

Orwell, G. (1949). *1984.* London, UK: Secker & Warburg.

Rowan, L., Knobel, M., Bigum, C., & Lankshear, C. (2002). *Boys, literacies, and schooling: The dangerous territories of gender-based literacy reform.* Buckingham, UK: Open University Press.

Simone, G. (2012). *Batgirl. Vol. 1: The darkest reflection.* New York, NY: DC Comics.

Smith, M.W., & Wilhelm, J.D. (2002). *Reading don't fix no chevys: Literacy in the lives of young men.* Portsmouth, NH: Heinemann.

Watson, A. (2011). Not just a "boy problem": An exploration of the complexities surrounding literacy underachievement. *Discourse: Studies in the Cultural Politics of Education, 32*(5), 779–795.

Weiner, S. (2002). Beyond superheroes: Comics get serious. *Library Journal, 127*(2), 55–58.

8

"THIS IS WHY WE TALK ABOUT RACE AND SEXUALITY, TOO"

Challenging White Feminism in and Through Literacies

Stephanie Anne Shelton and Shelly Melchior

The course on which this chapter reports was centered on feminist concepts and included a variety of readings and activities that presented gender as directly connected to a range of identities, including sexuality, race, socioeconomic class, gender expression, and able-bodiedness. Although the teacher had anticipated students having limited or no knowledge of feminism, she was unprepared for students' resistance to considering the ways that gender intersects with other identities and topics:

> These kids are really struggling with how feminism isn't just about gender. Like, when I bring up topics like race and class and sexuality, they're like, "Whoa! We thought this was a class on gender equality." And, so what I've got are kids who're unknowingly pushing "White feminism" as if it's feminism, and who understand gender as separate from other issues.

The teacher, Talia, (all names are pseudonyms) confided this reflection during an interview after the second day of a week-long course she had titled "Feminism 101" offered as a secondary English Language Arts class. She had planned the course to study the historical context for gender-rights movements based in the United States while also emphasizing literacy to examine gender within the context of other topics, such as racism, classism, heteronormativity, and transphobia.

From the beginning of these discussions however, she met strong resistance from her White female students who comprised most of her class, and she found herself addressing the concept of "White feminism" (Featherstone, 2016; Harris, 2016) through a range of literacy practices. White feminism is a claim of feminism by those women who most benefit from and, therefore, are most invested in the status quo. White feminism advantages "straight, white, middle-class American women," while ignoring or dismissing the realities and needs of other women, including women of color, socioeconomically disadvantaged women, transgender women, and queer women (Harris, 2016). This concept of White feminism was one that Talia identified as relevant to and pervasive in her course.

In response to this teacher's concerns, two questions guided our examination of Talia's teaching: how does the instructor describe students' understandings of gender and feminism, and how does the instructor's literacy instruction inform her students' understandings of gender and feminism as related to other aspects of identity? Our review of relevant literature examines scholarship related to the issue of gender as intersectional, and then provides a discussion of the contemporary issue of White feminism that Talia referenced as relevant to her classroom. Our choice to fully explore intersectionality as defined by Crenshaw (1989) is in line with current research initiatives that "demands that our scholarship be oriented toward accounting for the ways that race/ethnicity, class, gender, sexuality, religion, citizenship, ability, and age, among other things, shape the structural dynamics of power and inequality in social spaces and individual identities" (Tefera, Powers, & Fischman, 2018, p. viii).

Gender as Intersectional in Literacy Education

While the term "literacy education" might evoke images of classrooms or libraries, a substantial portion of the literature examining intersectional issues of gender in literacies are from the physical and mental health sciences. For example, Talwar (2010) applied an intersectional framework that included considerations of race, class, and gender in art therapy. Wood, Soudien, and Reddy (2016) focused on sexuality as connected to gender, and specifically to masculinity, in their work to provide HIV-related literacies; literacies that not only educate about HIV but incorporate an intersectional approach that advocates empathy as well as knowledge. McCloud, Jung, Gray, and Viswanath (2013) explored the best approaches to promoting literacy practices among cancer survivors by intersecting gender, race, and ethnicity in their research finding that "information avoidance may be driven, in part, by social determinants, particularly among those at the intersection of multiple social status categories" (p. 1949). In each instance, researchers worked to understand and acknowledge the ways that gender connects with other identity elements, such as race, ethnicity, and social class, and how those intersections mattered in advancing participants' knowledge of these intersections and the power and inequality often embedded within these structures, as well as self-advocacy.

Within the context of informal or formal schooling spaces, intersectional literacies are equally important but not as commonly explored. The largest portion of applicable scholarship does not overtly apply an intersectional perspective (e.g., Koonce, 2012; Mayo, 2014; Muhammad & Haddix, 2016); rather, most of these studies focus on a group or issue, such as Black girls' literacy needs (e.g., Price-Dennis, 2016; Shelton, 2018) or queer students' representations in texts (e.g., Blackburn, 2014; Miller, 2013). The few studies that explicitly examine gender as multifaceted did so to facilitate appreciations for the necessity for intersectional approaches to literacy education. Compton-Lilly, Hamman, Papoi, Venegas, and Schwabenbauer (2017) used intersectional literacy practices by supporting students' reflections on their personal identities during discussions on immigration and immigrants' experiences. Clark, Sapon-Shevin, Brimhall-Vargas, McGhie, and Nieto (2017) described how intersectional discussions, including considerations of gender, class, race, and sexuality, aided in curriculum planning and supporting students' considerations of social inequalities. Shelton and Melchior (2018) examined the affordances of intersectional literacies in a secondary teacher's efforts to facilitate students' discussions of social justice topics, including immigrant farming, heterosexism, and racialized sexism. Harter, Castor, Seigler, and Abrahams (2018) explored sites of privilege and oppression by considering the ways that religious beliefs in ethnic communities affected women differently than men, intersecting gender with race and religion. Long-standing literacy philosophies emphasize the value of students' identities and experiences in relation to reading and engagement; researchers extend and complicate these notions to emphasize the ways that multiple, overlapping identities and experiences matter in learning. This chapter further explores those affordances and possibilities by focusing on a teacher's efforts to both implement an intersectional pedagogy and to counter students' resistance to understanding gender as constantly being constructed through its various intersectionalities.

Contemporary White Feminism

The topic of intersectional literacies is inherently political in that curricula and pedagogies work to connect elements of identity or subjectivities to educational practices, presumably in ways that shape students' understandings and lives, and potentially the whole of society. Given that political element, the contemporary political landscape is an important context to examine particularly in relation to this chapter. Before Donald J. Trump's election as President of the United States, numerous polls had confidently predicted Hillary Rodham Clinton's win (e.g., Rhodan & Johnson, 2016; Westcott, 2016). After Trump's win, various groups began sifting through the election data, and discovered that White women had been a cornerstone of Trump's electorate, many of whom were college educated and at least middle class – the group of women least likely to be negatively affected by Trump's political platform (Featherstone, 2016; Scott, 2017). It seemed counterintuitive to many that a voting block of women would select Trump as their political voice, when "he was recorded bragging about . . . grab[bing] women's genitals without their permission . . . made degrading comments about a female political rival . . . [and] has a history of making sexist comments about his employees" (Scott 2017, n.p.). Following this finding, author Tamara Winfrey Harris (2016) wrote, "The triumph of President-elect Donald Trump represents the failure of many things. One of them is White feminism" (n.p.). While the concept of "White feminists" had certainly circulated prior to Trump's election (Featherstone, 2016; Harris, 2016), this moment provided a contemporary touchstone for the term.

Context

Talia was a faculty member in a highly selective summer-enrichment program for high school juniors and seniors. Students who were admitted to the program went through an interview process that included school, district, and state-level rounds of competition. Students who were admitted were offered a six-week, residential, on-campus experience, and were exposed to a range of academic and fine arts courses, including engineering, dance, Mandarin Chinese, and astronomy – 30 in total. Due to the nature of a summer enrichment program, no grades were given and faculty were encouraged to offer course topics not typically found in high schools (see also Shelton & Melchior, 2018 for additional context). Ultimately less than 1% of eligible students and only about 60 teachers in total joined the program each summer, producing a teacher to student ratio of approximately 1:10.

The Teacher

Talia had taught for five years in the English Language Arts Department with four other colleagues in this summer program. Her department was structured to offer multiple two-hour six-day-long courses based on texts and topics that the instructors chose and that a curriculum director reviewed, to ensure courses both challenged the program's intellectually and artistically gifted students and offered topics that were different from standard high school curricula.

Our Perspective

Crenshaw's (1989) concept of "intersectionality" is one view commonly adopted in feminist scholarship. Briefly, intersectionality examines the interconnectedness of people's multifaceted identities within systems of privilege and oppression Crenshaw (2004) argued that it was impossible to discuss sexism without simultaneously acknowledging the ways that "[r]ace, gender, and other identity categories" matter, too (Crenshaw, 1991, p. 1242). In her discussion of intersectionality, Crenshaw (1989) introduced the concept of a "single-axis framework" (p. 139), which we use as our perspective. The single-axis framework considers the implications of many well-meaning and social justice-minded individuals ignoring the multidimensional natures of individuals' experiences and identities and reducing those experiences and identities to "a single categorical axis" that unintentionally but undeniably emphasizes "otherwise-privileged members of the group" (Crenshaw, 2004, p. 140). For example, Crenshaw (2004) pointed out that research on Black girls' literacies in schools often "erases Black women [and girls] in the conceptualization, identification and remediation of race and sex discrimination" (p. 140) so literacy research either focuses on the single-axis of "girls" or the single-axis of "race," and thereby either privileges White girls or Black boys. As numerous scholars have noted, this approach ignores Black girls' unique and intersectional needs (e.g., Koonce, 2012; Mayo, 2014; Muhammad & Haddix, 2016). An example is the tendency to describe Black girls' class participation as "angry" and "loud," thereby using emotionally laden language commonly associated with women and girls in conjunction with a racialized tendency to see people of color in the United States as verbally aggressive (e.g., Koonce, 2012). The double focus on race and gender taps into long-standing tropes such as the "angry black woman" and risks silencing Black girls in ways that are different from either White girls' or Black boys' experiences (Smith, 1999).

Our Procedures

The first author, Stephanie, conducted six observations with half lasting for about one hour and the other half encompassing the full two hours of the course. During each observation, Stephanie took fieldnotes, "descriptive accounts of experiences and observations [. . .] capturing as closely as possible [. . .] overheard talk and witnessed activities" (Emerson, Fretz, & Shaw, 2011, p. 5). Stephanie typed her observation notes using an electronic tablet during class, and then, as soon as there was an opportunity, fleshed those notes out to narrative accounts.

In addition to these observations, Stephanie conducted interviews with Talia that were unstructured and conversational, emphasizing a non-standardized and unscripted interviewing approach (Lavrakas, 2008). These interviews were loosely structured so the interviewer and interviewee had the freedom to pursue various topics, ask for clarifications, and potentially deviate from the research questions and aims to produce interactions that were more informal and conversational than semi-structured or formal interview approaches. The interviews varied from 10 minutes to over an hour, depending on Talia's availability, with the goal of providing opportunities for Talia to introduce topics that we had not considered or anticipated, and to provide a form of participant review to provide the opportunity for clarification and, if necessary, further questioning by both interviewer and participant.

While Stephanie was involved in the observation and interviews, Shelly, the second author, joined the research at the data analysis stage – providing feedback and insight as a researcher removed from the data-collection site. Shelly's inclusion allowed for interrater reliability or cross checks when coding the data, as well as for thoughtful discussion on emerging themes and findings. Our analysis worked to preserve both Talia's narratives through her interviews, as well as the descriptive memos Stephanie created during her observations through Butler-Kisber's (2010) approach of "finding the story" (pp. 72–77). We read and reread the observations and interviews individually first, considering possible themes. We then conducted a cross-case analysis (Brooks, 2012) by comparing and contrasting repeated themes across the interview transcripts and the observations.

Our Insights

We identified two major themes or propositions across the classroom observations and conversational interviews that were framed by the teacher's own words: (1) "I'm having to fight them to see gender as multifaceted" and (2) "We're using writing and reading to challenge white feminism." When the summer program first started, Talia expressed concern to Stephanie that the course on feminism might not have enough students enrolled for it to be offered. She was surprised when several dozen more students requested the course than could enroll; she was excited that she would have an opportunity to explore gender topics with high school students, but she soon noted that students' dominant notions of gender were not intersectional.

"I'm Having to Fight Them to See Gender as Multifaceted"

On the first day of the Feminism 101 class, Talia began by providing an historical overview of the various waves of the Women's Rights Movement. After she drew connections between abolitionist efforts and suffragettes, she noted for the students, "A number of people felt the need to delineate between fighting racism and fighting sexism, so if you were a woman of color, you got left in the cold." As she transitioned to the second and third waves of historical feminist efforts, she again pointed to the issue of, as she put it for her students:

> Forcing people to choose a cause – so, like, in the 1980s when gay rights became a bigger issue: If you were a lesbian, you had to pick whether you were fighting for your rights as a woman or your right to love someone of the same sex; or, for a long while, if you were a Black woman, people were insisting that you pick challenging racism or sexism.

As her lecture contextualizing women's rights moved to contemporary matters, she brought up the #BlackLivesMatter Movement and the U.S. Supreme Court's ruling for marriage equality as "definitely moments that we need to talk about in this class, if we're going to do feminism right."

A girl, who had identified herself as White, cisgender (a person who identifies as the gender corresponding to their sex assigned at birth), heterosexual, and upper-middle class in a questionnaire that Talia had asked them to complete, raised her hand. When Talia nodded to her, she said, "I mean, I'm all about equality. Like, I think everyone in this class wants stuff to be equal in society."

She paused and looked around the room, as several students nodded in agreement. The student continued:

> But this isn't a class about social justice in the broad sense. That stuff's important, definitely, but I don't get why we're talking about slavery, the AIDS epidemic, and all that stuff. Yeah, it happened, and yeah, a lot of that was terrible and wrong, *is* terrible, but I don't get that we need to talk about that other stuff if we were going to learn about feminism. I mean, we've only got a week for this class, so I want to make sure that I learn as much as I can about women's rights.

Another girl raised her hand, and when Talia nodded, the second student said, "Yeah, like, all that stuff matters. I mean, I have gay friends, and I come from a really diverse high school, but this is Feminism 101 – like, I want to talk about gender equality." Several other students nodded in agreement, and nearly every set of eyes shifted to Talia for her reaction.

Talia took a deep breath, clearly surprised by the students' responses. She told them,

> So, like I said when I was showing you information on the third wave of the Women's Rights Movement, feminism isn't just about gender, can't be just about gender. In fact, even if this class was a gender studies class instead of one on feminism, it still couldn't only focus on gender. Because gender is *always* in connection to other identities. Like [she gestured to the first student who had spoken] when people see you, they see a woman or a girl, but they also see the brands of clothing you're wearing, that you're White; they assume that you're interested in men, that you're cisgender – people take in a lot of information and make a lot of assumptions about you in just a few seconds, and only part of that is your gender.

Several students' expressions indicated doubt, and more students raised their hands. For the rest of class, Talia maintained the need to intersect gender with other identity elements and social issues, and most of the students – notably all White, cisgender, heterosexual women – continued to push back. After class, as Talia and Stephanie stood at the faculty copy machine, Talia sighed heavily and said,

> You know, I was really excited about this class, and I think that I still am, but damn – I'm having to fight them to see gender as multifaceted. I know that it's because a lot of them don't deal with racism in their daily lives, don't deal with homophobia or transphobia, don't deal with classism, don't deal with disabilities. So, their realities are supposed to be everyone's. I guess it's going to be a fight, but that's fine. They'll push, and I'll push back. We're not going to examine gender in isolation. It's not going to happen.

Returning to Crenshaw's notion of a single-axis mindset is helpful here. As Talia and her students worked to understand issues of gender, even as Talia worked to intersect gender with race, ethnicity, sexuality, class, and ability, most students rejected these connections. Like Crenshaw (2004) describes, this tendency to dismiss gender as intersectional promotes the interests and experiences of "otherwise-privileged members of the group" (p. 140). Those students who heavily advocated for a strict adherence to gender alone already benefited from racial, sexual, and class privileges. As White, cisgender, heterosexual, upper-middle class young women, they enjoyed but seemed unaware of the ways that multiple facets of their identities afforded them opportunities and mobility that women unlike them did not enjoy. After the second day of the class, Talia noted, "What we're dealing with here is White feminism – they think they're feminists because they want to discuss sexism, but they're limiting what feminism can mean by making it only work for people like them."

"We're Using Writing and Reading to Challenge White Feminism"

On the third day, and at the halfway point in the six-day-long course, Talia began to shift from the class as discussion-based to asking the students to engage in a range of literacy practices. "I had wanted this class to be a seminar-style class," she said during an interview, "but it just turns into them versus me, and that's not what I want at all. That's not getting them or me anywhere good." On the third day, as Stephanie observed, Talia told the students,

> Okay, we're going to try a different approach today. First, I'm passing around a short reading. It's Peggy McIntosh's (2003) "Unpacking the Invisible Knapsack." What I want you to do is this: as you read it, make a star beside any statements that, if you're really honest with yourself, are true for you, and then jot a brief note about an example of when that was true.

Students began scanning the handout and making notes. After several minutes, Talia told them,

> Okay, several of you have indicated the need to focus on gender issues rather than racial ones, and I get that. I understand where you're coming from. You saw this class's title and felt like you had a clear idea of what it was going to go on in here, and I've taken you in a new direction. So, all I'm asking is that you give me a chance to show you how these intersections matter to all of us. So, you marked McIntosh's article. I want you to pick one item where you had an example of it being true, just one, and I want you, in a narrative format, to describe that moment. Just be sure that you're willing to let peers read what you write. That's all that I ask.

After students had had several minutes to write, Talia told them,

> Okay, trade papers with someone not physically near you, and after you've done so, I want that person to imagine your example and rewrite it as if it's happening to someone a different gender than you. Like, how would that matter? What would change?

The activity continued, until students had rewritten the narrative while adding and shifting to a range of different perspectives, including race, gender identity and expression, first language, class, and sexual orientation. At the end of the activity, Talia invited discussion. The conversation was significantly different from previous days' discussion. The student who had insisted on the first day, "I don't get that we need to talk about that other stuff" said, "I think I get it now. Gender's important, but these other topics really do matter." The student pointed to the McIntosh handout, stating:

> Like #26 about having bandages that match my skin. Y'all, sometimes I seriously pick a particular brand because I want to wear cute shoes or something, and it never occurred to me that all women couldn't just do the same. Like, that's gender and race together, and it's super silly, I know, but it kind of blows my mind.

As the week progressed, Talia continued to ask students to use a range of literacy skills and abilities, including narrative writing, re-writing, journaling, and art-making to have students engage in the intersections of gender with a range of other identities and issues. The latter portion of the week starkly contrasted with the former, as students readily and thoughtfully engaged with intersectionalities in ways that they had initially resisted. Talia said during an interview:

> There's been a huge shift. I didn't change what I wanted them to discuss – the topics are basically the same; I changed what I wanted them to *do*. Like, when I started to bring in the reading and writing together, it was like a switch flipped. White feminism was such a huge problem – this inability to see that women who weren't like them weren't experiencing gender in the same ways that most of them were. Now, we're using writing and reading to challenge White feminism, and it's going so well. They really are getting the need for intersectionality now.

Implications for Literacy Education and Cross-Disciplinary Fields

Talia entered the summer program with lesson plans in place for her Feminism 101 course, a plan that nearly immediately diverted from the path she had anticipated.

Presenting feminist history through intersectionalities with racism, classism, heteronormativity, and transphobia initially were received by Talia's students as decentering gender and whiteness, the two positions with which they were most comfortable. Reflecting on the course, and being adaptable and willing to adjust shifted the space from one that was seminar-centered to one that allowed individuals to engage directly with a host of identities and issues through their own narrative-writing, rewriting, and journaling. There is a crucial need for exactly the kind of critical, reflexive, transformational pedagogy that Talia exhibited; one that is not often supported, as programs focus instead on assessment measures, lesson planning, and educational foundations. It is equally imperative that there are professional development opportunities that advance these notions for teachers and others working with youth around literacy, closely following Lytle's (2006) "expanded notion of practice," that encourages "a deep belief in teachers as leaders in their own classrooms, as makers of knowledge about teaching and learning, and a parallel conviction that the walls of classrooms do not delimit their commitments and responsibilities as educators" (p. 261). Marlinda White-Kaulaity (2006) writes that "teachers play a huge role as decision-maker, change agent, and as determiner of whose voices are heard and experienced in the classroom. Essentially, pedagogy rests on values, and value issues infuse every classroom" (p. 8). As Talia's experience with the summer program demonstrates, a teacher's constructions of gender, class, and race inform pedagogy, often in unexpected ways. In today's increasingly volatile political climate, it is more important than ever that spaces are created to allow for the inclusion of all voices.

As Talia's experiences clearly indicate just the inclusion of all voices in learning is not nearly enough. Parents, teachers, academics, researchers, and those who interact with young people need to be mindful of the intersectionalities of the very voices that safe spaces need to include. Creating spaces of inclusion without addressing the myriad intersectionalities of these voices creates a mere echo where there should be a chorus.

As youth confront their own privileges and begin to look at issues from intersections outside their own, they must also be prepared to consider how family and friends might perceive and receive their newfound knowledge. Ellsworth (2005) speaks of this in terms of a "crisis of learning" as individuals let go of who they were to make room for this newly evolving self (p. 89). Navigating these new intersectionalities and their inherent discoveries often forces young people to enter unfamiliar territory. The creation of inclusive spaces that allow for self-reflection and becoming comfortable with confronting the uncomfortable is a necessary, yet often forgotten variable within transformational learning.

Disrupting narratives of privilege involves discomfort for everyone when opening a space for contemplation – to challenge, to explain, and to possibly evolve to a new way of thinking. To minimize these intersections or to not include them all makes education not liberatory as envisioned, but instead creates violence in their very erasure. This erasure is performed every day and has become commonplace because it is not often questioned nor challenged by those who, from their position of privilege, do not even recognize the need to do so.

References

Blackburn, M. (2014). Exploring literacy performances and power dynamics at the loft: "Queer youth reading the world and the word." *Research in the Teaching of English, 37*(4), 467–490.

Brooks, C.E. (2012). Retrospective understandings: Individual-collective influences on high achieving black students at a predominantly white institution of higher education. *Journal of Ethnographic & Qualitative Research, 6*, 123–144.

Butler-Kisber, L. (2010). *Qualitative inquiry: Thematic, narrative, and arts-informed perspectives.* Thousand Oaks, CA: Sage.

Clark, C., Sapon-Shevin, M., Brimhall-Vargas, M., McGhie, T., & Nieto, S. (2017). Critical multicultural education as an analytical point of entry discussion of intersectional scholarship: A focus on race, as well as class, gender, sexuality, dis/ability, and family configuration. *Taboo: The Journal of Culture and Education, 16*(1), 92–122.

Compton-Lilly, C., Hamman, L, Papoi, K., Venegas, P., & Schwabenbauer, B. (2017). Intersectional identity negotiation: The case of young immigrant children. *Journal of Literacy Research, 49*(1), 115–140.

Crenshaw, K. (1989). Demarginalizing the intersection of race and sex: A Black feminist critique of antidiscrimination doctrine, feminist theory, and antiracist politics. *University of Chicago Legal Forum, 1*(8), 139–167.

Crenshaw, K. (1991). Mapping the margins: Intersectionality, identity politics, and violence against women of color, *Stanford Law Review, 43*, 1241–1299.

Crenshaw, K. (2004). Intersectionality: The double bind of race and gender. *Perspectives Magazine.* Retrieved from www.americanbar.org/content/dam/aba/publishing/perspectives_magazine/women_perspectives_Spring2004CrenshawPSP.authcheckdam.pdf.

Ellsworth, E. (2005). *Places of learning: Media, architecture, pedagogy.* New York, NY: Taylor & Francis.

Emerson, R.M., Fretz, R.I., & Shaw, L.L. (2011). *Writing ethnographic fieldnotes* (2nd ed.). Chicago, IL: University of Chicago Press.

Featherstone, Liza. (2016, November 12). Elite, white feminism gave us Trump: It needs to die. *Verso Books.* Retrieved from www.versobooks.com/blogs/2936-elite-white-feminism-gave-us-trump-it-needs-to-die.

Harris, Tamara Winfrey (2016, November 16). Some of us are brave: The failure of white feminism. *Bitch Media.* Retrieved from www.bitchmedia.org/article/some-us-are-brave-0.

Harter, J., Castor, M., Seigler, C.P., & Abrahams, D. (2018). Navigating identity and privilege in multifaith engagement on a college campus. *Journal of College and Character, 19*(1), 4–17.

Koonce, J.B. (2012). "Oh, those loud black girls!": A phenomenological study of black girls talking with an attitude. *Journal of Language and Literacy Education, 8*(2). Retrieved from http://jolle.coe.uga.edu/wp-content/uploads/2012/10/Loud-Black-Girls.pdf.

Lavrakas, P.J. (2008). Conversational interviewing. In P.J. Lavrakas (Ed.), *Encyclopedia of survey research methods* (p. 152). Thousand Oaks, CA: Sage.

Lytle, S.L. (2006). The literacies of teaching urban adolescents in these times. In D.E. Alvermann, K.A. Hinchman, D.W. Moore, S.F. Phelps, & D.R. Waff (Eds.), *Reconceptualizing the literacies in adolescents' lives* (2nd ed., pp. 257–277). Mahwah, NJ: Lawrence Erlbaum.

McCloud, R.F., Jung, M., Gray, S.W., & Viswanath, K. (2013). Class, race and ethnicity and information avoidance among cancer survivors. *Journal of Cancer, 108*(10), 1949–1956.

McIntosh, P. (2003). White privilege: Unpacking the invisible knapsack. In S. Plous (Ed.), *Understanding prejudice and discrimination* (pp. 191–196). New York, NY: McGraw-Hill.

Mayo, C. (2014). *LGBTQ youth and education: Policies and practices.* New York, NY: Teachers College Press.

Miller, sj (2013). The broader contexts of bullying. In sj Miller, L.D. Burns, & T.S. Johnson (Eds.), *Generation bullied 2.0: Prevention and intervention strategies for our most vulnerable students* (pp. 131–145). New York, NY: Peter Lang.

Muhammad, G.E., & Haddix, M. (2016). Centering black girls' literacies: A review of literature on the multiple ways of knowing black girls. *National Council of Teachers of English, 48*(4), 299–336.

Price-Dennis, D. (2016). Developing curriculum to support black girls' literacies in digital spaces. *English Education, 48*(4), 337–361.

Rhodan, M., & Johnson, D. (2016, November 8). Here are 7 electoral college predictions for Tuesday. *Time.* Retrieved from http://time.com/4561625/electoral-college-predictions.

Scott, E. (2017, September 28). Millions of American women disagree with Michelle Obama: Donald Trump is their voice. *Washington Post.* Retrieved from www.washingtonpost.com/news/the-fix/wp/2017/09/28/millions-of-american-women-disagree-with-michelle-obama-donald-trump-is-their-voice/?tid=sm_fb&utm_term=.90789a3d4abd.

Shelton, S.A. (2018). From invisible, to ho, to magic: A narrative examination of the ways that literacies disenfranchise and empower Black girls. *Journal of Black Sexuality and Relationships, 4*(1), 3–24.

Shelton, S.A., & Melchior, S. (2018, in press). Valuing students' responses to implement a social justice pedagogy: A descriptive case study. *Journal of Language and Literacy Education, 14*(2).

Smith, P. (1999). Teaching the retrenchment generation: When Sapphire meets Socrates at the intersection of race, gender, and authority. *William and Mary Journal of Women and the Law, 6,* 53–65.

Talwar, S. (2010). An intersectional framework for race, class, gender, and sexuality in art therapy. *Art Therapy: Journal of the American Art Therapy Association, 27*(1), 11–17.

Tefera, A.A., Powers, J.M., & Fischman, G.E. (2018). Intersectionality in education: A conceptual aspiration and research imperative. *Review of Research in Education, 42*(1), vii–xvii.

Westcott, L. (2016, November 8). Presidential election polls for November 8, 2016. *Newsweek.* Retrieved from www.newsweek.com/polls-2016-presidential-election-trump-clinton-518280.

White-Kaulaity, M. (2006). The voices of power and the power of voices: Teaching with Native American literature. *The Alan Review,* Fall, pp. 8–16.

Wood, L., Soudien, C., & Reddy, V. (2016). Shaping social literacy through HIV in higher education curricula. *South African Journal of Higher Education, 30*(4), 156–170.

9

HOW GENDER AND INTERSECTIONALITY INFORM ADOLESCENT LITERACY

Kathleen A. Hinchman and Donna E. Alvermann

Multiple recent studies have described how youth enact such elements of identity as gender, race, ethnicity, and class as they communicate with one another in myriad social networks (e.g., Ehret, Hollet, & Jocius, 2016; Paris, 2010). This research results in recommendations that ask teachers to design literacy instruction that recognizes, respects, and responds to variations in youths' literacy practices (Alim, 2011; Duncan-Andrade & Mörrell, 2008), celebrates their counter-stories and out-of-school literacies (Kinloch, 2012; Yosso, 2005), or invites them to draw on their cultural resources to understand and reshape academic content through their eyes (Gutiérrez, Morales, & Martinez, 2009; Moje 2015). The similarities in instructional implications across these youth-oriented studies can sound like "just good teaching" to naïve readers who do not attend to the cultural nuances of the recommendations (Haddix, 2017; Miller, 2016). This, in turn, can marginalize youth whose identities do not well align with the identities of majority youth, including those whose race and gender identification doubly set them apart from their peers (Crenshaw, 2016).

An important construct, "intersectionality," was developed by Black feminist scholars to account for Black females' unique experiences of oppression at the *intersection* of race and gender to acknowledge the cultural dimensions of these women's experiences in more explicit ways (Cooper, 2015). This chapter draws on this construct to note that attention to the intersection of varied aspects of marginalized youths' identity with gender can help us to understand the oppressions they face from school and community literacy practices in new ways. The chapter begins by describing the origins and commitments of the analytic framework known as intersectionality. The chapter then draws on four studies of adolescent literacy to illustrate the commitments of intersectionality. The chapter ends with a discussion of how analyses that are true to the commitments of this construct can inform understandings of gender and adolescent literacy and provide a path to disrupting at least some aspects of inequity tied to adolescent literacy.

As this chapter's authors, we acknowledge at its outset that we are white, heterosexual, female scholars. We came of age in the relatively early days of large-scale female participation in the academy, experiencing both gender bias and microaggressions along with the privilege of our racial identification. Our understandings of intersectionality are necessarily limited by these experiences.

Origins and Commitments of Intersectionality

Almost three decades ago, Black feminist legal scholar, Kimberlé Crenshaw (1989), introduced the term, intersectionality, into the lexicon of legal scholars. Crenshaw used the term to critique antidiscrimination law, feminist theory, and antiracist politics that treated "race and gender as mutually exclusive categories of experience and analysis" (p. 139). She showed how scholarship tended to focus on the experiences of one or another of the more privileged members of each of the two categories, White women and Black men. This circumstance was likely exacerbated by the historical fact that "protection of white female sexuality was often the pretext for terrorizing the Black community" (p. 160) with lynching and other violence. These emphases effectively erased the systemic oppressions that were uniquely experienced by Black women. Crenshaw's framework instead highlighted Black women's position at the intersection of gender and race to more precisely name the location of their oppression and, thus, counter their marginalization.

More recently, Crenshaw (2016) explained that usage of the term had spread widely from these origins in Black feminism and critical race scholarship to many other areas of the social sciences concerned with identity issues. Patricia Hill Collins (2015) joined Sirma Bilge (2013) and other critical race scholars to critique recent appropriations of the term, describing misrepresentative and tokenistic applications that seemed to have lost sight of the construct's origins in Black feminist thought. Ann-Marie Núñez (2014) also critiqued analyses that emphasized individuality but ignored how systemic forces that perpetuate inequity oppress some individuals and not others. Núñez explained that reference to intersectionality should invite exploration of "how individuals experience privilege, marginalization, or both, according to various combinations of social categories" (pp. 85–86). This explicit anti-oppression orientation makes intersectionality theory different from feminist sociology or poststructural theories of multiple subjectivities, which describe how people's subjectivities push back against others' attempts to identify them as they move across discourse communities (Wheedon, 1997). Power is said to circulate in these enactments, too, but scholarship in this area does not typically explore how some social structures are calcified in ways that persistently privilege some groups of people while damaging others.

Women and gender studies scholar, Vivian May (2015), also acknowledged the misappropriations of intersectionality. May argued that intersectionality analyses would be more aligned with Crenshaw's original usage by recognizing and working against the patterns of oppression that result when the knowledge and power generated within social systems collide in individuals' experiences, creating dominant and subordinate relationships tied to gender, race, and class. She explained, "Intersectionality is a form of resistant knowledge developed to unsettle conventional mindsets, challenge oppressive power, think through the full architecture of structural inequalities and asymmetrical life opportunities, and seek a more just world" (p. xi). As a result, May suggested that studies in pursuit of intersectionality should maintain four deep commitments that were evident in Crenshaw's original work. These included commitments to an anti-subordination orientation, to meaningful engagement with human beings' inherent heterogeneity and divergence, to reading against the grain of dominant descriptions and oppressive structures, and to setting aside normative assumptions associated with identity categories.

Intersectionality, Gender, and Adolescent Literacy

Literacy scholars have long noted the seemingly gendered nature of adolescents' literacy practices. Early scholars in this area, like Margaret Finders (1997) and Meredith Cherland (1994), described girls' writing and reading, and Josephine Young (2000) and Michael Smith and Jeffrey Wilhelm (2002) described boys' enactments of masculinity in connection with literacy, though this scholarship was critiqued as being over-general, smoothing over difference within and across individuals to make assertions about boys and girls in general (Martino & Kehler, 2007). Recent studies have offered more complex renderings in an effort to counter critiques of essentialism (Franzak, 2006). For instance, Sarroub and Pernicek (2014) described how three boys' negative experiences with teachers, school academic and social structures, and relationships at home situated them as "struggling readers," but with significant differences among them. Delicia Greene (2016) explained that the Black girls in her study drew on their experiences, knowledge of society's neglect of Black girls, and social norms around literacy to create self-representations in a book club discussion. Latrise P. Johnson (2017) described how three Black queer youth navigated and interrupred literacy normativity through writing about themselves in an after-school book club.

sj Miller (2016) explained that use of the term "gender" to represent a unitary construct was troublesome, especially for individuals committed to queer theory. Miller described why being identified in terms of one's gender versus another could be particularly problematic for individuals for whom, "gender is fluid, or exists on a continuum, shifting over time and in different contexts" (p. 36). Some individuals identify as neither male nor female, which can be challenging for them when school and community literacy practices appreciate only traditional representations of gender as male or female.

Literacy is grounded in communication skills that grow from the normative structures of participants' discourse communities (Barton, 2008). Symbols represent language in varying ways, and recent research has begun to show how some individuals do not have easy access to important aspects of these systems via instruction. In the United States, for instance, male secondary school students of color may be seen as uncooperative, which can sorely undercut their opportunities for literacy support in school (Frankel, 2016). Exploring how the lived experiences of individuals situate them as disadvantaged at the intersection of gender, race, and literacy can yield added insight into the inequity experienced by some individuals in richer, more complex ways.

Of course, intersectionality-implicated literacy marginalization pales in comparison to the genocide experienced across the globe by people of color, often because of intersections with gender and sexual identification. However, lack of literacy and deficit-driven literacy instruction as it is experienced by some individuals position them as "less than" in ways that become enscribed on them, and that diminish their social futures. Such marginalization is exacerbated, as Frankel (2016) notes, at intersections of race, class, and gender.

Adolescent Literacy Studies Illustrating Commitments to Intersectionality's Origins

In this section, we summarize four studies that explored intersections of various aspects of identity with gender and adolescent literacy. We selected these studies as exemplars of the original anti-oppressive commitments attributed to Crenshaw and others, although we note the studies did not necessarily explicitly claim an intersectional lens. In our view each of these studies attended to all four of the commitments as May described them. Our summaries focus on each commitment in turn to delineate how attending to them adds to existing insights about gender and adolescents' literacies.

Anti-Subordination Orientation

In 2015, Gholnecsar E. Muhammad published a study in *Research in the Teaching of English* that explored the writings of eight urban African American adolescent girls ages 12 to 17. Entitled "Searching for Full Vision: Writing Representations of African American Girls," the article was grounded in sociohistorical and critical sociocultural theories. The girls referenced in the article's title were participants in an extracurricular literacy collaborative with goals of advancing their literacy proficiencies, making sense of their identities as African American females, nurturing their intellectual development, and helping them to gain authority over print via reading texts about inequities experienced by people like them and writing responses. Muhammad modeled varied ways to do this, sharing her writing publically as the girls did the same. Data included 16 pre- and post-collaborative interviews, 48 writing artifacts, daily participant-observation memoranda, and 33 hours of video observations.

The line-by-line thematic analysis, axial coding, and member checks considered how historically embedded dominant discourses were reflected in the girls' writings about identity, power, and agency. These youths used various forms of writing to correct popular negative community, cultural, individual, intellectual, kinship, and sexual representations of their identities. The analysis demonstrated how these youths' writing mirrored themes of African American women writers, like Mary Helen Washington and Anna Julia Cooper, who wrote against dominant discourses that silenced or pathologized them. This included writing to represent self, writing to resist or counter ascribed negative representations, and writing toward social change.

Muhammad's study design seemed an especially good example of the anti-subordination orientation May attributed to Crenshaw and her colleagues. Muhammad's approach treated the young people, their literacies, and their heterogeneity respectfully, suggesting that neither they nor their expressive literacies should be subordinated. Moreover, her intervention invited the young people to improve their writing even as they also learned to interrogate popular cultural stereotypes of people "like them," question normalized, colonial historical frames of African American women, and engage in the anti-normative action of developing literacy skills needed to fulfill life aspirations. She presented persuasive evidence for instructional practices that, like hers, could legitimize and build from youths' worldviews, teaching them to counter negative stereotypes. This argument contributes to research that suggests the agentive possibilities inherent in adolescent literacies developed at the intersection of gender and race – as opposed to research focused on developing narrowly conceived ideals of academic or personal writing whose purposes are not well understood by youth.

Meaningful Engagement with Heterogeneity and Divergence

In an article entitled "From Aquí to Allá: Symbolic Convergence in the Multimodal Literacy Practices of Adolescent Immigrant Students," which appeared in the 2014 *Journal of Literacy Research*, Michelle A. Honeyford conducted a study that approached meaningful engagement with heterogeneity and diversity that May described. This inquiry examined a multimodal photo essay completed by seventh- and eighth-grade immigrant students in an English as a New Language (ENL) class. The idea for the study emerged as a result of an ENL teacher's taking seriously her six students' concerns that they felt ill-prepared to enter high school. Beth, the teacher, worked with the six students to create a multimodal photo essay that was the culminating project of what the students called "the culture project." The study is an example of how intersectionality can inform literacy pedagogies when students' transnational cultural identities become the focus of inquiry and instruction.

Honeyford used the notion of symbolic convergence to explain her analysis. This concept was developed by Jenkins (2006) to reference how the roles of producer and consumer often blend into one in today's highly technologized media society (e.g., think iMovie or any of the more advanced apps that provide for creating, distributing, and consuming simultaneously). Honeyford analyzed data sources collected in a photo essay project to show how the group of six immigrant students' diasporic identities enabled them to appreciate their within-group differences. By acknowledging their already developing sense of hybrid identities, the students noted that they were better prepared to meet the challenges of moving into a new high school. Rather than being left with the identity of outsiders about to enter a pre-established culture that consisted of students who likely had read the same novels, attended the same movies, or listened to the same songs, Beth's group of six students, like Muhammad's in the previous study, was collectively able to reconceptualize their agency by representing symbolically through their photo essay how, as a hybrid youth group, they each had alternative identities to bring to the table. In this regard, Guerra's (2007) transcultural repositioning principle worked hand in hand with intersectionality's attention to how what is missed or left out of a curriculum initially need not remain invisible.

Opportunities to engage meaningfully with heterogeneity and divergence, as Honeyford did in her study, provide windows into how within-group differences manifest themselves in larger contexts. Experiences in navigating the local before attempting to do the same in larger contexts (e.g., entering a new school context) have implications for literacy instruction and beyond. For instance, transnational flows of people reflect physical border crossings as well as emotional and cultural ones. In an age when access to high-speed Internet coupled with an appropriate application can mediate a newcomer's anxiety, engaging with heterogeneity and diversity is a common occurrence.

Reading Against the Grain

In another 2015 article from *Research in the Teaching of English*, "'It's Like a Script': Long-Term English Learners' Experiences with and Ideas about Academic Reading," Maneka D. Brooks drew on Grosjean's (2008) conceptualization of people who use multiple languages, reading against the grain of an "idealized version of monolingual 'native speaker' proficiency in both languages" (p. 390). Brooks collected ethnographic observations in English language arts and biology classes, as well as multiple interviews with each of the five bilingual focal students. Her analysis described multiple social constructs and their relationships, including the youths' ethnicity as long-term English language learners, and instructional reading events, noting blurred lines across spheres of influence. This provided evidence for her critique of normative deficit notions that seemed to be held about the girls and their language abilities, as well as normative notions of suitable instruction given the nature of expected outcomes.

Brooks' study also showed how these young people were asked to subordinate their literacy expertise to a pervasive monolingual examination-driven school culture. Ironically, the instructional practice the youth most often experienced did not map onto the literacy expectations of this culture: Youth were usually asked to read aloud even though assessments of their reading required silent reading with discussion that authorized teachers' text interpretations over the students' interpretations.

The study's grounding in Grosjean's (2008) nonmonological approach to representing multilingual expertise was a deliberate effort to address what May (2015) called "epistemological injustice" (p. 238), in this case the grounding of "common sense" U.S. notions of multilingualism as deficient. The study's approach acknowledged the "'incommensurability' between speaking positions and worldviews" with an openness toward "opaque possibilities" "not explainable on conventional terms." The study worked what May described as the "intersectional matrix" (p. 239) and, as such, it allowed her, and readers, to recognize mismatches between espoused instructional goals and school tasks. This grounding makes Brooks' piece useful as an example of the intersectionality commitment to following opacities to read against the grain of normative structures. As such, it contributes novel views of youths' perspectives on the sedimentation of illogical instructional practice.

Setting Aside Norm Emulation

Mollie V. Blackburn and Caroline T. Clark published "Analyzing Talk in a Long-Term Literature Discussion Group: Ways of Operating within LGBT-Inclusive and Queer Discourse," in *Reading Research Quarterly* in 2011. This three-year study was conducted with participants in a lesbian/gay/bisexual/transgender (LGBT)-inclusive book group in a youth center. Half of the participants identified as lesbian, gay/bisexual, transgender, queer, questioning (LGBTQQ) and involved the youth in selecting and discussing books on LGBT-inclusive topics. They reviewed 18 transcripts of discussions of 24 books over three years using an ethnographic framework that Kamberelis and Dimitriadis (2005) developed from the work of Michel Foucault (1972) called knowledge/power defamilarization logic. The Kamberelis and Dimitriadis framework allowed the researchers to consider the nature of the book talk and whether the youths' discourse was liberatory and/or oppressive.

Blackburn and Clark (2011) discovered that elements of each discussion could be connected to one or more of the following norm groups: homophobia, homonormativity, and heteronormativity. Intersectionality's commitment to setting aside norm emulation was evident in that no discussion was a monolithic representation of any one norm group. Instead, intersectionality was the norm group, a finding that was useful to conducting discussions that were provocative but that did not shut down communication. An example from the Blackburn and Clark study that challenged May's commitment to setting aside norm emulation was an instance in which assumptions about single-axis logics were exposed. For example, consider the positionality of the individual who identified as following a homonarrative storyline – until he felt compelled to come out to straight friends in a manner that belied the comfort level he had assumedly experienced in being identified as queer in a homonarrative grouping.

Discussion

Studies of adolescents' literacy practices, like those described in this chapter, implicate gender and varied intersectionalities that can locate individuals as "less than" in schools and communities. All four studies maintained commitments true to the advocacy-oriented origins of intersectionality that May (2015) described. Their anti-subordination orientation, heterogeneity and divergence, reading against the grain, and setting aside normative assumptions, yielded more complex understandings of inequities that are embedded in literacy practices in school and across communities. These analyses also offered important insights for developing more inclusive approaches to adolescent literacy that acknowledge intersectionality rather than ignore it. When adolescent literacy scholars describe pedagogical moves that recognize and advance youths' ability to use literacies to push against their intersectional positions in society, their actions can also foster the youths' sense of agency, including the ability to disrupt the social order.

That said, naming points of intersectionality with two or three big categories could be viewed as ironic, putting a pin down on new identity categories that may colonize further those who are standing at these points in new ways. Moreover, it was not clear from the studies we described whether all the youths who participated in them felt well represented by the rhetoric used to describe them. "Girl," "African American," "queer," "immigrant," and "new speaker of English" are labels that can be just as delimiting as other labels. Scholars or others describing or working with adolescents should check with the individuals with whom they work about such representations.

Implications for Literacy Education and Cross-Disciplinary Fields

Exploring how historically grounded notions of intersectionality are reflected in research on gender and adolescent literacy allows limitations in many earlier studies' conceptualizations of adolescent literacy to become visible, in addition to highlighting the limits of many available literacy-related educational opportunities. Many such studies referred to such social aspects of young peoples' lives as age and race, but without noting others, such as gender identification, class, or sexual preference, and without understanding how intersectionality led to variations in youths' literacy practices or positioning as a result of these variations.

How can research on intersectionality, gender, and adolescent literacy offer support to teachers and others involved with adolescent literacy when most youth populations are more complex, intersectionality-speaking, than were contexts of the studies we reviewed in this chapter? That is, most schools and community-based programs do not just teach African American girls, like Muhammad did, or queer-sympathetic youth, like Blackburn and Clark. Indeed, many youth populations are incredibly diverse, including immigrants from many places who work alongside African American, European American, and mixed-race youth who conceivably also represent a full range of sexual identities. Even classrooms filled with students who appear to look alike hide much unrecognized intersectionality and accompanying oppressions with relative differences in degree and privilege. Gutiérrez and Penuel (2014) have noted that promising literacy instructional practices that seem to welcome heterogeneity are dialogic, grounded in youths' strengths, and advocacy oriented. The pedagogical features delineated at the outset of this chapter – literacy instruction that responds to variations in youths' literacy practices, celebrates their counter-stories and out-of-school literacies, or invites them to draw on their cultural resources to reshape academic content – can be orchestrated in a way that is true to Gutiérrez and Penuel's recommendation. But to be true to the commitments of intersectionality, they must be orchestrated in ways that make obvious to the youth through a range of individual and group interactions that their viewpoints, resources, and ways of being are expected, welcomed, and integral to the instruction and its anticipated outcomes.

Researchers who examine literacy practices in schools and communities can continue to detail the limitations, biases, and oppressions associated with the intersecting social identities of marginalized youth, including those who are marginalized by intersections of race, gender, dis/ability, ethnicity, or class. Practitioners in school and in out-of-school community contexts can work with researchers to develop project-based critical literacy teaching that appreciates and works to disrupt the ways individuals' multiple social locations position them as disadvantaged or advantaged in social hierarchies. However, May (2015, p. 15) offers the following caution about such research:

> Researchers may set out to do an intersectional study, but will not use intersectionality as an analytic lens to shape questions, design research models, or interpret data: it will, instead, be used only as a demographic or descriptive device (see Choo & Ferree, 2010; Harnois, 2013; Shields, 2008). In this way, its explanatory, political, and analytical capacities are abandoned: intersectionality is transmogrified into a descriptor of "difference," with no apparent utility for unpacking normative logics or challenging the workings of power and privilege therein. In fact, the sheer number of "slippages" away from intersectionality is fairly astounding, whether in critical or applied contexts.

This chapter demonstrates how expanding the meaningfulness of studies of gender and adolescent literacy involves explicit acknowledgment of the cultural nuances of the studies. Employing an intersectional lens requires recognizing how young people's social locations have material impact on their lived experiences. Who youths are, how they enact agency, and what they find important vary considerably by their mostly invisible intersectionalities. Making intersectionality visible can yield heightened understanding of oppressions and provide needed attention for encouraging young people's agency in the face of these oppressions. Use of an intersectional lens can highlight how youths' individualistic intersectional experiences with literacy practices situate them in society, and enable them to counter hegemonic practices and gain heightened equity.

References

Alim, H.S. (2011). Global ill-literacies: Hip-hop cultures, youth identities, and the politics of literacy. *Research in the Teaching of English, 35,* 120–146.

Barton, D. (2008). *Literacy: An introduction to the ecology of written language.* Hoboken, NJ: Wiley-Blackwell.

Bilge, S. (2013). Intersectionality undone: Saving intersectionality from feminist intersectionality studies. *Du Bois Review, 10*(2), 405–424.

Blackburn, M.V., & Clark, C.T. (2011). Analyzing talk in a long-term literature discussion group: Ways of operating within LGBT-inclusive and queer discourses. *Reading Research Quarterly, 46*(3), 222–248.

Brooks, M.D. (2015). "It's like a script": Long-term English learners' experiences with and ideas about academic reading. *Research in the Teaching of English, 49*(4), 383–406.

Cherland, M., (1994). *Private practices: Girls reading fiction and constructing identity.* New York, NY: Taylor & Francis.

Choo, H.Y., & Ferree, M.M. (2010). Practicing intersectionality in sociological research: A critical analysis of inclusions, interactions, and institutions in the study of inequalities. *Sociological Theory, 28*(2), 129–149.

Cooper, B. (2015). Intersectionality. In L. Disch & M. Hawkesworth (Eds.), *The Oxford handbook of feminist theory.* Oxford, UK: Oxford University Press. doi: 10.1093/oxfor dhb/9780199328581.013.20

Crenshaw, K.W. (1989). Demarginalizing the intersection of race and sex: A black feminist critique of antidiscrimination doctrine, feminist theory and antiracist politics. *Chicago Legal Forum, 140,* 139–167.

Crenshaw, K.W. (2016, October). The urgency of intersectionality. *TedWomen 2016.* Retrieved from www.ted.com/talks/kimberle_crenshaw_the_urgency_of_intersectionality.

Duncan-Andrade, J., & Morrell, E. (2008). *The art of critical pedagogy: Possibilities for moving from theory to practice in urban schools.* New York, NY: Peter Lang.

Ehret, C., Hollet, T., & Jocius, R. (2016). The matter of new meaning-making: An intra-action analysis of adolescents making a digital book trailer. *Journal of Literacy Research, 43*(3), 346–377.

Finders, M. (1997). *Just girls: Hidden literacies and life in junior high.* New York, NY: Teachers College Press.

Foucault, M. (1972). *The archaeology of knowledge and the discourse on language* (A.M.S. Smith, Trans.). New York, NY: Pantheon.

Frankel, K.K. (2016). The intersection of reading and identity in high school literacy intervention classes. *Research in the Teaching of English, 51*(1), 37–56.

Franzak, J.K. (2006). Zoom: A review of the literature on marginalized adolescent readers, literacy theory, and policy implication. *Review of Educational Research, 76*(2), 209–248.

Greene, D.T. (2016). We need more "us" in schools! Centering Black adolescent girls' literacy and language practices in online school spaces. *Journal of Negro Education, 85*(3), 274–289.

Grosjean, F. (2008). *Studying bilinguals.* Oxford, UK: Oxford University Press.

Guerra, J. (2007). Out of the valley: Transcultural repositioning as a rhetorical practice in ethnographic research and other aspects of everyday life. In C. Lewis, P. Enciso, & E.B. Moje (Eds.), *Reframing sociocultural research on literacy: Identity, agency, and power* (pp. 137–162). Mahwah, NJ: Lawrence Erlbaum.

Gutiérrez, K.D., Morales, P.Z., & Martinez, D.C. (2009). Re-mediating literacy: Culture, difference, and learning for students from nondominant communities. *Review of Research in Education, 33*(1), 212–245.

Gutiérrez, K.D., & Penuel, W.R. (2014). Relevance to practice as a criterion for rigor. *Educational Researcher, 43*(1), 19–23.

Haddix, M. (2017, November). Discussant remarks. Symposium presented at the annual meeting of the Literacy Research Association, Tampa, FL.

Harnois, C.E. (2013). *Feminist measures in survey research.* Thousand Oaks, CA: Sage.

Hill Collins, P. (2015). Intersectionality's definitional dilemmas. *Annual Review of Sociology, 41*, 1–20.

Honeyford, M.A. (2014). From aqui to allá: Symbolic convergence in the multimodal literacy practices of adolescent immigrant students. *Journal of Literacy Research, 46*(2), 194–233.

Jenkins, H. (2006). *Convergence culture: Where old and new media collide.* New York, NY: New York University Press.

Johnson, L.P. (2017). Writing the self: Black queer youth challenge heteronormative ways of being in an after school writing club. *Research in the Teaching of English, 52*(1), 13–33.

Kamberelis, G., & Dimitriadis, G. (2005). *On qualitative inquiry: Approaches to language and literacy research.* New York, NY: Teachers College Press.

Kinloch, V. (2012). *Crossing boundaries: Teaching and learning with urban youth.* New York, NY: Teachers College Press.

Martino, W., & Kehler, M. (2007). Gender-based literacy reform: A question of challenging or recuperating gender binaries. *Canadian Journal of Education, 30*(2), 406–431.

May, V.M. (2015). *Pursuing intersectionality: Unsettling dominant imaginaries.* New York, NY: Routledge.

Miller, sj. (2016). *Teaching, affirming, and recognizing trans and gender creative youth: A queer literacy framework.* New York, NY: Palgrave Macmillan.

Moje E.B. (2015). Doing and teaching disciplinary literacy with adolescent learners: A social and cultural enterprise. *Harvard Educational Review, 85*(2), 254–278.

Muhammad, G.E. (2015). Searching for full vision: Writing representations of African American adolescent girls. *Research in the Teaching of English, 49*(3), 224–247.

Núñez, A.M. (2014). Employing multilevel intersectionality in educational research: Latino identities, contexts, and college access. *Educational Researcher, 43*(2), 85–92.

Paris, D. (2010). Texting identities: Lessons for classrooms from multiethnic youth space. *English Education, 42*(3), 278–292.

Sarroub, L.K., & Pernicek, T. (2014). Boys, books, and boredom: A case of three high school boys and their encounters with literacy. *Reading and Writing Quarterly, 32,* 27–59.

Shields, S.A. (2008). Gender: An intersectionality perspective. *Sex Roles, 59*(5–6), 301–311.

Smith, M., & Wilhelm, J. (2002). *Reading don't fix no Chevys: Literacy in the lives of young men.* Portsmouth, NH: Heinemann.

Wheedon, C. (1997). *Feminist practice and poststructural theory* (2nd ed.). Hoboken, NJ: Wiley-Blackwell.

Yosso, T.J. (2005). Whose culture has capital? A critical race theory discussion of community cultural wealth. *Race Ethnicity and Education, 8*(1), 69–91.

Young, J.P. (2000). Boy talk: Critical literacy and masculinities. *Reading Research Quarterly, 35*(3), 312–337.

10

"OUTSIDE VOICES"

Justice-System Involved Adolescent Males Writing Their Identities

Thomas W. Bean, Judith Dunkerly-Bean, Barbara J. Guzzetti, and Julia Morris

In this chapter, we consider the written narratives of two justice-system involved youth who were awaiting sentencing in a co-educational residential group home in the southeastern United States. Each week, we held writing groups focused on their life stories and interests to create zines (self-publications created as alternatives to commercial magazines) featuring hip-hop lyrics, and sketches about their lives outside of the justice system. As part of a year-long critical ethnography (Madison, 2005) we share the stories of two youth – Dino and Marc (pseudonyms). Dino was a 17-year-old African American, while Marc was 18 and White. We frame their stories from the theoretical perspective of masculine theory and the performance of masculinity (Bean & Harper, 2007; Bean, Dunkerly-Bean, & Harper, 2014). For example, Noguera (2008) argues that, "black males learn at an early age that by presenting a tough exterior, it is easier to avoid threats or attacks" (p. 41).

The purpose of the overarching study was to explore how justice-system involved youth (pre-adjudicated) read, respond, and create alternative multimodal texts, such as zines, hip-hop lyrics, sketches and other arts-based responses to issues that are important in their lives. "A zine is a handmade, amateur publication that focuses on the particular interests of the publisher" (Gustavson, 2007, p. 29). Zines are typically produced as handcrafted hard copies that use photocopying and cut, paste, and staple construction (Guzzetti, & Lesley, 2017). The topics in zines can range from fan-fiction to social issues and parodies of popular culture. Zines, as well as sketches and lyric composition, offer a creative platform where youth have agency and voice to interpret and re-interpret issues, concerns, and ideas that matter to them. As incarcerated youth, both Dino and Marc's writing offers a candid and critical account of their life circumstances, including poverty, gang affiliation, armed robbery, and passing time in the crisis center awaiting their court cases. As the following statistics indicate, Dino and Marc are not alone.

The School-to-Prison Pipeline

Youth incarceration in the state in which this study took place includes 24 detention centers, 18 group homes, and two youth prisons (Durnan & Harvell, 2017). The public school system in this state has the highest number of student referrals to the juvenile justice system in the country. Black youth are overrepresented in the system and account for 71% of all admissions. The human and material costs are staggering. For example, the state spends more than $170,000 to incarcerate a youth offender for one year (Durnan & Harvell, 2017). The greatest percentage of crimes resulting in incarceration center on felony offenses (95%), particularly crimes against a person, and males dominate this figure at 93%. Adding to these dismal figures, Durnan and Harvell (2017) noted that: A significant proportion of youth committed to the Department of Juvenile Justice care recidivate" (p. 8) and "nearly four in every five were arrested for a new offense within three years" (p. 8).

At the national level, justice system-involved youth often do not have access to contemporary, high-quality educational opportunities compared to non-incarcerated youth (Farn & Adams, 2016). Despite the fact that less than 20% of youth attain a General Education Diploma (GED) while in custody, those that do are less likely to fall back into old patterns and be incarcerated yet again. In addition, other factors including poverty, truancy, trauma, and criminal behavior conspire to inhibit forward movement in school. Researchers have explored various ways to change the school-to-prison reality for far too many youth. The statistics are daunting yet there are promising programs aimed at disrupting the school-to-prison pipeline. This is no small task, as America has been called the "world's largest jailer, with 2.3 million people behind bars, or one in one hundred adults" (Dreisinger, 2016, p. 8).

Positionality of the Researchers

It is into this social context that we began our research into offering engaging pedagogies for youth aged 13 to 18 in a residential detention center located in an urban area of the southeastern United States. Two of us, local university literacy faculty in a college of education, were invited to visit three residential detention centers and create tutorial services for incarcerated youth who were perceived to be struggling readers. It became readily apparent to us in these initial visits where we observed existing tutoring practices that reading difficulties were rarely in evidence, despite the reportedly poor school-based literacy performance of the youth being held there. We were somewhat surprised by this due to the widely reported statistics that many incarcerated individuals struggle with literacy – yet another obstacle to success on the outside (Dreisinger, 2016; Farn & Adams, 2016).

In addressing our positionality as researchers, we are all White and from middle-class backgrounds. Judith's and Tom's research has focused on youth experiences at the intersection of social justice and literacy practices (e.g., Dunkerly-Bean, Bean, & Alnajjar, 2014). Both have had family members or close friends involved in the criminal justice system. Barbara is a professor from the southwestern United States who is well versed in studying how zines (low-cost do it-yourself publications) can be created to tell a life story to an expanded audience. She used Skype to join our sessions at the site. Julia is a white female doctoral student who became a favorite at the site because the residents felt comfortable confiding in her.

Our Perspectives

The sociocultural theories underpinning this research include Foucault's (1980) notions of speaking back to power, Gore's (1998) views on disciplining bodies, and sustainable pedagogies (Gutierrez, 2016), as well as youth critical literacies and multimodal arts (Bakhtin, 1986; Jocson, 2014; Rogers, Winters, Perry, & Lamonde, 2015). In addition, we viewed masculinity as a social performance that may range from day-to-day spaces where extreme masculine performance is called for (e.g., on the street), as well as forms of masculinity where sensitivity and emotions may be freely expressed through art, or in the case of this study, creating zines. As Jewkes and her colleagues (2015, p. 97) state:

> Masculinities are multiple, fluid and dynamic and hegemonic positions are not the only masculinities available in a given society. They may also be seen as positions that are occupied situationally, in that the position occupied, practices and values espoused in one context may be different from those of another.

In the center setting, however, masculinity was often an identity performance that reified a particular style of acting cool and street-wise (Bean & Ransaw, 2013). As Jewkes et al. (2015) noted, however, performance is contextual and frequently shifted as the youth in this study engaged in discussing their lives both inside and outside the justice system and through the creation of a variety of texts. Given that the youth wanted to share their "outside voices" while on the "inside," they created a platform that, despite their being incarcerated, provided a vehicle for broadening who they were as individuals, not just "incarcerated youth" (Certeau, 1984). In addition, we drew from theories that speak to using various semiotic expressions as a means of speaking back to power and oppressive societal structures and norms (Bakhtin, 1986; Jocson, 2014; Rogers et al., 2015; Steinberg, 2012). Thus, we took a critical stance to explore elements of inequality, oppression, struggle, and marginalization given unequal power relationships inherent in the juvenile justice system and its dependence upon law enforcement, public defenders, prosecutors, and the court system at large (Plaff, 2017).

Context and Participants

By the summer of 2017, we were approved by the Department of Juvenile Justice to begin working with one of the youth residential detention centers (ages 13–18). This residential center is unique in that it is the only co-ed facility in the area, and somewhat surprisingly, the only residential facility that accepts female youth offenders. It was constructed in the mid-1980s specifically to house incarcerated youth on a quiet neighborhood street with an expansive backyard, basketball backboard, and parking area. The inside great room where students can lounge on couches or sit at square tables adjacent to the kitchen is quite dark as all the windows have shades on them that are kept drawn at all times. The high walls of the cathedral-style ceiling are adorned with happy smiling dolphin murals courtesy of the local Rotary club. Various signs allude to the students' behavioral point system, and surveillance is announced on placards as well as by the obvious system of cameras and audio surveillance. A small conference room with a long table comprises an area for small group work but no smart boards or other technology typical of contemporary classrooms is there. It does feature a small white board and poster paper with a list of rules for participation in group therapy sessions.

The director of the center and staff at the center are friendly, caring, and tasked with trying to manage multiple students' needs when they are in the center after a day being bused to a local alternative school site about 10 miles away. They plan field trips and other activities to try to allay the inevitable boredom that accompanies incarceration. Although we typically worked with a fluid group of 6–15 residents each with their own stories to tell, we focus in this chapter on just Dino and Marc.

Dino

Dino was a 17-year-old African American youth who was small in stature but with a big, outgoing personality. Often smiling and kidding around with others in our weekly zine writing sessions, Dino's enthusiasm was contagious and engaging. He loved using our iPhones to play rap music to inspire his and the other students' art and writing. In one of our early sessions, Dino created the following autobiographical account after we asked students to write about their struggles.

"Real Shit" Struggle

My struggle as I was growing up is I had no Dad. My Mom had no job living in Maryland had a house with Bed Bugs. As a kid growing up with 4 young brothers 1 younger sister and an older brother didn't eat every night and barely had TVs and Wifi and clothes – wore the same stuff half the time, used to sleep in cars.

I did my own thing cause I got tired sleeping with bugs and nothing to
eat. Started stealing food to eat and when we moved to a neighborhood
   called May Oaks and was on section 8. Using EBT and started hanging
with the wrong people doing bad stuff. Joined a gang.
Out there people had guns smoking, robbing and that's when I started to
do that. Playing with guns and robbing people. Wish I never took that
route – because look where I'm at locked and I have nobody but myself.

Dino's story chronicles his history of living in low-income housing with inat-
tentive and neglectful parenting, presenting a context for some of the decisions
he has made. His words are reflective on shifts in his individual performance of
Black masculinities (Neal, 200; Kirkland, 2013). Dino demonstrates the complexity of masculinity though his text of emotionality by expressing his feelings
of regret and remorse, reminiscent of "the tears that black men spill on paper"
(Kirkland, 2013, p. 131).

Marc

Marc was a 17-year-old white male and, like Dino, Marc had an engaging personality and a small, wiry frame. What was striking to us about Marc was his
uncanny ability to code shift from Standard English to African American vernacular in a heartbeat. Indeed, Marc knew all the popular rappers and his street
cred was very apparent in that, as a white male, he was never criticized for his
code shifting into black dialect. Much like Dino, Marc was street smart and savvy
in his survival instincts. And, like Dino, Marc lamented his missteps but also took
full responsibility for them. He entitled his zine "Too Real."

My Struggle

I'm going to start with what I struggle with now. I currently stay in a
Motel. I've stayed in the same room for over ten years. I lived in this
city for about six years and got burned out of our house. So we moved
here and got stuck paying rent at a Motel. We had intentions of buying a
house but then that happened. My dad is the only one who works and my
mom stays at home to watch us so I hardly ever see my dad because he's
a workaholic.

I started off as a good kid but when I started getting in trouble for petty
stuff I stopped caring. I felt like I lost all hope. So then I just started running
cars and running into people's houses. I never got caught for it so I thought
I was invincible. So it finally got to where I was robbing people. That's
what I'm locked up for now. I guess my luck ran out and got caught with
a gun on me. I have three felonies over my head with two years upstate so
any mistakes I make I'm going upstate.

Right now I'm truly blessed to not be behind bars. That's when my parents just gave up on me. I had a court date to go to and they just left me and that's what got me here. I just went back to court on the 24th and my parents didn't want me back and told my P.O. to make me stay here. I'm 17 turning 18 next June so I gotta get straight so I can provide for myself but yeah, that's what I'm struggling with.

Like Dino, Marc writes of neglectful parenting in sharing his life story. He too expresses masculinity differently by writing of his crushed hopes and dreams and his regrets. Marc's personal narrative about personal relationships and emotions juxtaposed with his account of his crimes evidence the fluid performance of gender. Zining offered him a safe space to write of emotionality and to have agency to overcome hegemonic views and performances of masculinity (Bean & Ransaw, 2013), challenging dominant notions of masculinity and literacy performance (Kehler, 2013). For both of these youth, their identities are tightly entwined and mediated by environment and experiences – some within and others outside of their control. The way in which they selected to share some of those experiences with us, as well as with a larger audience we are attempting to reach with this chapter reflects not only their struggles but their evolving identities and masculinities as well. We turn now to a description of how our practices with Dino and Marc and all of the residents we have since worked with have been shaped and developed as a joint effort to share their "outside voices" with those that will listen.

Practices and Outcomes

As we spent our first few sessions with the residents including Dino and Marc, we began co-creating a curriculum for our weekly Friday afternoon sessions with them that centered on creating zines, sketching, creating hip-hop lyrics, painting, and artistic expression. This was a very conscious effort on our part to not duplicate the school curriculum as these youth were bussed to an alternative high school about ten miles away during the week. We deliberately attempted to create an environment where the youth would feel free to author their lives and share their stories that were not "school appropriate" through alternative forms of expression that are not often valued in schools. During one of these early sessions, the residents were talking about the different "voices" they had when they were on the "outside," meaning not confined to the governance of the justice system where their every word is literally monitored by staff and a surveillance system.

Indeed, the residents' artifacts, particularly their zines, offered a window on their experiences in the juvenile justice system, where they often found themselves incarcerated multiple times, sometimes for minor yet "repeat" offenses that are dealt with increasing severity. Perhaps because of this their zine stories and art were often directed to other youth and children who might be in danger of adopting a lifestyle of guns, fear, and street codes that would likely land them in the justice system, or as reflected in some residents' writings, shot and killed. For both Marc and Dino, these were very real and tragically far too frequent outcomes. Both had lost friends to violent death. Even as Dino opined that, "it was too late for him," he wanted to tell his story as a cautionary tale to others, as he did in the following rap:

> Never had a job
> All I did was rob
> Give up to me
> Or give up to God
> Lil kids wanna bang
> But really frauds
> Street life ain't no joke
> Always gotta keep a pole [a gun]
> Cause people would be after you
> Life tryna snatch
> Yo soul tryna score

In a previous rap, Dino ended his ode to his gang with the line: "I wish I could change my life around but it's too late." Indeed "snitching" in gang culture is the ultimate sin and loyalty is highly prized.

Thus, in concert with masculine theory, the creation of Dino's "struggle" account and a related rap provided a space where he could lament his tough guy street persona without being censored or criticized. In essence, Dino was able to at least question his pathway if not alter it. As we began writing this, Dino was arrested for the third time and sent to jail after an altercation with a teacher that resulted in numerous bandaged scratches and injuries to his small frame. Within the next week, however, it was determined that he was acting in self-defense and was back at his alternative high school and us at the center.

Similarly to Dino, Marc also wanted to share his story as a possible preventative measure for other youth who found themselves in similar situations. Marc wrote a number of raps that had a tough guy edge to them with guns and drugs and challenges to the value of a GED, which he ultimately wanted in order to get a job in the local ship building industry. He wrote the following rap to advise any kids about the street life and its consequences.

To Anyone Who Thinks This Is Fun

> This is to anyone who thinks this is fun
> Have you ever been locked in a small room
> And have someone let you in and out when they tell you?
> Ever been stuck in a small room so long you start to feel
> Like there's no hope and all you have to do is

Think about all the mistakes you've ever made?
You ever been forced to eat something you don't want to eat
But the only reason you do is because you don't want to starve?
This is basically all that happens when you get locked up
And this is only juvenile detention
So imagine how it is in jail
It is ten times worse
But sometimes it was really hard to keep my head on straight
I felt like I was going crazy
But the way I coped with it was just grip tight to what your
Waiting on when you get out

In this rap, Marc captures what Muth (2016) observed in working with fathers in prison creating murals with their children. That is, the prisoners in Muth's study talked about "looking down" to stay focused on getting by day to day versus "looking out" at the larger outside world to which there were denied access. In the last two lines, Marc captured that feeling that is very different from some of his raps where he carries a gun, does not snitch, and berates those who do not see his gangster street smarts. For example, one of his rap lines refers to packing a gun to go to the corner store in his neighborhood:

This real life this real facts
This ain't rap walkin to that corner store
We had to stay strapped

Thus, amid the bravado in some of their writing, both Dino and Marc found spaces to express their masculinities differently by letting their emotions run free in their zines and capturing a more complex range of masculine feelings.

Implications for Literacy Education and Cross-Disciplinary Fields

This critical ethnography centered on two incarcerated youth, Dino and Marc, and provides a glimpse of their lived experiences that led to their residing in the center. We sought to create a curriculum centered on the arts where these youth could step out of a hard exterior safety zone rooted in heteronormative, hegemonic masculinity (Bean & Ransaw, 2013) and tell their stories through poetry, hip-hop, singing, writing zines, and other multimodal expressive genres. As philosopher Crawford, (2015) notes: "External objects provide an attachment point for the mind, they pull us out of ourselves" (p. 27). Challenging masculinity as a social performance typically reinforcing male stereotypes can be critically deconstructed and reconstructed. For example, in a case study of a 36-year-old African American male from the south side of Chicago, Jonas was able to create zines for his infant son (to be read later) that interrogated his own upbringing with a cold and distant father (Guzzetti & Lesley, 2017). In one of his zines offering a counterpoint to the male edicts of his own father, Jonas wrote: "Pink for girls, blue for guys. No way. Pick whatever color you want" (p. 75). Other researchers working with incarcerated youth have noted that they often cling to who they were before being arrested and placed in a detention center as a way of preserving their sense of self (Pytash, 2014). Nevertheless, the arts and zines in particular, open up spaces where stereotypical forms of masculinity can be challenged.

Dino's and Marc's stories offer a temporary respite from their hyper-masculine personae and aim to inform an audience outside themselves about the realities of incarceration. A recurring theme in our ongoing research at the center is the "revolving door" that seems to cycle many of the youth we work with back into serving time there. The center has its own rules and a sort of family culture develops naturally in this space. Amid strict surveillance and a behavioral point system, the youth at the center actively engage in creating art that provides an outside voice for their struggles, advice, and creativity. Somewhat encouragingly, there is an ongoing effort to place youth in community placement programs closer to their home communities and pave the way for reentry services and successes. These efforts are not without a host of obstacles. For example, replacing the two existing youth prisons with smaller treatment-oriented facilities nearer to youths' home communities with mental health support staff is one vision designed to transform youth incarceration. Neighborhoods have been less than welcoming for youth incarceration facilities, however. As Dreisinger (2016) noted in her work with adults in her college writing program located in a New York prison: "Crime is driven by poverty and inequality, a fact realized in the United States, where income inequality is the highest it's been since 1928, and the richest fifth of families hold 88.9% of the country's wealth" (p. 196).

The road out of the juvenile justice system is fraught with potholes and obstacles. Gutierrez (2016) argues that educators badly need transformative learning ecologies for students from non-dominant communities. In our experience working with Dino, Marc, and other youth in the crisis center, the arts and the creation of zines offered a vehicle that moved out of the realm of standardized school curriculum. As a society, we need pedagogies of possibility to transform how youth in crisis center settings see themselves and the value of their lives and contributions once they are released. For example, in one session, Marc wrote a hip-hop lyric questioning why he would want or need a GED. Not long after that railing against the system, he mentioned wanting to work in the shipyards, welding and making a good living wage. The GED then became a way out of his prior life on the street, carrying a gun and robbing people to get money and food. Writing his zine, "Too Real" became a way to work through imagined futures and a different identity while bantering and code shifting into African American vernacular with his friend Dino. As far as we know, as we write this chapter, Marc is out of the juvenile justice system while Dino remains in the center with its heavy surveillance and close quarters with other youth confined there.

As Dreisinger (2016, p. 306) noted in her work with New York prisoners in writing their stories:

> The key is to keep marching. Justice work is ultimately a grand redundancy, restlessly demanding more of itself: More labor, more movement, more struggle, more victories and losses, and that work is powered by the potent thing I strap on daily, like a life vest, the thing that bouys me and keeps my spirit alive with mission and meaning: Hope.

It is our hope for Marc, Dino, and the thousands of incarcerated youth like them, that their stories be heard and that their "outside voices" influence and shape the ways in which all youth are heard and recognized.

References

Bakhtin, M.M. (1986). *Speech genres and other late essays*. Austin, TX: University of Texas Press.

Bean, T.W., Dunkerly-Bean, J., & Harper, H.J. (2014). *Teaching young adult literature: Developing students as world citizens*. Thousand Oaks, CA: Sage.

Bean, T.W., & Harper, H. (2007). Reading men differently: Alternative portrayals of masculinity in contemporary young adult fiction. *Reading Psychology, 28*(1), 11–30.

Bean, T.W., & Ransaw, T. (2013). Masculinity and portrayals of African American boys in young adult literature: A critical deconstruction and reconstruction of this genre. In B.J. Guzzetti, & T.W. Bean (Eds.), *Adolescent literacies and the gendered self: (Re)constructing identities through multimodal literacy practices* (pp. 22–30). New York, NY: Routledge.

Certeau, M.D. (1984). *The practice of everyday life*. Berkeley, CA: University of California Press.

Crawford, M.B. (2015). *The world beyond your head: On becoming an individual in an age of distraction*. New York, NY: Farrar, Straus, & Giroux.

Dreisinger, B. (2016). *Incarceration nations: A journey to justice in prisons around the world*. New York, NY: Other Press.

Dunkerly-Bean, J.M., Bean, T.W., & Alnajjar, K. (2014). Seeking asylum: Adolescents explore the crossroads of human rights education and cosmopolitan critical literacy. *Journal of Adolescent & Adult Literacy, 58*(3), 230–241.

Durnan, J., & Harvell, S. (2017). *Data snapshot of youth incarceration in Virginia*. Washington, DC: Urban Institute.

Farn, A., & Adams, J. (2016). *Education and interagency collaboration: A lifeline for justice-involved youth*. Washington, DC: Center for Juvenile Justice Reform.

Foucault, M. (1980). Prison talk. In C. Gordon (Ed., and Trans.), *Power/knowledge: Selected interviews and other writings by Michel Foucault, 1972–1977* (pp. 109–133). New York, NY: Pantheon.

Gore, J.M. (1998). Disciplining bodies: On the continuity of power relations in pedagogy. In T.S. Popkewitz & M.B. Brennan (Eds.), *Foucault's challenge: Discourse, knowledge, and power in education* (pp. 231–251). New York, NY: Teachers College Press.

Gustavson, L. (2007). *Youth learning on their own terms: Creative practices and classroom teaching*. New York, NY: Routledge.

Gutierrez, K.D. (2016). 2011 AERA presidential address: Designing resilient ecologies: Social design experiments and a new social imagination. *Educational Researcher, 45*(3), 187–196.

Guzzetti, B., & Lesley, M. (2017). Surviving: An African-American man Reconstructing masculinity through literacy. In T.S. Ransaw & R. Majors (Eds.), *Emerging issues and trends in education* (pp. 57–82). East Lansing, MI: Michigan State University Press.

Jewkes, R., Morrell, R., Hearn, J., Lundqvist, E., Blackbeard, D., Lindegger, G., . . . Gottzen, L. (2015). Hegemonic masculinity: Combining theory and practice in gender interventions. *Culture, Health, & Sexuality, 17*(suppl. 2), 112–127. doi: 10.1080/13691058.2015.1085094

Jocson, K. (2014). Critical media ethnography: Researching youth media. In D. Paris, & M.T. Winn (Eds.), *Humanizing research: Decolonizing qualitative inquiry with youth and communities* (pp. 105–123). Los Angeles, CA: Sage.

Kehler, M. (2013). Who will "save the boys"? (Re)examining a panic for underachieving boys. In B.J. Guzzetti & T.W. Bean (Eds) *Adolescent literacies and the gendered self: (Re) constructing identities through multimodal literacy practices* (pp. 121–130). New York, NY: Routledge.

Kirkland, D. (2013). Inventing masculinity: Young black males, literacy and tears. In B.J. Guzzetti & T. Bean (Eds.), *Adolescent literacies and the gendered self: (Re)constructing identities through multimodal literacy practices* (pp. 131–139), New York, NY: Routledge.

Madison, D.S. (2005). *Critical ethnography: Methods, ethics, and performance* Thousand Oaks, CA: Sage.

Muth, W. (2016). "A big circle of unity:" Incarcerated fathers being-in-text. *Journal of Literacy Research, 48*(3), 317–345.

Neal, M.A. (2003). *New black man.* New York, NY: Routledge.

Noguera, P.A. (2008). *The trouble with black boys: And other reflections on race, equity, and the future of public education.* San Francisco, CA: Jossey-Bass.

Plaff, J.F. (2017). *Locked in: The true causes of mass incarceration and how to achieve real reform.* New York, NY: Basic Books.

Pytash, K.E. (2014). "It's not simple:" The complex lives of youth in a juvenile detention facility. In P.J. Dunston, L.B. Gambrell, K. Headley, S. King Fullerton, & P.M. Stecker (Eds.), *63rd yearbook of the Literacy Research Association* (pp. 216–228). Altamonte Springs, FL: Literacy Research Association.

Rogers, T., Winters, K.L., Perry, M., & LaMonde, A.M. (2015). *Youth, critical literacies, and civic engagement: Arts, media, and literacy in the lives of adolescents.* New York, NY: Routledge.

Steinberg, S. (2012). Critical pedagogy and cultural studies research: Bricolage in action. In *Counterpoints, critical pedagogy in the new dark ages: Challenges and possibilities* (vol. 422, pp. 230–254). New York, NY: Peter Lang.

11

EMBEDDING THE COMPLEXITIES OF GENDER IDENTITY THROUGH A PEDAGOGY OF REFUSAL

Learning the Body as Literacy Alongside Youth

sj Miller

People in the United States are born into a culture still fastened to historical policing of gender and gender identities. While social and political movements have helped galvanize and afford some material, social, and economic gains about gender and gender identities, schools and many other institutions providing youth services remain as inheritors of gender norms and their subsequent attributions. Unfortunately, such changes have yet to be systemically addressed and rooted across or studied over time. Such gaps have left educators and those working with youth ill-prepared and ill-equipped to sufficiently address gender identity topics through coursework, curriculum, and pedagogy (Kosciw, Greytak, Diaz, & Bartkiewicz, 2016; Miller, 2016a, 2016b; Quinn & Meiners, 2011).

Schools have become a type of prison that mirror social, cultural, and economic modes of reproduction. Seen in this way, some bodies are instantiated with multiple forms of cultural capital or social currency (Bourdieu, 1980; Yosso 2005) while others have diminished capital. Specifically, some youth are vulnerable to experiencing gender identity insecurities that manifest as disproportionate rates of bullying, dropping out, truancy, lowered grade point averages (GPAs), mental health and substance issues (Kosciw, Greytak, Diaz, & Bartkiewicz, 2010; Kosciw, et al, 2016); pushout into the juvenile processing system (GLSEN, 2016; Ware, 2015); homelessness presence in foster care and/or group homes; and suicidal ideation. The numbers of these incidents are much higher for youth of color (Ybarra, Mitchell, & Kosciw, 2014). In addition, suspensions result in exclusion from classroom instruction and the school community. When these students are not present in school, everyone has diminished opportunities to learn and grow. These micro-aggressions and forms of gender identity-based violence could be disrupted if the schooling system and other youth-serving agencies were to embrace policies and procedures that shifted beliefs and practices about gender identity. Recognizing the impact of these disparities, teacher education programs become a lever in which teachers can develop capacities to disrupt and change these narratives and to share learning experiences with key stakeholders. This chapter shares the theoretical and pedagogical framing of a one-year study about how students with non-binary gender identities spoke to teachers, counselors, principals, school personnel, peers, and family members about what they needed to feel safe, included, and legitimized at school. This framing provides a context for ways educators can and should be interrupting disparities in gender identity insecurity.

Caring for Our Own

Young people with non-binary gender identities enter schools and other youth-serving agencies with gender identities they seem to already readily understand. These youth are highly attuned to how schooling practices mostly speak to binary gender identities and re-inscribe cisgender (those who identify with the gender associated with their biological sex) and gender identity normativity. Considering that access and recognition shape and inform identities, those with non-binary gender identities are positioned by their gendered relationality to school-based relationships that are co-constitutive of the other or those outside the norm. Their bodily awareness enables them to dislodge from the norms that many students are vulnerable to inheriting and embodying. As they move back and forth between their lives in and out of school, their bodies exhibit different forms of literacy. Outside of school, their gender identities are always in conversation as they simultaneously question gender construction, deconstruction, and reconstruction. When they are recognized through the eyes and/or words of another, their validation confers gender identity self-determination, and this legitimization generates emergent language, positioning them as agents of literacy. Their gender identities are complex and indeterminate and provide an opportunity to have a relationship with the body that is expressed through different manifestations of refusal. Expressions of their refusals that resist assimilation and enculturation posits them as both dexterous and agentive as they move from context to context.

A pedagogy of refusal emerged as a unifying concept for this study. Embodied enactments that refuse to be or to accept essentialized constructions of spaces, binaries, ideas, genders, bodies, or identities, are a form of resistance against the foreclosure of not becoming and being gender identity self-determined. This refusal is complex; it is a moving away from, or a refusal to be a predictable pattern. In other words, it is always in relationship to relationality – it is the act of queering binaries that manifest as indeterminate (Miller, 2016a). For example, a teacher assumes the cis-normative social positioning of a body when they say, "Hey guys, take out your notebooks." When a student corrects that teacher and responds with, "We are not all guys, and when you say that you position everyone to be male; *guys* means male or boys," the moment becomes a turning point for literacy learning and learning literacy. Stemming from this pedagogy, *gender identity* is the sense of how people feel about their gender, its expression, and its relationship to their bodies and how they want to be seen and legitimized by the world. Gender identity can therefore be the physical, emotional, and/or psychological embodiment that rejects gender (agender) altogether. It is a metric that signifies bodily location about gender identity that simultaneously questions its construction, the impacts of its social positioning, and its ongoing preparedness to participate in its reinvention. When educators put into practice a pedagogy of refusal, students not only see and feel themselves reflected and respected by a teacher's approach to the classroom, but their legitimization becomes both an academic motivation and a source of empowerment. Such empowerment that is situated in the body primes students as readily agentive, and as they move from context to context, they become change agents.

Schooling practices about gender and gender identity are built within hegemonic structures and essentialist or stereotypical notions of the male/man and female/woman binary. As the norm, this binary has, and more or less continues to, position and condition schooling practices and discourse (i.e., use and usage) to assume that bodies are cis- and gender identity normative. These cis- and gender identity-normative gazes apprentice students into linguistic and literacy practices that manifest in narrowing perspectives about the continuum of gender identities that are ever present, and diminish capacities for broadening understanding, recognizing, and legitimizing concurrent shifts in bodily expressions.

Identities seen through an intersection of cultural anthropology, feminist theory, and sociocultural theory suggest that "any given construction of identity may be in part deliberate and intentional, in part habitual and hence often less than fully conscious" (Bucholtz & Hall, 2005, p. 25). Known as the *partialness principle*, Bucholz and Hall reason that identity construction is relational, interactional, and social and cannot be individual if it is socially negotiated. They argue that it cannot be fully intentional if it is produced by practices and ideologies that may exceed conscious awareness, and it may be formed through contestation and negotiation because of others' preexisting perceptions that are linked to larger ideological and held beliefs. Therefore, when a person claims an identity, name, or pronoun, those choices are rooted in prior defaults indexed to ideologies and are conceived through negotiation and the desire to be gender identity self-determined. Understood this way, language used to name identity is connected by what is known as the *indexical principle*, which relies on how meaning is discursively produced through identity categories and labels; implications and presuppositions about one's or another's identity; evaluative positioning toward someone else's talk and their social roles; and, use of linguistic structures that are associated with specific people and groups (Bucholtz & Hall, 2005, p. 21). In other words, when school systems (or any other institution or person) positions or presumes someone's identity, that positioning is demonstrated or animated by difficult to sever or indissoluble ties to a heteronormative, patriarchal, hegemonic, cisgender/cissexual, ableist, classed system that has maintained and structured lives.

School systems, and especially teachers who perpetuate these ties, reinforce ideologies that sustain institutional and structural violence.

Yet, youth whose gender identities may seem incongruous with school and who are astute about their social positioning are vulnerable to how negative representations of gender identity impact mindsets and beliefs. Often left with no choice, and in search of positive recognition, young people are forced to turn to social media and to peer groups to educate and gain validation and recognition of and from each other (Adams, 2017; Byron & Hunt, 2017; Gieseking, 2015). These networks foster young people's *gender identity self-determination* (Miller, 2016a), whereby individuals are the ultimate authority on their own gender identity. A norm that has been established in non-binary gender identity communities has been to directly ask someone how that person self-identifies, how that person would like to be referred to, and what that person's claimed names and pronouns are or are not. Some people are pronouned, meaning they choose to not to use a pronoun. When people choose their names or pronouns and ask others to use a particular name and/or pronoun, it marks a major milestone in identity transition and being named or pronouned "correctly marks the moment in which a gender identity leaves the mind of a [trans] person and enters a new reality on the lips of an interlocutor" (Zimman, in press, p. 10).

For many trans*+ and gender non-binary people, naming one's identity is an inherently embodied principle of gender identity self-determination, in which individuals are the ultimate authority on their own gender identity. According to Stanley (2014) and Miller (2016a), gender identity self-determination constitutes "a collective praxis against the brutal pragmatism of the present, the liquidation of the past, and the austerity of the future" (p. 89). In this sense, "it is a form of resistance to normative structures of genital-based gender assignment. As a radical alternative to those normative systems, gender self-determination is realized first and foremost through the linguistic practice of self-identification" (Zimman, in press, p. 1). What is evidenced is a refusal to be essentialized or stereotyped, reified, codified, and trapped by institutionalized structures that impose an identity algorithm. While policies guide and shape mainstream practices and offer important protections, within these communities, there is a common (but not for all people) desire and need to self-identify in such a way that naming becomes imaginative and inventive. This act of resistance whether enacted by a young person or an adult like a teacher, vis-à-vis a refusal, mediates locating the self in second space (the imagined) (Soja, 1996, p. 10) and third space (coming together of the real and the imagined) (Gutiérrez, 2008; Soja, 1996, p. 10) sanctuaries where language can emerge as preservationist and coded, and yet also provide opportunities for bodies to invent and reinvent language. In these spaces what arises is "something new and unrecognizable, a new area of negotiation of meaning and representation" (Bhahba, 1994, cited in Soja, 1996, p. 11). What *arises* is that people determine how they want to be spoken about and understood. Butler (2004) reminds readers that "the body gives rise to language and that language carries bodily aims, and performs bodily deeds" even when, "not always understood by those who use language to accomplish certain conscious aims" (p. 199). When youth are not empowered for agentive moves, gender identity norms will remain static.

A view of gender identity is bound and tied to dynamisms of structural and institutionalized manifestations of power; identity is not immune from the desire to be recognized or even assimilated, and power relations illuminate presence, absence, and futurity (Bordo, 1993). For instance, Foucault (1980) and Bourdieu (1980) suggest that the effects of power and surveillance construct identities, and that the embodiment of identities is vulnerable as a result of power. Any absence of a range of identities, whether skin color, dress, ability, or non-binary, to name a few, reflects bias and microaggressive beliefs about bodies. To this Bordo (1993) attests: "the human body is itself a politically inscribed entity, its physiology and morphology shaped by histories and practices of containment and control" (p. 21). As students with non-binary gender identities enter school, their bodily enactments are ripe with opportunities to spatialize change as they educate their peers and adults about the ways in which they self-identify. For schools then, understanding that their bodies are *agentive*, means that educators can build from and on those dynamic assets for learning, and affirm and recognize that gender expression is flexible, on a continuum, and can shift over time and in context. These enactments can impact everyone in the school to become more aware of an ever-evolving continuum of gender identity (see examples in Miller, 2016a, 2016b, forthcoming a, b).

Situated within and stemming from a newfangled theory of trans*+ (Miller, 2016a, forthcoming b), which grew from students' resistance to static notions and embodiments of gender identities, trans*+ can be thought of as a mediator and practice for literacy learning. *A theory of trans*+ is built from the relationship between spatiality and hybridity theories (Miller, 2014b; Soja, 2010); geospatial theories (Nespor, 1997; Slattery, 1995; Soja, 2010); social positioning theories (Butler, 1990; Foucault, 1990; Leander & Sheehy, 2004; McCarthey & Moje, 2002); culturally responsive and relevant pedagogy (Gay, 2010; Ladson-Billings, 1995); culturally sustaining pedagogy (Pars & Alim, 2017); queer (Barrett, 2002; Butler, 1990; Leap, 2011; Motschenbacher & Stegu, 2013), trans (Davis, Zimman, & Raclaw, 2014; Zimman, in press), trans*+ (Miller, 2016a, 2016b, 2018); and sociocultural linguistics (Bucholtz & Hall, 2005; Ochs, 1992). Arising from this rhizome of theories then, trans*+ as a theoretical concept, not only is the connective tissue for these studies but uniquely suggests that students have agency in how they invite in, embody, and can be recognized by the self and other as they travel across contexts embodied by multitudinous identities that can be perpetually reinvented. Trans*+ as rhizome, situated within this framing, is a networked space where relationships intersect, are concentric, do not intersect, can be parallel, nonparallel, perpendicular, obtuse, and fragmented. It is both an invisible and visible space, which embodies all the forces co-constructing identities. Such spaces cut across borders of space, time, and technology and generate pathways into different contexts. It also recognizes that histories have spatial dimensions that are normalized with inequities hidden in bodies whereby bodies become contested sites that experience social justice and injustice both temporally and spatially. Gender identity, situated within a trans*+ theory is trans-sectional (Miller, forthcoming a, b, c) because it is always in perpetual construction and deconstruction (Miller, 2016b, p. 4).

Drawing upon a refusal of pedagogy for learning literacy and literacy learning, educators and other influential adults can challenge expectations that re-inscribe gender identity normativity. Ensuing shifts prime educational spaces for a deepening understanding, recognition, and increased capacity about teaching and welcoming youth who have dynamic gender identities. A goal is to minimize discontinuities between literacy learning and learning literacy inside and outside of school. Ongoing embodiments, long-term practice and applications of refusal in and across school, can deepen human awareness and provide meaningful and intentional opportunities to shift deeply entrenched binary understandings of highly nuanced complexities about gender identity.

A pedagogy of refusal is an enactment and engagement of learning that opens space for ideas, concepts, and the indeterminate to be part of the process of learning. Answers are not compartmentalized into the binary of the *yes* or *no*, and answers can shift back and forth, be between, imagined, futuristic, and fragmented. As youth come to understand and recognize these possibilities through participation and practice, a pedagogy of refusal can grant bodied communications to be made legible and become legible to others. Bodies and minds become emerging forms of and for understanding and teaching. Therefore, this theory of trans*+ suggests that for new knowledge to emerge, learning spaces must be thought of and taught as a networked space where relationality and one's relationship to relationality is continually reinvented based on where both students and *educators* are in their awareness about gender identity (Miller, 2014a). A theory of trans*+ *is* a critical consciousness about how we read and are read by the world (Freire, 1970) and a refusal and divesting from essentializations (Miller, 2016a, 2017b). Since language helps us locate and discover gender identities, the education process has opportunity to learn from students' relationships to the complexity of their gender identities and discover how to approach a re-invention of language through policy, pedagogy, and curriculum.

Why Shifts in Relationship to Young People's Gender Identities Matter

Today's youth with non-binary gender identities are increasingly visible within schools and youth-serving agencies and can be extraordinarily creative in negotiating the politics that seek to suppress, repress, and occasionally eradicate and erase their very being. Yet, while youth have an innate sense of how gender identity norms function as modes of surveillance, they are locked into a system that does not fully understand, recognize, or know how to support them. As a result, young people are forced into silence, and often experience isolation or marginalization. Resultant, they often seek social validation and recognition in each other outside of school (Miller, Lugg, & Mayo, 2018). In these moments, the *extraordinary* occurs. Their very embodiment is the construction and production of literacy wherein new meaning/knowledges emerge. If schools and other learning institutions were prepared to embrace and build on these generative moments of literacy production, opportunities could be created for youth to advance their psychological, social, and academic well-beings, increasing capacities for all to disrupt microaggressions and rationales that produce stereotypes, bullying, and violent behavior. These changes can manifest as incorporating more inclusive forms of address that explicitly invite students to self-identify; allowing students to use bathrooms and locker-rooms that match their claimed gender identity or having those spaces be inclusive of all or non-gendered; going beyond the gender binary when teaching, speaking, making announcements, having causal conversation; putting up signs that enumerate all forms of identities in hallways and classrooms; and always introducing oneself by claimed name and pronoun; (Miller, 2016a, forthcoming a).

Bullying and vitriolic language evidenced by the current political climate and removal of the *Federal Guidance* that protected trans[*+] and youth who are gender/gender identity non-binary have brought gender identity topics into critical focus, warranting immediate attention. Not only have educators and other adults been summoned to understand how schools and other youth-serving institutions delimit boundaries of gender identity normativity, sanction certain configurations of gender, and reinforce cissexism, they are challenged to disrupt resocialization, efforts that cannot be tokenized but cultivated and embodied for systemic transformation.

Trans[*]+-Cultural and Trans[*]+-Culturaling

Awareness of how language helps to locate and discover gender identities can assist in imagining, inventing, and reinventing language. Seen this way, language becomes a critical agentive nexus for bridging various contexts. Self-identification, legitimization, and recognition, when embodied, present possibilities to impact and inform local, national, and international communities dedicated (even unknowingly) to discursive and dialogical processes between the intersections of gender identity and emergent language. I call this process *trans[*+]-cultural*, while the action or movement as bodies move from space to space, *trans[*+]-culturaling*. Trans[*+]-cultural is the broader conceptualization of complex gender identity formation as bodies trans-sect with technologies, spaces, times, contexts, cultural identifiers, and language and simultaneously produce both material and symbolic meanings that give rise to literacy practices. Trans[*+]-cultural then is the transsection, i.e., the rhizome or networked space whereby relationships intersect, are concentric, do not intersect, can be parallel, nonparallel, perpendicular, obtuse, and fragmented (Miller, 2014b, 2016b). It is both an invisible and visible space that embodies all the forces co-constructing gender identities that traverse borders of space, time, and technology, and carves out and generates pathways into different contexts where gender identities are formed and generated. Trans*+-culturaling is the process, activation, and realization of such gender identity formations. Gender identity, when validated by another, highlights its visibility, ontology, and affirms its social positioning.

Embedding the Complexities of Gender Identity through a Pedagogy of Refusal: The Body as Literacy

The high-leverage literacy practices embodied by youth provide rich examples of strategies that can become folded into educational spaces. Adolescents are tomes of information that present possibilities for bridging in and outside of school literacy practices that are waiting to be un-sedimented so they can be embedded. They are the walking, breathing, living agentive embodiments that can not only change literacy practices in schools or youth-serving agencies, but simultaneously be educative for all people in all schooling contexts. Adolescents' understanding of *being refused* prompts them to use refusal as a means for resistance and survival. These assets, when built *with* can help to restructure approaches to engage and activate literacy learning and learning literacy as a co-constitutive process. All people are on a learning curve and each one enters this work at differential stages of understanding and applications of knowledge. Many want to learn about how to support youth with non-binary gender identities. It will take folding in the literacy lives of young people for changes to systemically occur. This means *listening to* and *being in* the work with youth.

Young people must make a stance if change is to occur. They know this, and they take on roles that the adults around them should assume. Youth are the true teachers. They each are self-advocates for both small and large school-wide and community change. They are parenting each other and providing love, understanding, support, and encouragement. They are teaching each other and developing their literacy practices. Together, they are finding ways to navigate through the complex obstacles that each must face.

This work will deepen, expand, and advance capacities to fold young people's literacy practices across curriculum, practice, and policy. Both adults and youth should not be forced to survive during a school day or hide who they are to placate others' discomfort; that is not what school should be about. For true systemic transformation to occur, more research should attend to how youth create, use, and vary linguistic practices in different cultures and social groupings; how youth use their rich and innovative gender identity funds to create and recreate language and literacy; how gender identity language and literacy practices vary by demographics; and how trans*+-culturaling shifts and deepens understanding about language and literacy practices in local, national, and international contexts.

Together, these studies can be informative of the dynamism between language and literacy and how they evolve, shift, and are re-invented. As these identities become empowered vis-à-vis recognition and affirmation in schooling practices, there is a greater possibility to spatialize change and expansion across different educational contexts. Such change will strengthen schools in their efforts to move away from presuming the cis- and gender identity-normative default and be reset through a trans-sectional gaze.

While strides have been made and change is happening, many resort to self-hate or tolerate their misrecognition or erasure because of a system that is *failing* them. Educators – *err*, the entire schooling process – are charged with paying attention to students' agentiveness; to their knowledge that they bring into schools; and attend to how that knowledge can push schools forward to expand what literacy can be by teachers and other adults learning alongside youth. As adolescents continue to fashion indeterminate gender identities, and as adults come to see how a pedagogy of refusal can move away from policing gender identity norms, schools and other educational institutions will be better prepared to embed the literacy practices continually unfolding. Many of those in teacher education, K-12 schools and other youth-serving institutions are deeply committed to sustaining those changes. The current default can move away from how hegemony structures and centers standards and outcomes normed within white, middle-class, monocultural, mono-linguistic, cisgender, and gender-normative schooling processes and practices. Paris and Alim (2017) in their powerful work on culturally sustaining pedagogies provoke questions about not only how linguistic, literate, and cultural pluralism must be changed, embedded, and sustained in schooling practices, but how these efforts can bring about social transformation. It is also important to consider how sustaining trans*+-cultural identity (Miller, forthcoming c) "is increasingly necessary given the explicit assimilationist and antidemocratic monolingual/monocultural educational policies emerging" (Paris & Alim, 2014, p. 88), and how there remain remnants of colonization. The power of the collective comes to mind so that trans-sections of identities becomes a starting point for the work. As this work progresses, gender identity (among all trans-sections of identities) will be unhinged from the word "issue," and self-determination will become evidence of its embedment.

Implications for Literacy Education and Cross-Disciplinary Fields

What will it take for teachers and those who interact with youth around literacy to be able to learn with and from young people about gender? Some practices that comprise this kind of work that can be done by teachers, administrators, service providers, and youth inside of the high-leverage practice of specifying and reinforcing productive behavior include studying policies, texts, and films together to be more attentive to gender. For example, the titles of after-school gender and sexual diversity clubs can be renamed so gender identities are enumerated in their titles. On an individual level, teachers and youth service providers can begin with the presumption that all young people's identities are trans-sectional and reconfigure their approaches to pedagogy, curriculum, and policy accordingly. They can inquire and dialogue with youth on a regular basis about what they need related to their gender identities. Guest speakers of all ages who have non-binary gender identities can be invited to speak about their life journeys, interactions with others, their own experiences in and out of school, and the triumphs they have experienced and observed. Finally, teachers and youth leaders can commit to ongoing self-reflection on their own and youths' views about gender.

Teachers and others who work with youth will need training and education related to gender. Professional development opportunities for teachers, administrators, counselors, and youth service providers can be tailored to their specific needs. These informal sessions may include seminars on such topics as a changing culture and climate, trans*+-ing classrooms and curriculum, creating strategic action plans, identifying specific action steps, and learning about and practicing discourse that recognizes and affirms gender identities (Miller, 2016b, forthcoming c).

School staff and youth service agency personnel will need to develop intake forms and resources that are inclusive of self-claiming gender identities, offering choices regarding demographic information that include categories of male, female, female-to-male, male-to-female, gender non-specified, or self-identified gender choices. (The word "other" should not be included as a choice on these forms because these students are already "othered" or seen as outside the norm.) Counselors, nurses, and administrative office staff will need to have updated and accurate information to distribute to young people and their parents about where to get medical care, counseling, peer-support groups, and provide lists of community organizations that do outreach, faith-based support, and offer safe homes. Staff in schools and youth-serving organizations can create resource packets that include glossaries of terms related to gender; lesson plans that address gender issues; lists of websites related to gender; bibliographies of texts that present alternative representations of and information about gender; biographies of trailblazers and others of interest; telephone contacts for suicide help lines; gender inclusive and pronoun posters; sample course syllabi statements; and descriptions of current and relevant federal policies, such as guidance for ensuring the civil rights of transgender youth that were issued jointly by the U.S. Departments of Justice and the U.S. Department of Education (Miller, forthcoming b; U.S. Department of Justice, 2016). It is my hope that these suggestions will guide those who work with young people to recognize and affirm their powerful and evocative representations of gender identities.

References

Adams, C. (2017, March 25). Social media, celebrities, and transgender youth. *CBS News*. Retrieved from www.cbsnews.com/news/social-media-celebrities-and-transgender-youth.

Barrett, R. (2002). Is queer theory important for sociolinguistic theory? In K. Campbell-Kibler, R.J. Podesva, S. Roberts, & A. Wong (Eds.), *Language and sexuality: Contesting meaning in theory and practice* (pp. 25–43). Stanford, CA: CSLI Press.

Bordo, S. (1993). *Unbearable weight: Feminism, Western culture and the body*. Berkeley, CA: University of California Press.

Bourdieu, P. (1980). *The logic of practice*. Stanford, CA: Stanford University Press.

Bucholtz, M., & Hall, K. (2005). Identity and interaction: A sociocultural linguistic approach. *Discourse Studies*, 7(4–5), 585–614.

Butler, J. (1990). *Gender trouble: Feminism and the subversion of identity*. New York, NY: Routledge.

Butler, J. (2004). *Undoing gender*. New York, NY: Routledge.

Byron, P., & Hunt, J. (2017). "That happened to me too: Young people's informal knowledge of diverse genders and sexualities. *Sex Education*, 17(3), 319–332.

Davis, J., Zimman, L., & Raclaw, J. (2014). Opposites attract: Theorizing binaries in language, gender, and sexuality In L. Zimman, J. Davis, & J. Raclaw (Eds.), *Queer excursions: Retheorizing binaries in language, gender, and sexuality* (pp. 1–12). New York, NY: Oxford University Press.

Foucault, M. (1980). *Power-knowledge: Selected interviews and other writings, 1972–1977*. New York, NY: Pantheon Books.

Foucault, M. (1990). *The history of sexuality*. New York, NY: Vintage.

Freire, P. (1970). *Pedagogy of the oppressed*. New York, NY: Continuum.

Gay, G. (2010). *Culturally responsive teaching: Theory, research, and practice*. New York, NY: Teachers College.

Gieseking, J.J. (2015). "For Leelah: queering+ spaces of education." Presentation in Presidential Plenary "Toward what justice? Describing diverse dreams of justice in education" with M. Dumas, N. Erevelles, L. Patel, E. Tuck, & K.W. Yang. Chicago, IL: American Educational Research Association.

GLSEN (2016). *Educational exclusion: Drop out, push out, and school-to-prison pipeline among LGBTQ youth*. New York, NY: GLSEN.

Gutiérrez, K. (2008). Developing a sociocritical literacy in the third space. *Reading Research Quarterly*, 43(2), 148–164.

Kosciw, J.G., Greytak, E.A., Diaz, E., & Bartkiewicz, M. (2010). *The 2009 national school climate survey: The experiences of lesbian, gay, bisexual and transgender youth in our nation's schools*. New York, NY: GLSEN.

Kosciw, J.G., Greytak, E.A., Giga, N.M., Villenas, C., & Danischewski, D.J. (2016). *The 2015 national school climate survey: The experiences of lesbian, gay, bisexual, transgender, and queer youth in our nation's schools*. New York, NY: GLSEN.

Ladson-Billings, G. (1995). Toward a theory of culturally relevant pedagogy. *American Educational Research Journal*, 32(3), 465–491.

Leander, K., & Sheehy, M. (Eds.) (2004). *Spatializing literacy research and practice*. New York, NY: Peter Lang.

Leap, W.L. (2011). Queer linguistics, sexuality, and discourse analysis. In J.P. Gee & M. Handford (Eds.), *The Routledge handbook of discourse analysis* (pp. 558–571). London, UK: Routledge.

McCarthey, S., & Moje, E. (2002). Identity matters. *Reading Research Quarterly*, *37*(2), 228–238.

Miller, sj (2014a). Hungry like the wolf: Gender non-conformity in young adult literature. In C. Hill (Ed.), *The critical merits of young adult literature: Coming of age* (pp. 55–72). New York, NY: Routledge.

Miller, sj (2014b). Spatializing social justice research in English education. In C. Compton-Lily & Erica Halverson (Eds.), *Time and space in literacy research* (pp. 122–133). New York, NY: Routledge.

Miller, sj (Ed.). (2016a). *Teaching, affirming, and recognizing trans and gender creative youth: A queer literacy framework*. New York, NY: Palgrave Macmillan.

Miller, sj (2016b). Trans*+ing classrooms: The pedagogy of refusal as mediator for learning. *Social Sciences*, *5*(34), 1–17.

Miller, sj (2018, February). *Embedding the complexities of gender identity through a pedagogy of refusal: Learning the body as literacy alongside our students*. Ann Arbor, MI: TeachingWorks, University of Michigan School of Education.

Miller, sj (forthcoming a). *Gender identity justice: Sowing seeds for transformation in education*. New York, NY: Teachers College Press.

Miller, sj (forthcoming b). Gender identityWOKE: A theory of trans*+ for animating literacy practices. In M. Sailors & D. Alvermann (Eds), *Theoretical models and processes of literacy* (7th ed.). New York, NY: Routledge.

Miller, sj (forthcoming c). *Navigating trans*+ and non-binary gender identities*. London, UK: Bloomsbury

Miller, sj, Lugg, C., & Mayo, C. (2018). Sex and gender in transition in US schools: Ways forward. *Sex Education*. Retrieved from http://dx.doi.org/10.1080/14681811.2017.1415204.

Motschenbacher, M., & Stegu, M. (2013). Introduction: Queer linguistic approaches to discourse. *Discourse & Society*, *24*(5), 519–535.

Nespor, J. (1997). *Tangled up in school: Politics, space, bodies and signs in the educational process*. Mahwah, NJ: Lawrence Erlbaum Associates.

Ochs, E. (1992). Indexing gender. In D. Alessandro & C. Goodwin (Eds.), *Rethinking context: Language as an interactive phenomenon* (pp. 335–358). Cambridge, UK: Cambridge University Press.

Paris, D., & Alim, H.S. (2014). What are we seeking to sustain through culturally sustaining pedagogy? A loving critique forward. *Harvard Educational Review*, *84*(1), 85–100.

Paris, D., & Alim, H.S. (2017). *Culturally sustaining pedagogies: Teaching and learning for justice in a changing world*. New York, NY: Teachers College Press.

Quinn, T., & Meiners, E.R. (2011). Teacher education, struggles for social justice, and the historical erasure of lesbian, gay, bisexual, transgender, and queer lives. In A. Ball & C. Tyson (Eds.), *Studying diversity in teacher education* (pp. 135–151). Lanham, MD: Rowman & Littlefield.

Slattery, P. (1995). *Curriculum development in the postmodern era*. New York, NY: Garland.

Soja, E. (1996). *Thirdspace: Journeys to Los Angeles and other real-and-imagined places*. Malden, MA: Blackwell.

Soja, E. (2010). *Seeking spatial justice*. Minneapolis, MN: University of Minnesota Press.

Stanley, E.A. (2014). Gender self-determination. *Transgender Studies Quarterly*, *1*(1–2), 89–91.

U.S. Department of Justice (2016, May 13). *U.S. Departments of Justice and Education Release Joint Guidance to Help Schools Ensure the Civil Rights of Transgender Students*. Retrieved from www.justice.gov/opa/pr/us-departments-justice-and-education-release-joint-guidance-help-schools-ensure-civil-rights.

Ware, W. (2015). Rounding up the homosexuals: The impact of juvenile court on queer and trans/gender non-conforming youth. In Eric Stanley & Nat Smith (Eds.), *Captive genders: Trans embodiment and the prison industrial complex* (2nd ed., pp. 97–104). Oakland, CA: AK Press.

Ybarra, M.L., Mitchell, K.J., & Kosciw, J.G. (2014). The relation between suicidal ideation and bullying victimization in a national sample of transgender and non-transgender adolescents. In P. Goldblum, D. Espelage, J. Chu, & B. Bognar (Eds.), *Youth suicide and bullying: Challenges and strategies for prevention and intervention* (pp. 134–147). New York, NY: Oxford University Press.

Yosso, T. (2005). Whose culture has capital? A critical race theory discussion of community cultural wealth. *Race, Ethnicity and Education, 8*(1), 69–91.

Zimman, L. (in press). Trans identification, agency, and embodiment in discourse: The linguistic construction of gender and sex. *International Journal of the Sociology of Language.*

12

BREAKING GENDER EXPECTATIONS

Adolescents' Critical Rewriting of a Trans Young Adult Novel

Rob Simon and the Addressing Injustices Collective: benjamin lee hicks, Ty Walkland, Ben Gallagher, Sarah Evis, and Pamela Baer

> Hello ugly children, this is your community radio station, 90.3 KZUK, the Z that sucks. Today we're talking about stereotypes and gender roles. The world has expectations for gender, what women should do and be and what men should do and be. It's like being put in a box, no way out. But we want to break out of those boxes, break your boundaries and do what you feel is right for you. So let your B-side show.

This voiceover opens a music video that adolescents in our project, Leah, Tali, Kayla, Grace, Sydney, and Ava made as a group response to the young-adult novel, *Beautiful Music for Ugly Children* (Cronn-Mills, 2012). The group of eighth-grade students from an ethnically diverse public school in downtown Toronto, along with teacher candidates from the Ontario Institute for Studies in Education of the University of Toronto (OISE), spent several months investigating ideas about gender and change, working to construct curriculum together that addressed their reactions to the novel. Our work is part of the Addressing Injustices project: a multiyear research collaboration that invites adolescents and educators to explore issues of social justice in response to young adult novels and co-research that process (Simon et al., 2018). The authors of this chapter are co-investigators who work alongside youth and teacher candidates and document our participatory research. Each year, we select novels like *Beautiful Music* that students and teachers use as openings for inquiries into identity, culture, and power.

Beautiful Music tells the story of Gabe, a teenage disc jockey and music lover, who tries to come to terms with who he is and how he fits into the world. He explains to readers,

> My birth name is Elizabeth, but I'm a guy. Gabe. My parents think I've gone crazy and the rest of the world is happy to agree with them, but I know I'm right. I've been a boy my whole life.
>
> *(Cronn-Mills, 2012, p. 8)*

"Beautiful Music for Ugly Children" is also the name of the late-night radio show that Gabe hosts on a community radio station. Music and records are a recurring metaphor in the novel. Gabe says,

> When you think about it, I'm like a record. Elizabeth is my A-side, the song everybody knows, and Gabe is my B-side – not heard as often, but just as good. It's time to let my B-side play.
>
> *(Cronn-Mills, 2012, back cover)*

The group's opening voiceover adopts the language of radio and records from the novel and uses it to frame their own frustrations with the gender stereotypes imposed on them as adolescents. They have a sense of the world's expectations for their behavior, and the ways in which those expectations can act as restraints. These words highlight adolescents' resistance to what they viewed as "stereotypical" portrayals of female characters in the novel, and their desire to "contribute to breaking gender expectations as a whole." The voiceover captures much of what we aim to explore in our chapter: the pedagogical implications of students' resistance, the consequences of adopting an inquiry stance (Cochran-Smith & Lytle, 2009) in and outside of the classroom, the importance of supporting a multiplicity of responses to texts, and the critical potential of opportunities for the creative redesign (Janks, 2010) of literature.

Queer-in-Content YA Literature and Queering Educational Space

Our co-inquiries with youth and teachers follow those of other educators and researchers who have explored critical approaches to teaching queer-in-content young adult (YA) literature and queer approaches to teaching and teacher education. While queer content is sometimes addressed in classrooms, homes, or other informal learning spaces, the introduction of literature with queer characters or subjects does not guarantee that texts are taken up using queer pedagogies. As Blackburn and Clark (2011) explain, the history of introducing queer-in-content texts within classrooms has often been framed around inclusivity, a limited concept that can narrow who is heard, seen, and acknowledged as "queer." This practice may unintentionally re-establish homophobic discourses or center cisgender identities – individuals whose gender identification corresponds with the sex assigned to them at birth – since it hinges on heteronormative conceptions of the "normal."

Blackburn and Clark (2011) distinguish between an accommodating approach to queer content and a "queered" pedagogy, which emerges collaboratively through "ways of thinking, talking, feeling, acting, and being that are both linguistic and textual" (p. 224). Clark and Blackburn (2009) advocate for deliberately foregrounding the *pleasures* of reading queer-in-content literature, "to promote a wide array of responses" (p. 30), as an aspect of critical literacy, which involves examining how texts reinforce or critique established social orders (Janks, 2010). In other words, *queering* pedagogy involves more than text choice, but also shifting how those texts are interrogated. In this way, a queered approach to queer-in-content literature resonates with the New Literacy Studies, which regards both literacy and identity as culturally constructed and multiple (Street, 1995). As Krasny (2013) noted, taking up YA literature to explore the social construction of gender, and the possibilities of subverting those constructions, does not "dismantle the actual power relations that construct difference" (p. 17). Following Blackburn (2003), we invite youth and adults to work through the tensions that may exist between reinforcing and destabilizing notions of gender in their responses to queer-in-content literature.

In our research, we have found that our understanding of what it means to queer educational spaces and curriculum is continually enriched and challenged by young people's powerful, creative, and even subversive responses to the texts we choose for them. Queering educational space entails working more consciously to expect and prepare for individuals of multidimensional gender identities, sexualities, and family structures (hicks, 2017a). A queering-space perspective challenges the limitations of "anti-transphobia education" by problematizing this framework, as well as the terminology that supports it (Airton, 2013). This ongoing process of questioning is central to a queer pedagogy because, although anti-homophobia and anti-transphobia approaches have been developed with the intention of opposing violence and supporting inclusion, there is an aspect of inclusion that is binary: that defines some people as "in" and others as "out" (hicks, 2017a). Queering educational space means challenging the passive use of words like "inclusive" and "accommodating" by questioning how these determinations are made, by whom, and for what purpose. It also involves risk-taking: challenging previously uninterrogated institutional standards with the awareness that current approaches to anti-homophobia and anti-transphobia education are frequently ineffective in altering the felt experience of being a trans/gender diverse person in schools (hicks, 2017b; Taylor et al., 2011).

Our approach to queering instructional spaces has parallels to Hilary Janks' (2010) conception of critical literacy education, in particular to her observation that attempts to define the world are never neutral. Janks notes that "both the word and the world embody human choice" (p. 227) and calls for reimagining educational structures. Janks' (2010) four-part critical literacy framework emphasizes the function of *power*, conceptions of identity and *difference*, individuals' *access* to socially valued materials and discourses, and the role of *design* as a means for young people to engage in redesigning, rewriting, or remaking the world (Freire, 1970/2005).

Co-Researching, Co-Teaching, and Co-Constructing Curriculum

The inquiry process that produced the video featured in this chapter draws upon Freirean (1970/2005) problem-posing and problem-solving education, which invites youth and adults to make power dynamics visible with the goal of addressing inequitable conditions in their schools, communities, and society (Picower, 2007). This work involves critical practitioner research, which positions educators as researchers, knowledge generators, and agents of social and educational change (Cochran-Smith & Lytle, 2009), and participatory action research, which involves research collaborations among educators, youth, and community members (Cammarota & Fine, 2008). Both methodologies foreground the epistemic value of situated experience and reciprocal connections between research and practice. In our work together, youth and teacher candidates are co-researchers whose questions, affective responses, and experiences of societal inequities inform the research process. We invited participants to use *Beautiful Music* as a basis for exploring their own identities, the social construction of gender, and the role of allies in the enactment of an equitable, all-gendered future. We intended this to be a starting point for the disruption of transphobic, homophobic, and misogynistic discourses and practices in schools and society: a way to "queer" curriculum, teacher education, and educational spaces (Butler-Wall, Cosier, & Harper, 2015; Goldstein, Collins, & Halder, 2008; hicks, 2017b).

In total 30 middle school students, 19 teacher candidates, and the 6 members of our research team came together to discuss our responses to *Beautiful Music*, to explore our experiences of gender and transition in our lives, and to use these conversations and activities as a basis for designing arts-based critical literacy projects. We collected videotaped and audiotaped classroom discussions, interviews, written reflections, creative work, and photographs. The goal of our larger project was to provide opportunities for youth and teachers to co-construct social justice curriculum that challenges top-down hierarchies and standardized curriculum development (Shor, 1996) while exploring the potential of collective research for actualizing social change.

This chapter was co-authored by six people who represent a larger research collective: Rob Simon, teacher educator and principal investigator of the project; benjamin lee hicks, artist, activist, and primary teacher, who organized gender workshops for youth and teachers; Ty Walkland, an experienced equity educator, who coordinated the project; Ben Gallagher, a community-based arts educator, who helped organize and analyze data; Pamela Baer, a filmmaker who oversaw digital storytelling workshops and directed a film about this research (available at www.addressinginjustices.com); and Sarah Evis, educator and activist, who co-directed our research with eighth-grade students as their teacher. Our work together was part of the curriculum in Sarah's eighth-grade class and assignments in Rob's literacy methods course.

Youth and teacher candidates were invited to read and reflect on *Beautiful Music* in their own classes before meeting as a large group. We opened our first session together with an activity called "Big Paper," which facilitates a silent conversation through writing in response to quotes from the source text, as well as from other resources related to gender and equity. These initial impressions and questions were taken up throughout the remainder of our work. In the tradition of critical literacy educators like Hilary Janks (2010) and Linda Christensen (2017), we invited all participants to place their life experiences in conversation with our shared readings. Youth and teachers participated in creative workshops, led by benjamin and Pam, in which they developed found poetry from words generated collectively in conversations about their own experiences of identity and change. Participants used versions of these poems to create collaborative scripts for digital story-making.

Small groups of teacher candidates and students also designed three curriculum activities in response to the book. Curriculum-making provided teacher candidates with ideas for their future classrooms. Students chose one of these co-planned activities and worked together to produce a project addressing an area of interest for them related to gender equity. These projects included a rainbow mural with mosaic fish representing gender creativity, which is now on permanent display in the middle school; a project that involved rewriting *Beautiful Music* as a choose-your-own adventure online roleplaying game; a YouTube channel exploring gendered language and representation; a life-size diorama that addressed ideas related to identity and change; and the music video that we discuss in the remainder of this chapter.

(Re)making *Beautiful Music*

The three-minute music video, edited on students' iPhones, documents their response to the gendered ideals of femininity they encounter in their lives and saw reproduced in *Beautiful Music*. It opens with students performing feminized gender stereotypes – gazing at themselves coquettishly in a bathroom mirror and wearing high-heeled shoes (Figure 12.1) – reinforced by the soundtrack, "Stacy's Mom," by Fountains of Wayne (Collingwood & Schlesinger, 2003), which sexualizes a friend's mother from the perspective of a teenaged boy.

FIGURE 12.1 Shoes that represent conventional ideals of femininity.

Halfway through the song, Leah "flips the record over," and the music changes to Beyonce's "Pretty Hurts" (Coleman, Furler, & Knowles, 2013). Like the previous song, this selection is specific and intentional. The director of the "Pretty Hurts" music video, Melina Matsoukas, noted in an interview for MTV News that the song explores "all the pain and struggle that we go through as women to maintain this impossible standard of beauty" (Vena, 2013, n.p.). The group echoes this sentiment in their voiceover:

> Wait, wait. Why does the world portray women like this? All the words rushing through our heads telling us not to act dumb, but don't be too smart. Be fit, but don't be too good at sports. It shuts us in a box and tapes it closed. Women are strong and powerful in their own ways. If you could break that box, what would you do?

In the next scene, Sydney steps into a box that reads "A-side" wearing a full-length dress and heels. She jumps out wearing jeans, and literally smashes this box with a hammer (Figure 12.2).

The second half of the film shows what students call, following the central metaphor in *Beautiful Music*, their "B-sides": images of students as artists, bakers, drummers, and friends. Sydney and Ava dance in front of a chalkboard, decorated with rainbows, stars, hearts, and peace signs, that reads: "Let my B-side run free: Let your freak flag fly." As the students' conversations described in the following section and students' project plan illustrate, the completed video draws together many of the group's collectively negotiated ideas for responding to the text, such as "smashing boxes, hate labels, etc.," using the "elements of music video" to "show people can have multidimensional A-sides and B-sides."

FIGURE 12.2 Sydney smashing her "A-side" box.

Resistant Readings for Critical Rewriting

In their initial small-group conversations about the book, students wondered whether they could deviate from what they perceived to be our expectations as teachers – in their words, "go off the sheet" and pursue their own areas of interest tangential to the novel. It was in one of these early planning sessions that the group members first articulated their critique of the binary gender stereotypes they noticed in *Beautiful Music*. Tali was vocal about the specific plot and character elements that frustrated her:

> I disliked it because, first of all, I thought the plot was, like, really, really slow and not a lot happened . . . And then I also just felt like a lot of the characters and scenarios were like really, really cliché. It felt really done before.

From here, the group launched into an analysis of the female characters in the novel and voiced the ways in which these characters felt two-dimensional or unrealistic, especially compared to their own more nuanced sense of themselves.

What could easily have been construed as resistance to the assignment, a rejection of the book itself, or a "risky" conversation because of the heated emotions that ensued, became the focus of a brainstorming session that inspired the project plan for the music video. As students continued to work through their ideas, the group deepened their critique of the novel and envisioned their creative response. They not only saw how Gabe's transgender identity was being labeled and stereotyped by some of his classmates, but also how Gabe as a male-identifying person was actively complicit in perpetuating stereotypical ideas about his female friends and crushes. For the girls in the group, who were simultaneously reflecting on their own experiences of change, the project became a way for them to discuss and enact what it might mean to break through the labels and stereotypes they themselves felt burdened by.

Initially, students voiced a strong desire to "break boxes" by physically smashing some cardboard boxes in Leah's backyard. Fairly quickly, the boxes took on a symbolic weight, as Sydney said, "Boxes? No, we're *breaking* the boxes, we're breaking the boundaries." At the same time, they also considered the potential responses of authority figures. Tali said, "We're supposed to be, like, a *safe* space, not *breaking*," and Kayla worried about their teacher's reaction: "I'm not sure if Sarah would be so into it, just like, 'here are haters.'" While they expressed a desire to resist authority, they were uncertain about how that would be perceived. Others reassured Kayla that breaking boxes was a symbolic action, representing positive images of femininity and allyship: "We're talking about getting *rid* of hate: We're just *hating hate*."

The group also hoped to make space in this project to showcase their creative abilities, and initially discussed plans that included writing a song, hosting a podcast, or choreographing and performing a dance. This list led to a discussion of feminism, the Bechdel test (Bechdel, 2008), which critiques films in which female characters talk only about men, and the movie *Mean Girls* (Guinier, Messick, Michaels, Rosner, & Shimkin, 2004), ultimately returning to the discussion of gender stereotypes that became central to all subsequent conversations. From their perspective, the female characters in the novel seemed one-dimensional, and in the eyes of the protagonist, Gabe, they were, as Kayla put it, merely "sex objects with nice lips."

As the group continued to negotiate a shared project they could agree on, they launched into a discussion about the book's cover. They articulated that covers are another metaphor for thinking about stereotypes. And in reimagining the cover, they hit on the idea of recreating the female characters of *Beautiful Music* in ways that were less stereotypical. After the many twists and turns of a sometimes-heated brainstorming process, including frustrations about having to discard project ideas that they were excited about, the group decided to combine all their ideas into one: a music video that features boxes representing stereotypes that must be destroyed for a more nuanced self to emerge. Their subsequent exchange was a whirlwind of overlapping voices:

Tali: I don't know, I liked our original idea of including all of our talents and personalities into the video, so it's like, she'll be baking . . .

Kayla: [*interjecting*] I'll make *genderbread* men!

Tali: And it's embracing our own femininity and sexuality, personality, showing our talents and interests . . .

Leah: [*overlapping*] We'll be smashing boxes and punching . . .

Kayla: stand-up twerking . . .

Sydney: We'll be showing our talents.

Grace: Exactly.

When inquiry invites simultaneous and different responses, the possibility of conflict increases as well. For example, during the filming of the music video, some members of the group needed to step away from the project. Their post-production reflections gave voice to the challenges they experienced when the video began to evolve in directions they had not initially intended. In her final interview, Tali said:

> It got to the point where I just, I had to quit halfway through. And on the last day, I mean, we all sort of talked it out, we kind of made up. But, I don't know, it was like we didn't really work through it. I mean, people just kept working and I just went on to help other groups with their projects. It was a difficult process.

Later in the same interview, as she tried to reconcile the interpersonal difficulties of the creative process with a final video that her classmates responded well to, Tali also said that her "take-away was [that she] can't really have expectations for other people":

> I have to just, you know, roll with it, play off stuff. You know? Yeah, I think I really related to the project. And it was frustrating to have to leave halfway through. But I think I need to learn to give people more chances.

This was difficult learning – not just for Tali and her group members, but for us as teachers and researchers as well. Involving young people in constructing their own learning experiences invites conditions where everyone involved wrestles with difference and conflict, with the uncontrolled and the unknown. The risks are integral to the inquiry process.

(Re)reading the Music Video

Sarah's rereading of the group's video, from her perspective as their teacher, helps to shed light on the world from which these adolescents' words and images evolved:

> At first glance, it is a charming, clever, and entertaining take on the A-sides and B-sides of six Grade 8 students; a student film, made entirely on an iPhone, with a rocking soundtrack. Peel off a layer, using the transcribed conversations that led up to the creation of this project, and we see a care-fully thought out and nuanced response to the gender binary stereotypes in the novel.

When we look carefully at what is going on in the scene of their collective dressing-up time in the bathroom, we see the students giggling and genuinely hamming it up for the camera. But they are also gazing at themselves in the mirror. This is not a coincidence. Part of what they want us to see is that they are watching themselves – they are both the actors and the audience. The performers are standing in for the stereotypical male gaze that they found so problematic in the book. They seem to be thinking: We are showing you what you want to see, but we are on to you, and so we are also disrupting what you think you see – a conventional dressing-up and decorating of "femininity": make-up, hair, tight dresses, and fancy shoes (see Figure 12.1).

Let's move to the action, flip the record over. Sydney doing what she was so keen to do in the group's original discussion about what their project should look like – smashing the box (see Figure 12.2), and with a vengeance!

The clothing changes, the students' real selves emerge. Kayla making *gender-bread* cookies in the kitchen, Ava making art, Leah, the cameraperson, drumming, then Sydney and Grace and Ava – wearing her Girl Power jacket! – dancing, gently supporting each other.

I am never able to watch this section of the video without recalling the first time the group showed it to me, sitting at my desk, in the middle of English class. Tears streaming down my face, threatening to erupt into sobs of joy and amazement.

Because the final layer peels away to reveal what can happen when a group of students with difficult and complicated relationships with being at school feel supported in their strong desire to address damaging social constructs, and be their true selves, all within the framework of a novel study assignment.

As Sarah's analysis suggests, the music video illustrated how students took up the research team's content, questions, and ideas about trans identity and allowed a story of gender transition to speak to experiences in their own lives that have felt similarly mismatched. The video also demonstrated students' natural facility for interpreting and remaking texts from their own feminist perspectives (Appleman, 2014).

Several group members interpreted their video as a response to the ways that gender roles were imposed on them by the world at large. Grace was struck by the way the novel did not fully resolve the negative impacts of stereotyping. She said, "We wanted to show that if you're trying to break stereotypes, then why are you stereotyping people in the book?" For Tali, the portrayals of women in the novel spoke to her own felt-experience of being boxed and labeled by others. She said, "We really related to that, always being stereotyped into being, you know, *basic*, and having this white rich girl personality – that we're all supposed to be exactly like that." Reflecting on the message they wanted to send about their resistance to stereotypes, Leah noted, "Not all girls want to be like that. They have different opinions on how they want to act and how they want to live their life."

As we described previously, the group presented social stereotypes as the "A-side" of a record, while their more deeply personal selves became the "B-side." Some members of the group were suspicious of this metaphor, because they felt aware of the pervasiveness of binaries within it, even as they hoped to disrupt them. Tali, however, argued, "You can have a *multidimensional* A-side and a *multidimensional* B-side." For us as researchers this idea offered a frame to interpret the group's analysis of gender that speaks to the difficulty of stepping outside of binary constructs – linguistically, conceptually, socially, and institutionally – far enough to "queer" them. Although it does not address trans lives specifically, the concept of multidimensionality highlights how the music video directly challenges systemic patriarchy and misogyny that allow gender binaries, stereotypes, and inequities to persist.

At first glance, the students' inquiry may seem removed from the focus of a book with a transgender main character. On closer inspection, however, students' own work is strikingly similar to the process that the protagonist, Gabe, experiences in *Beautiful Music*. Their message reveals an increasingly common and vocal rejection of the binary, gendered language that perpetuates gender stereotypes. The resistance that these young people demonstrate is therefore also queer, just as this ongoing process of pedagogical inquiry is queering.

By embodying how their self-knowledge challenges the ways they feel "boxed in and labelled" by others, these young people articulated their demands for self-determination. This insistence creates a spaciousness within which the limiting questions we may ask about gender are eclipsed by many possibilities for a future in which gender diversity is celebrated. By asking their audience, "If you could break that box, what would *you* do?" the group powerfully implicates all viewers – including their classmates, teachers, and ourselves as researchers – in the work of "breaking gender expectations as a whole."

Implications for Literacy Education and Cross-Disciplinary Fields

The examples we present in this chapter suggest how taking an inquiry stance (Cochran-Smith & Lytle, 2009) on gender involves negotiating difference and discomfort, working across multiple viewpoints, modes of expression, and even points of contention, toward imagining and working toward an alternative future. This entails reframing adolescents' resistance as forms of critical engagement, with the potential to enliven rather than impede their learning, as well our own learning as educators, parents, caregivers, and scholars in literacy and other fields. The adolescents' inquiries presented in this chapter offer one example of what exploring gender through critical literacy can look like.

Although we locate this work in a classroom and draw upon frameworks from literacy studies and education more broadly, this exploration of the intersection of gender diversity, identity, and power may resonate with scholars and activists who work in other sites and fields of study. Our research particularly suggests how listening to and learning from young people's experiences and perspectives can be a starting point for raising questions, making connections, and opening conversations about gender. Recalling Janks' (2010) framework, the music video evolved through conversations in which students took up critical perspectives on *power* relationships in society – including relationships to texts, teachers, and normative constructions of gender. Negotiating different approaches to responding creatively to *Beautiful Music* invited a *diversity* of perspectives and increased *access*, allowing all group members to participate. Yet it was not an easy or foolproof process. The eventual shape of the final project was revealed by holding the multiplicity of young people's perspectives in focus. Recalling Clark and Blackburn's (2009) discussion of the pleasure of inviting multiple responses as a way of queering educational spaces, in or outside of school, this demonstrates how pleasure and conflict can occur simultaneously in youths' inquiries and are themselves not binaries either.

As these students considered the words of *Beautiful Music* together, they were able to parse, deconstruct, debate, and reform some of the ideas that challenged them. In doing so, they showed, shared, and came to understand more about their own gendered experiences in the world. This could be read as a political project of making students who are comfortable resisting authority, including the authority of educators or other adults. From another perspective, it presents an opportunity to engage in the emotional labor required to accept – even celebrate – students' resistance. In supporting Krasny's (2013) call to demonstrate how to dismantle the power relations that construct difference, educators, researchers, and concerned adults must also be prepared to play an active role in dismantling our own (assumed) power.

In spite of our collective encouragement for adolescents to recreate words and worlds (Freire, 1970/2005), we remain cautious about attributing this group's creative efforts solely to our research design or theoretical approaches. The middle school students we worked with came with their own pre-existing group dynamics relationships, and critical perspectives. The music video featured in this chapter is about being understood in ways that resonate with young people's experiences of themselves and their world. It is also about developing more empathic perspectives of others. As Janks (2010) suggests, creative rewriting is a way of empowering students to change the world, and developing empathy and understanding in the process.

When teachers first introduce books with queer content in classrooms or concerned adults invite adolescents into conversations about gender, it can feel imperative to define words like *transition* and *transgender*, to talk directly about stereotypes and myths that some people carry about queer lives and trans communities, and to discuss the details of policies that aim to disrupt transphobia and cis-centrism. This was a significant beginning for us as researchers as well. Yet, in our ongoing work together, we recognize there will always be a next layer of questioning to consider in the practice of queering. Mirroring in some respects youths' own process of rewriting gender, we continue to work through how rewriting curriculum to queer the physical and emotional landscape of learning environments may differ from introducing content that is queer in story or theme.

We began this project in the hope that we could support youth and teacher candidates to explore non-binary understandings of gender in ways that were free of limitations. Two years later, we face the humbling recognition that stories told in reaction to a dualistic system are still constructed in reference to that system. We invited middle school students to read this novel with a transgender main character in the hope that maybe they would think about gender and the future of gender differently. With so much more depth and multiplicity than our own gendered upbringings had prepared us to expect, these students responded beyond binaries.

References

Airton, L. (2013). Leave "those kids" alone: On the conflation of school homophobia and suffering queers. *Curriculum Inquiry, 43*(5), 532–562.

Appleman, D. (2014). *Critical encounters in high school English: Teaching literary theory to adolescents* (3rd ed.). New York, NY: Teachers College Press & Urbana, IL: NCTE.

Bechdel, A. (2008). *The essential dykes to watch out for.* New York, NY: Houghton Mifflin Harcourt.

Blackburn, M. (2003). Exploring literacy performances and power dynamics at The Loft: Queer youth reading the world and word. *Research in the Teaching of English, 37*(4), 467–490.

Blackburn, M., & Clark, C. (2011). Analyzing talk in a long-term literature discussion group: Ways of operating within LGBT-inclusive and queer discourses. *Reading Research Quarterly, 46*(3), 222–248.

Butler-Wall, A., Cosier, K., & Harper, R.L. (Eds.) (2015). *Rethinking sexism, gender, and sexuality.* Milwaukee, WI: Rethinking Schools.

Cammarota, J., & Fine, M. (2008). *Revolutionizing education: Youth participatory action research in motion.* New York, NY: Routledge.

Christensen, L. (2017). *Reading, writing, and rising up: Teaching about social justice and the power of the written word* (2nd ed.). Milwaukee, WI: Rethinking Schools.

Clark, C., & Blackburn, M. (2009). Reading LGBT-themed literature with young people: What's possible? *English Journal, 98*(4), 25–32.

Cochran-Smith, M., & Lytle, S.L. (2009). *Inquiry as stance: Practitioner research in the next generation.* New York, NY: Teachers College Press.

Coleman, J., Furler, S., & Knowles, B. (2013). Pretty hurts. Recorded by Beyoncé Knowles. On *Beyoncé* [CD]. New York, NY: Columbia Records.

Collingwood, C., & Schlesinger, A. (2003). Stacy's mom. Recorded by Fountains of Wayne. On *Welcome interstate managers* [CD]. New York, NY: S-Curve Records.

Cronn-Mills, K. (2012). *Beautiful music for ugly children.* Mendota Heights, MN: Flux.

Freire, P. (1970/2005). *Pedagogy of the oppressed.* New York, NY: Continuum.

Goldstein, T., Collins, A., & Halder, M. (2008). Anti-homophobia education in public schooling: A Canadian case study of policy implementation. *Journal of Gay and Lesbian Services, 19*(2), 47–66.

Guinier, J., Messick, J., Michaels, L., Rosner, L., Shimkin, T. (Producers), & Waters, M. (Director). (2004). *Mean girls* [Motion picture]. Hollywood, CA: Paramount Pictures.

hicks, b.l. (2017a). Gracefully unexpected, deeply present and positively disruptive: Love and queerness in classroom community. In D. Linville (Ed.), *Queering education: Pedagogy, curriculum, policy*. Occasional Paper Series 37. New York, NY: Bank Street College of Education.

hicks, b.l. (2017b). *ALL-WAYS in transition: De-sensationalizing beliefs about trans identities in schooling through participatory action research*. Master's thesis. Retrieved from https://tspace.library.utoronto.ca/handle/1807/79127.

Janks, H. (2010). *Literacy and power*. New York, NY: Routledge.

Krasny, K.A. (2013). Taking patriarchy to task: Youth, YouTube, and young adult literature. In B.J. Guzzetti & T.A. Bean (Eds.), *Adolescent literacies and the gendered self: (Re)constructing identities through multimodal literacy practices* (pp. 13–21). New York, NY: Routledge.

Picower, B. (2007). Supporting new educators to teach for social justice: The critical inquiry project model. *Penn GSE Perspectives on Urban Education, 5*(1). Retrieved from www.urbanedjournal.org/node/147.

Shor, I. (1996). *When students have power: Negotiating authority in a critical pedagogy*. Chicago, IL: University of Chicago Press.

Simon, R., hicks, b.l., Walkland, T., Gallagher, B., Evis, S., & Baer, P. (2018). "But in the end, you are all beautiful": Exploring gender through digital composition. *English Journal, 107*(3), 39–46.

Street, B.V. (1995). *Social literacies: Critical approaches to literacy in development, ethnography and education*. New York, NY: Longman.

Taylor, C., Peter, T., McMinn, T.L., Schachter, K., Beldom, S., Ferry, A., . . . Paquin, S. (2011). *Every class in every school: The first national climate survey on homophobia in Canadian schools: Final report*. Toronto, ON: Egale.

Vena, J. (2013, December 18). Beyonce's "Pretty hurts": Find out how the video was supposed to end. MTV News. Retrieved from www.mtv.com/news/1719326/beyonce-pretty-hurts-video-alternate-ending.

13

DEFINING GENDER AND SEXUALITY IN LGBTQ MEMOIRS

Kate E. Kedley and Jenna Spiering

The lived experiences of youth in increasingly diverse educational spaces embody a complex reality that is not always present in the literature, texts, and materials within classrooms, schools, and libraries. Memoirs can serve as an important genre for considering the lived experiences of youth as they relate to narratives of growing up and coming of age and negotiating expressions of gender and sexuality within the individual's culture and society. Furthermore, memoirs can serve as significant sites for youth and adults to examine the socially constituted (or alternatively, naturally occurring) nature of gender and sexuality. These types of books offer a way to examine expressions of gender and sexuality as they are defined through the complex negotiation of forces outside the individual parents, family, friends, school, religion, culture, nation, and society.

In this chapter, we examine two recently published LGBTQ (lesbian, gay, bisexual, transgender, and queer) memoirs: *Being Jazz: My Life as a (Transgender) Teen* (Jennings, 2016) and *Saving Alex: When I was Fifteen I Told My Mormon Parents I Was Gay, and That's When My Nightmare Began* (Cooper, 2016). Using the theoretical framework of queer theory (Butler, 1999; Halberstam, 2005; Rich, 1980), we consider how youth define, describe, and reflect on their own gender and sexuality within these memoirs. These memoirs are specifically written by and about LGBTQ youth and introduce new ways of challenging and disrupting discourses that both create and limit possibilities for understanding and discussing gender and sexuality with youth in English Language Arts (ELA) classrooms, library spaces, youth service programs, homes, and beyond. In this chapter, we explore two questions: (1) How do queer youth define their own gender and sexuality through memoir? (2) In what ways does memoir provide space for conversations about gender and sexuality in classrooms, libraries, homes, and other educational and reading spaces?

LGBTQ Young Adult Literature

LGBTQ young adult literature (YAL) can serve as an important site for generating challenging questions about gender and sexuality. Several scholars suggest that these texts deserve more prominent spaces in classrooms (e.g., Blackburn, 2011; Clark & Blackburn, 2009). Blackburn and Smith (2010) however, note that simply including LGBTQ texts in a classroom, library, or home does not do enough to push young people to think differently about gender and sexuality. These authors suggest that teachers and those interreacting with youth around literacy must attend to issues of heteronormativity and intersectionality while teaching and engaging with LGBTQ texts. Intersectionality theory (Crenshaw, 1991) considers various and overlapping forms of oppression that result from intersections of race, gender, and social class. For example, women face challenges in our society in terms of sexism, access to equal earnings, and discrimination. The rubric of "women" is not a homogeneous category, however. For example, black women face a different kind of oppression than white women because black women are also marginalized in terms of race. This is not a double oppression (i.e., race and gender), but a different type of oppression altogether.

In addition to including LGBTQ literature in the curriculum and into home reading materials, educators, parents, and others interacting with young people must also think about questioning strategies that invite queer readings of texts by troubling standard or mainstream readings of texts. While several scholars have engaged in analyzing LGBTQ YAL by looking for complicated depictions of gender and sexuality (e.g., Kedley & Spiering, 2017; Linville, 2015; Thein & Kedley, 2015), little attention has been paid to the ways these themes present themselves in nonfiction texts produced both by and for youth audiences. This chapter addresses this gap by looking at examples of contemporary LGBTQ memoirs that are authored *by* young adults *for* young adults.

Contemporary Critique of Memoirs

An article in the online edition of the *New Yorker* noted that the memoir has often been thought of as the "black sheep of the literary family" (Mendelsohn, 2010). Memoirs, the author claims, are full of "unseemly self-exposures, unpalatable betrayals, unavoidable mendacity, a soupcon of meretriciousness," all motivated by the "need to be the center of attention" (p. 68). A year later, a *New York Times* book reviewer concurred, and labeled the entire genre of memoirs as representing the "lost art of shutting up," indicating that not everyone's life story should necessarily be written (Genzlinger, 2011). Nevertheless, the memoir genre persists, and a quick search on the online book retailer Amazon (www. amazon.com) will provide hundreds of new memoir releases, and a plentitude of "how-to" books on writing memoirs that will potentially allow a person to create a legacy, make money, and become a best-selling author. Although memoirs are heavily criticized, in a more recent online article Nolan (2013) noted that it is a "demoralizing truth . . . that there is a huge appetite for first-person essays" in the form of memoirs.

Young Adult Memoirs

Memoirs created by youth constitute an emerging trend in young adult publishing – there is increased desire for stories authored by and for youth. LGBTQ memoirs offer readers insight into the sometimes fraught and complicated or alternatively sometimes rewarding and liberating processes of discovering the individual's sexuality, coming out of the closet, or self-defining gender. Memoirs provide scholars with texts that represent "real" and authentic stories in which youth (often aided by a ghost writer or some sort of invisible adult, guiding influence, or editor) are provided space to author their own gender and sexuality in ways that may run counter to the dominant discourses circulating at a societal level.

While studies have suggested that memoirs can be important sites for reproducing *and* resisting dominant discourses about youth (Rogers & Marshall, 2012), there is also research that suggests the form and structure of young people's memoirs might limit or narrow the ways in which publishers define the kind of stories and trajectories that youth have access to (Thein, Sulzer, & Schmidt, 2013). Little scholarly attention has been paid specifically to LGBTQ memoirs and the way in which youth define, describe, and represent their own gender and sexuality, however. Therefore, we suggest that those working with young people, literature studies, education, or gender, women's, and sexualities studies to look to memoirs to engage youth in critical conversations about gender and sexualities in identity development.

Our Perspectives: Queer Theory

Queer theory is not one unified field of study (Britzman, 1995; Butler, 2004; Sedgwick, 1990; Sykes, 2011). In our analysis of LGBTQ memoirs and their use in classrooms and informal educational settings, we focus on the often-conflated concepts of gender and sexuality identity. An individual's sexuality is frequently assumed by others based on a person's gender presentation, actions, or clothing. For example, a person who was labeled male at birth, but who exhibits what is normally thought of as "feminine" traits may be perceived by others as gay. A person who was labeled female at birth, but who exhibits what are normally thought of as masculine traits may be perceived by others as a lesbian. Queer theory explains, however, that there is no link between gender and sexual identity or practice (Butler, 2004). A female is no more inclined to be feminine than masculine, and a male is no more inclined to be masculine than feminine (even though people may assume these are natural inclinations). A male who is masculine is not more suited to heterosexuality any more than homosexuality, and a female who is feminine is not more suited to heterosexuality either. Sexuality appears to naturally stem from gender identity, but the presumed link is influenced by social constructions of feminine and masculine.

Second, queer theory proposes that gender and sexuality are unstable and temporal categories (Butler, 2004; Marcus, 2005). Societal definitions and individual performances of gender and sexual identities change over the course of a lifetime, through time and over place, from generation to generation, and from context to context. The definition of "woman" today in the United States is different than it was a century ago, and even that definition varies significantly between cultures, regions, and even families. Homosexuality as an identity category is a fairly recent concept (see D'Emilio & Freedman, 2012). Homosexual practice has always existed, but the category of a homosexual (or an LGBTQ) identity is a contemporary label in U.S. society and its meaning is different across cultures and regions.

For the sake of clarity in this chapter, we use the term gender to indicate male or female. Although queer theory provides a clear distinction between sex (based on genitals) and gender (based on social and cultural norms, and presented through an individual's identity, performance, or presentation), we limit our use of gender to describe a character's gender presentation (that readers can see through visuals and images in a text) or gender identity (that readers can read through thought bubbles or narrative in a text). As authors, when we use the terms sexuality, sexual identity, or sexuality category, we refer to a character's capacity for or preference for intimate and romantic partnership. We do not use this definition as limited to sexual practice alone.

Heterotrajectory

We define a *heterotrajectory* (Kedley & Spiering, 2017) as the assumed trajectory or course a person is expected to take, over time, in a heterosexual romantic partnership and in a society that values heteronormativity. As the well-known playground song suggests: "first comes love, then comes marriage, then comes the baby in the baby carriage." We live with unspoken yet powerful traditions and customs that dictate the expected stages of heterosexual relationships, including the acceptable order of these stages. In this manner, those who perform and enact a different trajectory, including those who remain single or those who have more than one partner simultaneously even if they are heterosexual, are relegated to the margins.

If any – hetero or homo – romantic partnership does not follow this expected trajectory, the couple and their relationship are subject to: (1) confusion, e.g., "Why don't you get married?" or "How will you explain to your parents that you're living together without tying the knot?"; (2) intimate questioning about sexual behavior or shock, e.g., "When are you two having kids?" and "You're not having kids?"; (3) suspicion about the authenticity of the relationship from others, e.g., "If he/she isn't ready to settle down, give her/him an ultimatum"; and (4) suspicion about the authenticity of the relationship from a member of the couple, e.g., "If he/she isn't ready to commit to marriage this month, I need to move on."

There are, of course, perpetual and innumerable exceptions to the heterot-rajectory, and much like stable gender and sexuality categories, few people or partnerships meet the standard society prescribes as acceptable and desirable. Part of dismantling restrictive gender and sexuality categories is identifying them to challenge them. The same objective holds true in attempting to disrupt the heter-otrajectory. An important part of disrupting the heterotrajectory within literature for young adults (including memoirs), and with youth is identifying these trajec-tories and discussing how they limit (or expand) individual choice and police (or liberate) variations from the norm.

Our Study

We began our research by reading several LGBTQ memoirs written by and for youth and became interested in the way in which these young authors represented their life stories through published texts. We also began noticing commonalities in the form and structure of these narratives. We narrowed our inquiry on two memoirs: *Being Jazz: My Life as a (Transgender) Teen* (2016) by Jazz Jennings and *Saving Alex: When I was Fifteen I told my Mormon Parents I was Gay, and That's When My Nightmare Began* (2016) by Alex Cooper with Joanna Brooks.

While both memoirs feature LGBTQ teens who are "coming of age" and defining their own gender and sexuality, the individual experiences they relate to their audiences are quite different. Jazz Jennings, a teenage girl famous for her reality television show on cable television, shares her experiences and struggles growing up as a transgender girl with a fairly supportive family and friend support system. Her memoir is described on the back cover of the book as being "about accepting yourself, learning to live an authentic life, and helping everyone to embrace their own truths."

Alex Cooper's story, however, is about her life as a teenager, growing up in a Mormon family and community, who eventually realizes she is gay and comes out to her parents. This bothers Cooper's parents so much that they force her to live hours away with a couple named Johnny and Tiala Siale. There, Cooper and other youths are subjected to a kind of gay conversion therapy that is so abusive that Cooper eventually sues the Siale family and attempts to legally restrict her parents from trying to influence her sexuality.

After reading each memoir, we made a second pass through each text looking for, marking, and coding passages where each author self-defines and describes his or her own gender or sexuality. As researchers, we then compared our codes and notes and engaged in narrative coding (Saldaña, 2012) of the identified pas-sages for topics and themes related to gender and sexuality. These thematic codes focused primarily on self-representation (Rogers & Marshall, 2012), and benevo-lence/malevolence toward people and institutions. Three themes across the two texts resulted from our analysis; we identify these themes and offer examples of them from each of the two texts.

Self-Defining Sexuality and Gender Through Memoir

There is a significant debate in U.S. society about whether sexuality is self-authored or if sexuality is culturally nurtured. The same debate holds true for gender identity: is gender identity intrinsic or are individuals influenced by society? Nevertheless, and perhaps even more importantly, it is imperative to intentionally bring those discussions to classrooms and to out-of-school learning spaces, including homes. Doing so provides opportunities for people who have been traditionally marginalized to share their stories and allows young people to see themselves (or their potential selves) in texts and to build their understandings of diverse genders and sexualities.

The genre of memoir allows young people to directly share their own experiences through narrative reflection and allows the readers to engage directly with the authors' stories. Long (2007) suggests that youth when presented with memoirs can "find emotional connections between their own lives" (p. xv). Youth and adults may use the memoirs of Cooper, Jennings, or others to prompt discussion about the question of whether gender and sexual identity are a matter of self-definition or if they are identities that society coerces individuals into in one way or the other, or a combination of the two. Individuals may examine what forces prompt a belief in one or the other. Who does each belief serve or hurt?

In both memoirs we examined, Jennings and Cooper spent a significant amount of time presenting their sexuality (in Cooper's case) and gender (in Jennings' case) as something that they have known from early childhood. They frequently offer evidence to prove this, such as early preferences for a type of clothing or toys, or early masculine or feminine behavior that didn't "match" with the sex they were labeled at birth. Jennings, for example, said that as a baby she turned her onesie into a dress and frequently mentioned early preferences for all things glittery, sparkly, and purple, which as she noted, are typically linked to young girls in contemporary U.S. society. Cooper also frequently reflected on how she was never a typical girl, but instead demonstrated traits associated with a boy (therefore linking her to a lesbian sexuality): she was "rowdy and independent (p. 6), "impatient and a handful" (p. 9), and "hard headed and difficult" (p. 19). Our readers may ask: What do stories like these mean for those who identify as LGBTQ but who do not have these early experiences? How do these stories influence the way gender and sexuality are understood? Are individuals "born this way"?

As noted earlier, the heterotrajectory (Kedley & Spiering, 2017) is the assumed trajectory or course a person is expected to take over the course of life within a heterosexual romantic partnership and in a society that values heteronormativity. Heterotrajectory often manifests itself in the relationships of LGBTQ-identified people and occupy a prominent place in the fight for equality. For much of the early 2000s and 2010s, the focus for LGBTQ rights focused on marriage equality, or the right for same-sex couples to marry and attain the benefits that came with legal coupling.

Adults and youth may begin to think about heterotrajectory relative to these texts. How does heterotrajectory influence individuals' understandings of Jennings' and Cooper's marginalized gender and sexual identities? Does heterotrajectory influence Jennings or Cooper as they self-define themselves? Furthermore, as youth may begin to critically examine their own lives, how are they influenced by hetero-norms and the heterotrajectory, rather than simply accepting them as the "natural" way of growing up and becoming an adult or having a family?

Benevolence and Malevolence

Both Jennings and Cooper in these two LGTBQ memoirs frequently reflect on the way family members react to their journeys. They also often note how social and cultural institutions restrict or enable their own representations of their gender and sexuality. Perhaps because of the nature of a memoir – a story that inherently involves real people, and material consequences for the author's lived experience after publication – both Jennings and Cooper exhibit a kind of benevolence toward individuals who did not understand (and sometimes, did not accept) their gender or sexuality. For example, Cooper, a teen raised in a Mormon family and community, is at times incredibly critical of her family's religion. At the same time, Cooper is very sympathetic to the role of religion in shaping her parents' thinking and actions about her sexuality. Consider the following passage from the final pages of Cooper's memoir:

> I know that what I've been through has been rough on my parents as well. Being a parent of an LGBT kid can be challenging. Especially when you have a child as spirited as I've been – as I've had to be to survive my circumstances. When you believe there is no place in God's plan for gay people and that God's plan is the only way to keep your family together, for your own child to come out as a lesbian must turn the whole world upside down. I know they believed that they had to change me to save me, to save our whole family's chances of being together in heaven. It is incredible that any family, any child, should be under so much pressure. It is awful that there are people who take advantage of that fear and pressure to sell parents on the idea that sending their kids away to live with strangers in boot camps and treatment centers will somehow help.
>
> *(Cooper, 2016, p. 243)*

Cooper explains that a belief of those in the Mormon faith is that families, after being sealed in the church, will spend eternity together. Cooper romanticizes this idea and describes comfort in knowing that even as she struggled through her rebellious teenage years, at some point she would return to the community of the Mormon Church and be with a family forever. A family, as defined in her parents' faith, does not include LGBTQ-identified people, however. She sympathizes with her parents' desire to maintain this kind of family and understands that by living as a lesbian, she represents a threat to that desire and plan. Cooper notes that the pressure her family must have felt when she came out influenced how they reacted toward her, but Cooper places the onus for these restrictions on her parents' reactions within the church. In her mind, individuals in the Mormon faith, like her parents, passively accept what they have been taught and all that they know, and therefore they are not ultimately to blame. Cooper describes the Mormon faith as a force that took advantage of her parents' potential fear. Again, she cedes blame from her parents onto the church, suggesting her parents are completely controlled by their faith and the institution. Cooper does not question why her parents are so steadfast in their faith, even after she tells her parents about the abuse she is enduring as she undergoes the Siale family's version of converting Cooper back into a heterosexual youth.

Jennings' memoir describes a decidedly more positive experience as a youth and member of the LGBTQ community. Jennings is surrounded by, and reminds the reader frequently, of the parents, siblings, and friends who accept her for who she is. She acknowledges throughout the text that she is in a supported position that many transgender teenagers do not find themselves in: "I believe the truly brave ones are all the transgender kids out there in the world who go about their daily lives without the kind of love and encouragement that I have" (Jennings, 2016, p. 163).

Rather than focusing on her parents and siblings, Jennings critiques societal institutions and regulations that seek to marginalize transgender youth, such as youth and adult sports teams segregated by gender, and by bathroom policies based on a person's genitals. She suggests these critiques should be done in a civilized manner, however, with an appropriate time and a place for celebrating, and a separate time and place for protesting. In one anecdote, Jennings describes her visit to Washington, DC to meet U.S. President Barack Obama for the White House's Pride Month celebration. While there, a "heckler" – a transwoman of color and activist named Jennicet Gutiérrez – interrupted Obama's remarks to protest the treatment of undocumented and detained transgender immigrants. While Jennings is sympathetic to Gutiérrez' position, Jennings makes sure to note that she feels the protest was disrespectful:

> I thought it was nice enough that Barack Obama was inviting the LGBTQ community to his house for this reception, and I didn't think she should disrespect him, especially after all the support he's shown for the community. Her message was definitely valid – the latest number from the US department of Justice reported that almost 40 percent of transgender inmates are sexually assaulted – but I didn't think she delivered it the right way, especially on such a day of celebration. Sure, there is always more work to be done when it comes to activism and advocacy, but I also think that a party should just be a party, and insulting the host isn't going to help a cause.
>
> (Jennings, 2016, p. 204)

While Jazz remains benevolent toward the cause and former President Obama in this anecdote, the reader sees that Jennings also makes complex negotiations about the nature of advocacy, progress, and behaving in a civilized manner. While Jennings agrees with the protestor, she does not agree with the protestor's method. She believes she can celebrate victories for the transgender community, while continuing to advocate for more progress in other spaces.

Limitations of the Memoir Form

Memoirs as Public Service Announcements

While memoirs provide a space for youth to share their stories and define their own narratives about gender and sexuality, there are also significant limitations to the genre. One example is evidenced in both the memoirs. In *Saving Alex*, Cooper refers to Brooks as a ghostwriter, but Brooks is also named on the cover. *Being Jazz*, on the other hand, was not written with a ghostwriter, but readers can assume that a teenage author would have received significant editing and marketing guidance throughout the production of this book, especially as a first foray into authoring a book. In both instances, these are the stories of youth, released to a youth audience, but always through an adult gatekeeper, such as an editor. Readers of memoirs written by youth might want to explore why an adult gatekeeper seems to be the norm in this genre and what limitations or strengths an adult gatekeeper gives to a reader's interpretation of the text. Readers might consider the question: How do youth voices change when filtered through or viewed through the lens of adults?

Both Memoirs Reflect Aspects of Adult Control

While a memoir is supposed to convey a personal experience and reflection about that experience, both Cooper's and Jennings' stories contain elements that include narrative insertions to teach (rather than to tell) the audience about the experiences of gay and transgender youth. For example, Cooper interrupts an anecdote about another teen – Dante, who had had just moved in with the Siale family as another one of their foster children – with this statistic: "LGBT kids like Dante and me end up in state custody more frequently than straight kids. Thirteen to fifteen percent of the kids in the juvenile justice system identify as LGBT" (p. 143). An interjection about the persistence of LGBTQ teens in the justice system is certainly relevant to the experiences of LGBTQ youth in the United States, but is not part of Cooper's individual story and would not typically be found in a memoir or as a reflection on experiences. While youths' experiences within the juvenile justice and foster care systems are important to the text, the timing and statistical nature of the information feels pedantic and inauthentic.

In another example from *Being Jazz*, Jennings explains how her own sister reacted to the news that Jennings was transgender:

> She was nine at the time and wasn't too happy to suddenly have to share the family princess status. But after my dad explained to her that many transgender kids have really difficult lives and that more than 50 percent try to kill themselves at some point because they aren't loved and accepted, she started to cry and promised him she'd be the best big sister ever.
>
> *(Jennings, 2016, p. 20)*

Once again, the insertion of statistical information into Jennings' anecdote about identifying as transgender speaks to the kind of messages that are being conveyed through these texts. The heavy-handed nature of the messaging in these memoirs disrupts the conversation that Jennings and Cooper have with their readers and situate the youth reader in a position where they are being taught something (rather than being told a personal story or shared experience) with this text.

Implications for Literacy Education and Cross-Disciplinary Fields

This chapter lays the groundwork for incorporating and discussing LGBTQ youth memoirs in and outside of classrooms. These texts can serve as vehicles for examining the socially constituted nature of gender and sexuality through literature and offer youth and adults the chance to examine how gender and sexuality are represented through individual reflection and narrative. Memoirs can be used in educational spaces and informal settings to examine how culture and society reflect and shape gender and sexual identity.

LGBTQ youth memoirs offer the opportunity for adults and youth to incorporate individual stories into critical discussions about gender and sexuality. Teachers, educators, scholars, parents, and others can consider various tenets of queer theory as they engage with LGBTQ-themed memoirs. If memoirs are presented as a single story (or a series of single stories), they may be taken up as *the* story of LGBTQ experiences, furthering stereotypes and offering an incomplete picture of the range of LGBTQ lived experiences (see Chimamanda Ngozi Adichie's 2009 TED talk entitled "The Danger of a Single Story"). Memoirs as educational material should be used to consider and work through such questions as: Are gender and sexual identity intrinsically developed (i.e., "born this way") or are they socially constructed? Or are gender and sexual identity a combination? How do society and culture (specifically, religion, schools, family, regions, etc.) define gender and sexuality? Or do they not at all?

Responsibly using an LGBTQ memoir includes the inclusion of other relevant texts in addition to memoirs to support learning about gender identities. These supplemental texts can offer context to memoirs about gender and sexuality, a topic that is often left unexamined for young people, especially in educational contexts. Furthermore, supplemental texts are necessary to engage with many of the historical, cultural, and religious events mentioned by memoir authors.

Without sufficient supplemental reading, students will walk away with incomplete stories of the lives and experiences of LGBTQ youth, relying on individual stories for limited and narrow understandings. Adults in libraries, families, classrooms, and other educational spaces may offer youth the chance to critically examine book reviews both praising and critiquing each memoir and discuss the implications of those reviews (Spiering, 2017). News articles about various events reported in these texts, such as the incident concerning Jennicet Gutiérrez and President Obama (mentioned earlier in this chapter), or the so-called "bathroom bills," which either limit or provide access to public bathrooms based on one's genitalia or one's gender identity, can give young people the context they need to understand the lived experiences of those who author memoirs. By ensuring readers of youth memoirs – in homes, schools, libraries, and other formal and informal learning spaces – have access to a range of reading support and frequent opportunities for discussion, critical readings of LGBTQ youth's stories can broaden social understandings of the role gender and sexuality play in society.

References

Adichie, C.N. (2009). The danger of a single story. *TEDGlobal*. Retrieved from www. ted.com/talks/chimamanda_adichie_the_danger_of_a_single_story.

Blackburn, M.V. (2011). *Interrupting hate: Homophobia in schools and what literacy can do about it*. New York, NY: Teachers College Press.

Blackburn, M.V., & Smith, J.M. (2010). Moving beyond the Inclusion of LGBT-themed literature in English language arts classrooms: Interrogating heteronormativity and exploring intersectionality. *Journal of Adolescent & Adult Literacy, 53*(8), 625–634.

Britzman, D. 1995. Is there a queer pedagogy? Or, stop reading straight. *Educational Theory, 45*(2), 151–165.

Butler, J. (1999) *Gender trouble*. New York, NY: Routledge.

Butler, J. (2004). *Undoing gender*. New York, NY: Routledge

Clark, C.T., & Blackburn, M.V. (2009). Reading LGBT-themed literature with young people: What's possible? *The English Journal, 98*(4), 25–32.

Cooper, A. (2016). *Saving Alex: When I was fifteen I told my Mormon parents I was gay, and that's when my nightmare began*. San Francisco, CA: Harper One.

Crenshaw, K. (1991). Mapping the margins: Intersectionality, identity politics, and violence against women of color. *Stanford Law Review, 43*(6), 1241–1299.

D'Emilio, J., & Freedman, E.B. (2012). *Intimate matters: A history of sexuality in America* (3rd ed.). Chicago, IL: University of Chicago.

Genzlinger, N. (2011). The problem with memoirs. *New York Times*. Retrieved from www.nytimes.com/2011/01/30/books/review/Genzlinger-t.html.

Halberstam, J. (2005). *In a queer time and place: Transgender bodies, subcultural lives*. New York, NY: NYU Press.

Jennings, J. (2016). *Being Jazz: My life as a (transgender) teen*. New York, NY: Crown Books for Young Readers.

Kedley, K., & Spiering, J. (2017). Using LGBTQ graphic novels to dispel myths about gender and sexuality in ELA classrooms. *English Journal, 107*(1), 54–65.

Linville, D. (2015). Creating spaces of freedom for gender and sexuality for queer girls in young adult literature. In D.L. Carlson & D. Linville (Eds.), *Sex education in beyond borders: Queer eros and ethos (ethics) in LGBTQ young adult literature* (pp. 123–128). New York, NY: Peter Lang.

Long, J.E. (2007). *Remembered childhoods: A guide to autobiography and memoirs of childhood and youth.* Westport, CT: Libraries Unlimited.

Marcus, S. (2005). Queer theory for everyone: A review essay. *Signs, 31*(1), 191–218.

Mendelsohn, D. (2010) But enough about me: What does the popularity of memoirs tell us about ourselves? *The New Yorker.* Retrieved from www.newyorker.com/magazine/2010/01/25/but-enough-about-me-2.

Nolan, H. (2013). Journalism is not narcissism. *Gawker.* Retrieved from http://gawker.com/5972454/journalism-is-not-narcissism.

Rich, A. (1980). Compulsory heterosexuality and lesbian existence. *Signs, 5*(4), 631–60.

Rogers, T., & Marshall, E. (2012). On the road: Examining self-representation and discourses of homelessness in young adult texts. *Journal of Adolescent & Adult Literacy, 55*(8), 725–733.

Saldaña, J. (2012). *The coding manual for qualitative researchers* (2nd ed.). Los Angeles, CA: Sage.

Sedgwick, E.K. 1990. *Epistemology of the closet.* Oakland, CA: University of California Press.

Spiering, J. (2017). Reviewing to exclude: Critical discourse analysis of LGBTQ book reviews for school librarians. *The ALAN Review.* Blacksburg, VA: Digital Library and Archives.

Sykes, H. (2011). Hetero-and homo-normativity: Critical literacy, citizenship education and queer theory. *Curriculum inquiry, 41*(4), 419–432.

Thein, A.H., & Kedley, K.E. (2015). Out of the closet and all grown up: Problematizing normative narratives of coming-out and coming-of-age in young adult literature. In D. Linville & D.L. Carlson (Eds.), *Beyond borders: Queer eros and ethos (ethics) in LGBTQ young adult literature.* New York, NY: Peter Lang.

Thein, A.H., Sulzer, M.A., & Schmidt, R. (2013). Evaluating the democratic merit of young adult literature: Lessons from two versions of Wes Moore's memoir. *English Journal, 103*(2), 52–59.

PART IV

Gender, Sexualities, and Adult Literacies

14

PERFORMING AND RESISTING TOXIC MASCULINITIES ON SPORTS NEWS COMMENT BOARDS

Erik Jacobson

Recent developments in gender politics give credence to the hopes of those who see the Internet and social media as a potential force for good in society. For example, countless numbers of women have found in the #MeToo campaign a place to come forward with their own stories of sexual abuse and a way to engage others in addressing the problem of systemic violence against women. Other people are also taking advantage of the open nature of social media to name and gender themselves as they wish, with many explicitly rejecting traditional binary categories of male and female. In cases like these, political and technological progress appear to be mutually supportive.

The Internet has also fostered a number of communities of men who assert ideas that directly confront and push back against more progressive ideas on gender, however. For example, the #GamerGate controversy began as an accusation of conflict of interest against a female video game reporter and soon escalated into misogynistic name calling and threats of sexual violence against the reporter. When these threats were brought to light and criticized, many male gamers asserted that they were being misunderstood by those outside their community who did not understand that this was just the way gamers talk. As another example, men identifying themselves as *incel* (short for "involuntary celibate") had a forum on Reddit in which they discussed such topics as the "evil" nature of women and why rape should not be considered a crime. These virulent expressions of a violent male chauvinism take place in self-selected online forums (e.g., within 4-Chan, a message board that allows anonymous posting) that mark men who participate as overtly misogynistic. Participants in these spaces police and reject challenges to their shared ideological framework, creating near uniformity in terms of acceptable expression.

In contrast, because interest in sports cuts across many ideological lines, the comment boards for sports news stories are spaces where men with diverse opinions about gender (among other topics) gather and debate each other. Despite not being a barrier to participating in the site, these ideological commitments do remain active and can surface at any time. This means that a comment board for a story about a given player's historic accomplishment can become an occasion for the expression of misogynistic vitriol disconnected from the story itself. These off-topic eruptions also include the use of racist, homophobic and other biased language. There are, however, also individuals on sports news comment boards who critique this type of language and publicly reject sexist, racist, and homophobic thinking. Thus, in comparison to other more self-selected and hermetic online communities, sport news comment boards are places where competing versions of masculinity collide. This chapter will focus on the nature of that collision and what the implications may be for the field of literacy studies.

Gender, Language, and Writing

Analyses of sports media suggest that it is highly gendered. Not only do sports played by men receive more attention than those played by women, but sports that are associated with traits traditionally seen as masculine – power, strength, violence – have more prestige (Kian, Clavio, Vincent, & Shaw, 2011). For this reason, Connell, (2005, cited by Kian, 2015) and others believe that actively identifying as a fan of these sports is a way to express a hegemonic masculinity that values aggression and assertiveness. Talking about sports in similarly aggressive and assertive ways can become a stand-in for actually playing the sport. Cleland, Magrath, and Kian (2018), suggest that, "a practice of exaggerated hypermasculinity can occur as message boards allow for boys and men to engage in discourse that creates opportunity to raise their masculine capital" (p. 103). Not surprisingly, this masculine capital is often raised by demeaning others, particularly women and gay men (Kian et al., 2011), but other heterosexual men are also subject to these overt attempts to establish some type of superiority. According to Butler (1997), these public displays of particular types of interests and use of a shared language of chauvinism can be best understood as the performance of gender. Raising masculine capital by overtly deploying and celebrating familiar tropes of masculinity (e.g., interest in aggressive sports, the use of demeaning language) is one way for an individual to assert to themselves and others that they are identifiable as men.

In recent times, this type of behavior has come to be referred to as toxic masculinity, which speaks directly to the cost of establishing hypermasculinity to the individual, others they interact with, and society as a whole. Anderson (2009) suggests that resistance to hegemonic masculinity can be found in more inclusive models of masculinity. Per Butler, it could be expected that the language used to perform these two models would differ, with more inclusive models of masculinity marked by an embrace of diversity and a rejection of violent, demeaning language. Therefore, it is not only the choice of topics to discuss that could be used to express and establish a masculine identity (e.g., sports that are more or less violent), but the nature of the discussion could also be crucial to expressing a gendered identity.

In addition to topic and tone, competing concepts of masculinity may draw on very different understandings of individual words. What a self-identified *incel* (men who describe themselves as "involuntary celibate" and who place the blame for their situation on women in general) denotes when he uses the word *woman* is very different than what a self-identified feminist does when using the word. In the same way, commenters on sports news sites argue for the primacy of their own understanding of particular words, both explicitly (statements along the lines of "this means . . .") and implicitly (by modeling a particular use of that word). For example, different understandings of the word *sports* can lead to contrasting expectations for the nature of discussion within a comment board – "It's sports – no talking about politics here!" versus "Sports, as part of society, are inherently political!" Within comment boards, any word can potentially become a flash-point for struggle over meaning given the right conditions. For example, rather than focusing on the technical demands of the activity, discussions about whether or not auto racing should be considered a sport often develop into heated debates about the social class and regional identity of fans.

Bakhtin (1981) suggests that this volatility in meaning is due to the ideological nature of language. For that reason, he sees in language, "the co-existence of socio-ideological contradictions between the present and the past, between differing epochs of the past, between different socio-ideological groups in the present, between tendencies, schools, circles and so forth, all given a bodily form" (p. 291). Thus, although governments, schools, and other powerful institutions have a large influence on the use of language, particularly in regard to what is considered acceptable speech and correct usage, competing groups within society push for their own ways of using words. As such, an analysis of language use in spaces like sports news comment boards may reveal the ways in which older and more contemporary ways of talking about masculinity and gender battle for primacy. At any given time, the meaning of a word is shaped by the contest over its use, and its meaning can never be finally resolved.

One important aspect of sociocultural analyses of literacy is how individuals come to be members of communities that engage in distinct reading and writing practices. Although formal literacy instruction plays a key role in many people's lives, much of what individuals learn to do with literacy happens outside of school and in association with being members of particular groups and networks. For this reason, Barton and Hamilton (1998) (among many others) stress the importance informal learning plays in the development of new literacy practices. Members of online communities that come into existence and are sustained through writing do not typically receive explicit training in that space's set of expectations for rhetoric, style, or vocabulary. For example, although there may be posted guidelines for contributions, there is generally no formal training in how to write a comment board message. Individuals master these vernacular literacy practices by trial and error and through socialization, often in the form of feedback from more experienced members of the online community.

Increased knowledge of students' and adults' vernacular literacy practices may provide insight into what value they find in literacy, particularly when they seem disinterested in traditionally academic or school-based literacy practices. Gustavson (2013, following Heath, 1997) suggests that teachers need to recognize that students take their out-of-school leisure pursuits seriously and that these pursuits may provide important insights into how they learn and grow. In addition, from a lifelong-learning perspective, identifying the vernacular literacy practices of adults (such as writing on comment boards) highlights how adults may develop new literacy practices over the course of their lives.

The Analysis

This chapter draws on data from an ongoing project that examines the nature of writing and communication within sports news comment boards. The primary research questions for this analysis were: (a) What types of language are used by comment board writers to raise their masculine capital? and (b) What are the nature of comments that critique expressions of toxic masculinity? Other studies of comment board writing have looked for the amount of particular types of comments, such as the level of homophobia present on particular sites (Cleland et al., 2018). By comparison, this study was focused on identifying the variety of comment types to better understand the ways that hegemonic or toxic masculinity might be performed and what the language of a more inclusive masculinity might look like.

Data collection for the project began with a convenience sample. Over the last four years, the author has archived sample discussions taken from comment boards for articles he read as part of following sports news (one of his own leisure pursuits). For the last year, data collection has included purposeful sampling by selecting specific news articles covering sports that involved varying levels of aggression and violence (e.g., mixed martial arts, curling) and news items that dealt with explicitly gendered or gender stereotypical topics (e.g., testing female athletes' levels of testosterone). To date, the archive consists of samples from 60 articles. The number of posts on each of the comment boards ranges from two dozen to over 400. Most of the samples were taken from a popular sports news website, espn.com, chosen because of the heavy traffic the site receives.

Following other studies of comment board messages, a textual analysis of the data was conducted (Cleland et al., 2018; Kian et al., 2011). As each sample was collected it was given an original code (e.g., "Chill Dude!" for when somebody was rebuked for being overly enthusiastic) and a running list of codes was created.

I returned to the data to review existing codes to refine them and note associations between codes, thus moving from open coding to axial coding (Strauss & Corbin, 1998). Finally, this second set of codes was revised again, with some codes being collapsed and others and deleted because they did not address the research questions. This was often because the comment board post addressed the writer of the news article rather than engaging another comment board contributor.

The Results of the Study

Reinforcing Discourses of Hegemonic Masculinity

On most sports news comment boards, argument structures typically consist of a writer posting a response to an article, and then subsequent writers engaging to either amplify the first writer's comments or to question them. Discussions can end after one or two more iterations between the initial dyad, or it could go on for dozens of comments that begin to draw in other contributors. For example, below is an exchange in the comment board for an article titled, "Tom Brady vs. Michael Jordan for Greatest GOAT: The Scorecard" (ESPN, 1/26/18). [Writers' names have been redacted for these posts and all other posts in the chapter. All posts are reproduced verbatim.]

W1: Tom Brady has had a great career and has established himself as the greatest QB in NFL history to this point. However, at every point of his career, there has been a legitimate argument for another QB being better than him at the time – Peyton Manning, Aaron Rodgers, Drew Brees. Over the course of Jordan's career, from the beginning of his third season until the day he retired for the second time as a Bull, there was no time where you could make anything approaching a valid argument that he wasn't the best player in the NBA.

W2: Drew Brees has never been considered better than Brady and Manning was a media favorite, but lacked the true winner gene, same as Rodgers. Rodgers is a great quarterback but not on Brady's level of sustained winning + excellence.

Here, W1 is asserting that Tom Brady cannot be compared to Michael Jordan because he never defined the standard for excellence while he was playing. W2 disagrees, suggesting that Brady's contemporaries never were at his level. The argument here stays on topic, draws on evidence (subjective as it is), and sets up a basis for debate that can be explored (i.e., a player's excellence needs to be judged in context). This exchange suggests that sports can be discussed in ways that are productive and respectful, lending support to those who believe the Internet can provide spaces for "reasoned debate without regard to rank or status (Luscombe, Walby, & Lippert, 2017, p. 748).

Sports news discussion boards are also marked by ad hominem attacks on other writers, however. Rather than acting as a counter-hegemonic response to the media (Toepfl & Piwoni, 2015, cited by Luscombe et al., 2017), much of the content of sports news comment boards works to reinforce existing discourses that inform hegemonic ideals of masculinity. Three types of ad hominem attacks were prominent in the analysis conducted here: expressions of homophobia, explicit misogyny, and the use of cuckold as an insult. Each appeared to be deployed in an attempt to establish the types of privileged positions associated with hegemonic masculinity

Studies of comment boards for new articles about gay male athletes have noted high levels of homophobic language (Kian, 2015: Kian et al., 2011), though others have suggested that this may be changing due to a growing acceptance of homosexuality on the part of sports fans (Cleland et al., 2018). Nevertheless, homophobia is present in many stories that are unrelated to discussions of gay rights, and homophobic attacks are deployed regardless of context. For example, below is an exchange from an article, "Gregg Popovich: LeBron James May Have More Impact Off Court Than On" (ESPN, 2/25/18). The article focuses on outspoken NBA coach Gregg Popovich's belief that LeBron James' public statements (e.g., denouncing racism and systemic police violence against African American males) and his philanthropy (e.g., providing college scholarships to children in Akron) is more important than his basketball career. After many suggestions that Popovich and James should remain silent on non-basketball matters, two commenters began to go back and forth about whether James' philanthropy is genuine or a publicity stunt. Their exchange finally reaches a breaking point:

W1: He's the sixth most charitable athlete. You are the #1 idiot.
W2: [. . .] wipe Lebron's man juices off your chin & lips.

W1 begins by referring to a measurable statistic, and then rhetorically uses the idea of rankings to castigate his opponent in this argument. W2 responds with a graphic homophobic taunt. At this point, the debate has moved from being about the value of James' and Popovich's views to the value of the writers engaged in the debate. W2 attempts to trump W1's putdown of his intelligence by suggesting W1 is gay, with the implication being that fact renders anything he has to say irrelevant.

Explicit expressions of misogyny are also a key aspect of toxic masculine discourse, and they are present in sports news comment board arguments in different forms. The comment board for the article, "Jay Feely Says Picture with Gun, Daughter was a Joke" (ESPN, 4/23/18), provided several different examples. The article focused on the controversy caused by a picture that former NFL player (Jay Feely) shared of him standing between his daughter and her prom date, with Feely holding his daughter around the shoulder with his left arm and grasping a pistol in his right hand. A number of commenters felt that given the level of gun violence in the country, the photo was insensitive. Some also believed that with the brandished gun, Feely was asserting a patriarchal "ownership" of his daughter. Commenters who thought the photo was simply a funny joke or celebrated the message they thought Feely was sending directly attacked the masculine identity of those who took offense.

W1:   Dude. Tampax is the product that you need in your life. Sounds like a heavy flow kind of day.

W2:   He shouldn't have to apologize for anything. He's a celebrity who made a joke. Liberals and vaginas are pu$$ys.

In comments like these, the message is clear. People, that is, men, who were offended by the photo (and possibly gun culture) are so soft as to be women. This association between perceived weakness and femininity is prevalent in the sports world, such as with the well-known phrase "You throw like a girl" and when athletes who cannot play through an injury are called "girls." For W1 and W2 the argument is now presumed to be over because for them, the perspectives of men who act like women are not worth considering.

A third form of ad hominem attack drawing on discourses of hegemonic masculinity was the use of cuckoldry as an insult. For example, as part of a comment board discussion of whether or not a play in an NFL game should have resulted on an interference penalty on the defender ("Rob Gronkowski Hit in Head, Misses Second Half," ESPN, 1/21/18), one writer attacked those who believed it should have been a penalty in this manner:

W1:   Keep smoking that legal pot in Colorado, and kissing the illegal immigrants – and wondering why the Denver professional teams suck so much. You wouldn't know pass interference from when another guy takes your wife home for sex, would you.

This response has nothing to do with the NFL rule book about what constitutes interference, and instead is a string of insults. The comment includes a political dig ("kissing the illegal immigrants"), an insult directed at a region, and the questioning of the other writer's masculinity. Here, since the commenter being attacked is so clueless as to be cuckolded, his views on the football play in question are meaningless. Such attacks are also visible in current AltRight discourse, where the word cuck" (short for cuckold) is used as a slur to demean fellow conservatives who don't have the courage to be "true" to their beliefs.

In addition to homophobia, misogyny and the cuckold label, writers in sports news comment boards also use other means to try to demean others. Contributors to comment boards cut short discussions by ascribing to their opponents an inferior body type ("have another donut"), inferior employment ("says the guy working behind a counter") and inferior levels of maturity in terms of living conditions ("how's life in your parents' basement?"). There are also a variety of terms used to denote other contributors who are deemed too sensitive. These include the seemingly ubiquitous *snowflake*, but also *cupcake* and *napkin*. These terms are deployed to make the case that language and writing that articulates and supports homophobia and misogyny are natural expressions of traditional masculinity, and thus those who would critique them are not acceptably masculine.

Literacy Skills as an Avenue of Attack

There were also attacks that drew on the written nature of these interactions. Although not typically associated with discourses of hegemonic masculinity, comments about reading and writing skills were also used as ways to assert superiority and to demean others. Some of these were more generalized attributions of poorly developed skills, such as reading ("Let me guess, you failed remedial English due to lack of reading comprehension") but some focused on the writing of the comments themselves.

One common example of this is pointing out poor spelling on the part of somebody being engaged in argument. For example, below is an exchange from one article ("NBA Suspends Warriors G. Shaun Livingston, Referee for Incident," ESPN, 12/4/17) covering an on-court altercation between an NBA player and a referee.

W1: They should suspend some for the games they reg., difinately one sided! 19 free throws to 38? Come on, so games are so one sided. I agree the commissioner has it in for the Dubs! Cavaliers 22 free throws in 1 quarter??? Refs should be held accountable.

W2: "difinately"? You mean "definitely"? Your Warriors won the game and will win the championship again this year, so spend less time complaining and more time learning how to spell.

W2 uses his rejoinder to try to shame W1 about his poor writing skills and paint W1 as a whiner. Incorrect spellings abound online and in social media, but W2 still finds this to be an opening to demean W1.

In addition to spelling errors, mistakes regarding conventions of print were also used to assert superiority over other writers. An example can be found in, "Coin Toss, Catch Controversy Heighten Drama of Cardinals Win" (ESPN, 1/18/16), a story about an NFL game and confusion about what constitutes a recognized catch.

W1: [Self-identified as being from University of Arkansas in their photo] "I don't know what the hell a catch is anymore," the Packers coach said,,,,,,,,,,,,,,Sure you do coach. A catch is what Larry Fitzgerald had to end your season. Take the 75 yard catch that he had,,,,or the final catch,,,,you know,,,,the five yard catch for a TD. Those were catches coach. Enjoy your summer.

W2:   Why are you separating your thoughts with commas and why don't your periods come right after your terribly constructed attempts at a sentence? Instead, you have a space between them, kind of like what's between your ears. Oh, wait, I see you went to the University of Arkansas,,,,,,,,,, .

College rivalries have long been a big part of sports, but here W2 is using the admittedly odd choices W1 made with regards to comma usage to disparage W1's university rather than the performance of their sports teams.

Public rebukes of other commenter's writing also involved word usage. In the comment board for the article, "Patriots DC Matt Patricia Expected to be Next Lions Head Coach" (ESPN, 1/14/18), there was the following exchange.

W1:   Funny how ALL the teams and fans say we cheat . . . yet they want to sign our coaches to take over their team.

W2:   What is your job title within the Pats organization?

Here W2 is sarcastically critiquing the habit of some sports fans to use terms like "we" and "us" when referring to the teams they root for. As Bakhtin (1981) suggests, competing attempts to assert the meaning of words and what can be considered correct usage creates a situation in which critiquing the presence of the word "we" becomes a means to raise masculine capital. In each of these cases, the second writer does not address the topic of the article, but instead attempts to embarrass the first writer in a public forum on the basis of his their literacy skills. This type of ad hominem attack displays the same type of assertive and aggressive language use associated with toxic masculinity, even if they do not directly reference the object of ridicule's gender or sexuality.

Resisting Toxic Masculinity

There is also evidence of the more inclusive models of masculinity that Anderson (2009) suggests are developing. Often, this is visible when people directly push back against expressions of hegemonic masculinity. These writers demonstrate that they take the topics under consideration seriously and believe, despite the presence of mean-spirited attacks, that these forums are places to address these volatile issues. For example, one commenter responded to a jab about another's body by writing, "Hey, ****, I hope making fun of another man's physique made you feel better about yourself! Positive vibes to you!"

In recent times, the sports media landscape has increasingly had to cover accusations of domestic violence committed by players. As teams and leagues debate how to treat athletes that are accused or found guilty of the crime, fans do as well. These self-identified as male commenters on the following article – "Red Sox Pitcher

Steven Wright Still Being Investigated by MLB [Major League Baseball] After Domestic Violence Case "Retired" (ESPN, 12/22/17) – came to very different conclusions about the incident described in the article.

W1: MLB needs to stay clear of this; "verbal abuse" is not nice behavior, but it does occur at times in a marriage, when one or both are under pressure from other issues and the fuse blows. As long as they are reconciled, no physical abuse was involved and it is not a recurring thing, it is nobody's business but theirs.

W2: Charges involved more than "verbal assault." Your attitude towards the issue is part of sports figures entitlement issues. He should face the consequences of his actions.

W3: Rationalizing that verbal abuse is less harmful than physical abuse doesn't adequately address the problem which is engaging in unacceptable and potentially psychologically damaging behavior towards women. In the era of the #MeToo movement, men should be especially sensitive to and careful not to exceed any boundaries concerning this.

Here, W2 and W3 explicitly reject any suggestions that verbal abuse is natural or acceptable within a marriage or relationship. They also make it clear that to tolerate it in any way is part of a larger issue of violence towards women.

In a similar fashion, there is evidence of writers who are willing to confront other types of attacks. An example can be found in the comment board for the article, "Jalen Ramsey Guarantees Super Bowl Win to Jags fans" (ESPN, 1/16/18). Ramsey, a player for the NFL's Jacksonville Jaguars told fans of the team that they would win the championship.

W1: Someone should tell this street thug who cann't speak english that he has nothing to be cOcky about, the Steelers dropped 42 points on them!

W2: Funny you say he can not speak and you spell can't with two n's and cOcky. Lmao. And just because he is black doesn't make him a street thug. What a sad person you are the hate is strong in this one.

W3: Thug? What makes Ramsey a thug? Oh, that's it, he's black and people don't like him because he talks so he's automatically labeled a thug. Got it, my mistake.

In this exchange, W2 begins by pointing out the hypocrisy of W1's criticism of Ramsey's language skills when in his own comment he has several spelling mistakes. Both W2 and W3 then call W1 on his use of the word *thug*. According to Bakthin (1981), to understand the various connotations of the word *thug* it is necessary to examine influential discourses of current and historical racism and the ways coded language has been used to communicate racist ideas in contexts that presumptively proscribe them. Here, W2 and W3 have already begun that work.

Other commenters pushed back on the use of literacy skills as a means of demeaning someone. For example, in "Patriots CB Malcolm Butler Signs RFA Tender" (ESPN, 4/19/17), there is an exchange between three commenters:

W1: The Pats, the best team in football, are going to reap at least a 2nd rounder in a trade with a team trying to win now who may be able to sign him. If no trade happens, Butler will play his butt off in order to get paided next year, and the Pats will let him walk after another SD run and possible victory.

W2: Paided? How does one get paided? And why would NE run to San Diego?

W3: I think it is obvious what he meant. Why do you feel the need to point out spelling errors and typos on a message board? Seems like a waste of time.

Here W3 takes W2 to task for what he sees as an unnecessary dig. He suggests that "paided" is clear enough, and that the typo – SD instead of SB (for Super Bowl) – can also be understood in context. W3 closes by suggesting that these types are comments are not productive, and the implication is that they do nothing to raise W2 masculine capital.

At times, commenters also used these spaces to directly perform a more inclusive masculinity by their comments on the topics of articles and their use of language. For example, in response to the article "Kevin Love Discusses Suffering Panic Attack During Game" (ESPN, 3/7/18) there was the following exchange:

W1: As a psychologist, I am thrilled to see these men dealing with their mental health challenges I hope they are an inspiration to others.

W2: What's your advice for finding a psychologist that fits my needs?

Here W1 praises athletes for being open about their mental health issues, going against models of hegemonic masculinity that value being silent about emotions and psychological well-being. W2 follows this lead and risks ridicule by expressing his own vulnerability. There were similar exchanges focused on looking for treatment for behavioral health issues. Although the variety of these types of comments was more limited than those reinforcing hegemonic or toxic masculinity, there is enough to suggest that these are not isolated incidents.

Implications for Literacy Education and Cross-Disciplinary Fields

The two research questions framing this study were: (a) What types of language are used by comment board writers to raise their masculine capital? and (b) What are the nature of comments that critique expressions of toxic masculinity? Based on the analysis above, there are several implications for literacy education and cross-disciplinary fields.

The Importance of Examining Out-of-School Literacies in School

For some time, educators have been intrigued by the potential to learn from their K–12 and adult students' use of digital resources outside of the classroom (e.g., students using video cameras to make their own narrative or documentary films). This study suggests that a key question both teachers and students need to examine is how students are being socialized into gendered literacy practices in informal learning spaces. Sports news comment boards are just one example of unsupervised locations where students experiment with performing gender in different ways, and indeed, experiment with performing different genders. Formal education can play a role in students' productive use of these out-of-school spaces by helping students develop the analytical language needed to recognize and resist discourses of toxic masculinity (among other things), particularly when these discourses utilize coded language (i.e., words that appear uncontroversial but that are meant to serve as an implicit signal to those who share the speaker's or writer's ideological beliefs).

Toxic Masculinity Is Protean in Nature

Previous studies suggested that the discourse of toxic masculinity was heavily homophobic in nature. Not surprisingly, the sports news message boards in the study also showed evidence of misogynistic language. The use of literacy skills as a means to publicly humiliate opponents in an argument was unexpected. This suggests that toxic masculinity is protean in nature, and that there are any number of ways that it can be expressed or performed. Thus, although reviewing examples of toxic masculinity online is not pleasant or seems unnecessary ("we already know comment boards are full of hateful voices"). I would suggest that it is important to understand the shifting contours of its discourses. Gaining specificity when it comes to the performance of toxic masculinity may help in combatting it.

Developing and Promoting the Language of Inclusive Masculinity

Finally, despite the fact that these comment boards can be filled with hateful language and disturbing invective, there are commenters who choose to stay and critique toxic masculinity. Of course, somebody caring about equality and calling out oppression of any form is liable to be accused of being overly sensitive (e.g., "you're just some kind of stupid SJW!" [social justice warrior]), thus increasing the amount of hostility. This dynamic makes the idea of spending time on comment boards seem both unpleasant and a waste of energy. Nevertheless, in the ongoing ideological struggle over the meaning of words, whether *male, woman, sports*, or *we*, those who do push back against expressions of toxic masculinity on comment boards are doing necessary work in the trenches of language use. More work needs to be done to see how to support this kind of endeavor rather than simply writing off comment boards as swamps of vile behavior. We need to model inclusive masculinity in multiple contexts and develop language that will convince those invested in a toxic masculinity to rethink what damage they are doing to themselves and their communities.

References

Anderson, E. (2009). *Inclusive masculinity: The changing nature of masculinity*. New York, NY: Routledge

Bakhtin, M. (1981). *The dialogic imagination: Four essays* (C. Emerson & M. Holquist, Trans.). Austin, TX: University of Texas.

Barton, D., & Hamilton, M. (1998). *Local literacies*. New York, NY: Routledge.

Butler, J. (1997). *Excitable speech: A politics of the performative*. New York, NY: Routledge.

Cleland, J., Magrath, R., & Kian, E. (2018). The internet as a site of decreasing cultural homophobia in association football: An online response by fans to the coming out of Thomas Hitzlsperger. *Men and Masculinities, 1*, 91–111.

Connell, R.W. (2005). *Masculinities* (2nd ed.). Berkeley, CA: University of California.

Gustavson, L. (2013). Influencing pedagogy through the creative practice of youth. In C. Lankshear & M. Knobel (Eds.), *A new literacies reader* (pp. 101–122). New York, NY: Peter Lang.

Heath, S.B. (1997). Culture: Contested realm in research on children and youth. *Applied Developmental Science, 1*(3), 113–123.

Kian, E. (2015). A case study on message board-media framing of gay male athletes on a politically liberal web site. *International Journal of Sport Communication, 8*, 500–516.

Kian, E., Clavio, G., Vincent, J., & Shaw, S. (2011). Homophobic and sexist yet uncontested: Examining football fan postings on internet message boards. *Journal of Homosexuality, 58*, 680–699.

Luscombe, A., Walby, K., & Lippert, R. (2017). Readers' comments as popular texts: Public opinions of paid duty policing in Canada. *Canadian Journal of Communication, 42*, 745–765.

Strauss, A., & Corbin, J. (1998). *Basics of qualitative research*. Thousand Oaks, CA: Sage.

Toepfl, F., & Piwoni, E. (2015). Public spheres in interaction: Comment sections of news websites as counterpublic spaces. *Journal of Communication, 61*(4), 465–488.

15

TRANSNATIONAL WOMEN'S ONLINE LITERACIES

Writing as Social Action

Jin Kyeong Jung

The recent #MeToo movement against sexual harassment and assault has impacted the global society by sharing previously unrevealed personal stories across nations. This social movement has amplified many women's voices and experiences of oppression through their personal accounts on social networking sites or by their anonymous writings in other online communities. Computer-mediated technologies create opportunities not only to share individuals' lived experiences and make multiple voices heard across time and space, but also to engage collaboratively in social actions. Digitally networked communities are vital for transnational women who may experience varying levels of gender inequality in addition to cultural isolation and racism across borders.

While transnational feminists have examined women's issues from a global perspective (e.g., Grewal & Kaplan, 1994), this chapter adds consideration of the literacy practices of transnational women to this research by examining how Korean American women facilitated online discourses for social change across the local and the global as they built an active multiliterate community together. Transnational women's border crossings with digital technologies and complex intersections among ethnicity, race, legacies, class, sexualities, languages, national boundaries, immigration, and cultures have impacted how they make sense of their identities. To study this issue, I investigated a Korean American women's online community based in the United States, MissyUSA (MissyUSA.com) and how one Korean American woman used the online community to change society by mobilizing her literacy practices both within the community and the outside world. This chapter attempts to build greater awareness of how digital literacies open up access for transnational women to engage in social issues and position them as social changers without reifying their labels and invoking stereotypes through a non-Westernized lens.

My inquiry on transnational online communities is grounded in rethinking stereotypes toward diversity. I focused on women of Asian heritage. Asian Americans are perceived as perpetual foreigners in the United States even if they were born and raised in the United States (Lee, Park, & Wong, 2017). They are continuously stereotyped as being less visible and silent (Paek & Shah, 2003). In English-language classrooms, Asian students are viewed as being "obedient to authority," demonstrating a "lack of critical thinking skills," and not participating in classroom interactions (Kumaravadivelu, 2003, p. 710). These stereotypes are doubled against Asian women, who are thought to be submissive, passive, or controlled (Arisaka, 2000; Mayuzumi, 2015; Pyke & Johnson, 2003). For example, a recent Facebook video of Asian American news anchor Nydia Han's shows a driver shouting to her on the street based on her Asian appearance as the driver perceived her to be "not part of America." Her response to the racist comment, "This is America," was instantaneously circulated on social media as an illustration of talking back to negative stereotypes (Han, 2017).

Transnational women may face various levels of oppression based on their gender, race, social class, culture, age, nationality, marital status, and ethnicity. Although digital literacies lower the barriers and open the possibility to hear multiple perspectives, there seem to be fewer voices from women, particularly those from certain regions. For example, Brandtzaeg (2017) noted inequalities in civic engagement by the poster's gender and country origins by analyzing the "Likes" posted on Facebook, a feature that allows readers to approve of a post. Women participants were more invisible than men, especially in non-Western countries (i.e., in Asia and Africa) in expressing civic engagement online. Brandtzaeg concluded that women's civic engagement is less visible on Facebook because women "Liked" political and informational Facebook pages less often than did men.

This study explores how Korean American women make meaning together in a discussion forum on social issues in a women's online community through multimodal and multilingual literacy practices for social change. The inquiry centers on writing as social action in the digital era and is guided by the research question: How do Korean American women mobilize their literacy practices toward social change through an online transnational community?

Digital Literacies for Transnational Women

This research employs the New Literacy Studies (Gee, 2010; Street, 2006), perspective, which is grounded in a sociocultural view of literacies and a perspective of transnational feminism (Parisi & Thornton, 2012) that draws attention to the complex interplay of gender and cultural identities. Social views of literacy (Street, 1984) posit that literacy practices can differ along with power dynamics in time and space, from one context to another, and from one culture to another. This perspective calls attention to the human mind and the diversity of a culture in terms of languages, modes, and multicultural issues, such as race, gender, ethnicity, sexuality, and economic status. The New Literacy Studies appreciates the diversity and influences of various sociocultural factors on literacy practices. Therefore, a transnational perspective resulting from proliferating digital technologies must be one of the primary focuses in research.

Within the debate in the New Literacy Studies regarding relationships between the local and the global, it is necessary to unpack the importance of global flows (Appadurai, 1996) in literacy education (Brandt & Clinton, 2002; Hansen, 2014; Stornaiuolo & LeBlanc, 2016; Street, 2006). Street (1984, 2006) asserts the importance of the context in which literacy practices occur whereas Brandt and Clinton (2002) criticize this emphasis for "exaggerating the power of local contexts" (p. 338) and possibly limiting the scale of literacy practices. As the categories of the local and the global are not fixed (Stornaiuolo & LeBlanc, 2016) and have been explored only modestly, how often and how much global flows are embedded in daily life and how they complicate borders between the local and the global, especially through digital media, must be recognized. This complication can be illuminated by transnational communities' literacy practices online, including what borders they cross and how they reconstruct their identities through online border crossings.

Why should transnational women's literacy practices be investigated? To answer this question, consider the meaning of "transnational," the relationship between literacy and civic engagement, and unequal opportunities for women to experience civic engagement. Transnational women extend across national boundaries and construct this extension as a part of their identity. The multifaceted social view of literacy can embrace civic engagement through literacy practices. Literacy can be powerful "rhetorical action as a demonstration of will in asserting a right to agency and authority in the negotiations of our lives using language and literacy as vital and flexible tools" (Royster, 2007, p. 5). Civic engagement through literacy practices can contribute to how to "read the word and the world" critically (Freire & Macedo, 2005). Unfortunately, the traditional guidance, scaffolding, and interest in civic engagement have not been equally implemented and encouraged for women of color.

Transnational feminist civic engagement (Parisi & Thornton, 2012) is a useful addition to the New Literacy Studies by differentiating a transnational perspective from a global (international) feminist perspective. The transnational perspective focuses on "flows across borders and the differential gendered, racialized, classed, and sexualized impacts of these processes" (p. 217). The international feminist approach views the local and the global as more distinct concepts rather than an intertwined concept. The transnational feminist lens helps to rethink how women in different contexts may face oppression by not assuming all women's issues are universal.

Scholars in digital literacies conceptualize literacies as situated in diverse contexts with multiple forms (e.g., Buckingham, 2006). Reading and writing skills and abilities are still at the core of literacy, but digital literacies require additional technical skills and abilities. The New London Group (1996) described what these additional technical skills refer to in the current interconnected world: it is not only knowing how to use technology for reading and writing but also about how to make meanings by leveraging digital technologies for social justice. Those who engage in the new literacies must see themselves as "active participants in social change, as learners and students who can be active designers-makers-of social futures" (p. 64). Virtual contexts of learning interrogate the boundaries of reader-writer, text-modes, and time and space with the potential to disseminate literacy practices as social change. This perspective is appropriate for this study as it situates this research in expanding meaningfulness to multiple literacies, especially for transnational women who constantly cross multiple borders but remain underrepresented.

Studying Transnational Women Online

This study employed an online ethnography (Garcia, Standlee, Bechkoff, Cui, & Ya, 2009) as a way of expanding the methodological repertoire in literacy research in this digital era and developing ecological perspectives on learning. Since the 1990s, ethnography has gained popularity in research on online communities (e.g., Hine, 2008; Lammers, 2016) as a method to trace the new kinds of cultures that are emerging from participatory media or those new media that allow for content creation, and has been used to examine how literacies are situated as social practice. As contemporary literacy practices and daily experiences are inseparable from computer-mediated communications, online ethnographic research enables researchers to examine lived experiences, identities, and subcultures as a part of human action and social life (Garcia et al., 2009). By crossing boundaries as both the researcher and the user of online spaces, ethnographers can explore online spaces while simultaneously learning about others' lived experiences and contexts. This study views online communities as sites of civic engagement in terms of convenience of usage across time and space and the fact that members can express themselves comparatively freely with anonymity.

An Online Community for Korean American Women for Civic Engagement

I chose MissyUSA because it is one of the largest online communities for Korean American women in the United States. As a Korean woman, I have participated in the community as a member of this discussion group where the discussions are publicly available. MissyUSA is usually used by women of Korean heritage in the United States, as well as by repatriates to South Korea, but membership is also open to other women (e.g., Japanese or Chinese women married to Korean men and living in the United States). If women can communicate in the Korean language regardless of their residence, race, nationality, and ethnicity, they can engage in discussions on the site. The majority of MissyUSA members are married Korean American women who are living in the United States. Members of the community communicate in Korean, English, or a mixture of both languages. They post stories with photos, images, graphics interchange formats (gifs), and links to videos, news articles, and other websites.

Within this discussion group, I examined a forum called "Hot Issues/Society/Politics" hosted in the Talk Lounge on the site. The Talk Lounge has active multiple forums, such as Living Q&A, "Sokpuri" (where users vent their innermost feelings about their lives), Poem/Novel/Essay/Book Reviews, Heartwarming, and Entertainment. All the postings and comments in the forum are anonymous and are publicly available. As a member of the community, I visited the forum multiple times almost every day for five years. My participant observation included posting my own stories, reading and commenting on others' postings, or interacting with other users in a small group. These reciprocal actions helped to deepen my understanding of transnational women's meaning-making practices online and I accumulated knowledge of the community as I engaged in layered interactions within it.

I collected posts from the online forum from January 2018 to April 2018. In total, 61,658 writings were posted on the Hot Issues/Society/Politics forum during that period. Comments on the postings and responses to previous comments were also collected to investigate how members of the community interacted with one another. I selected posts that showed how participants participated in civic engagement through their literacy practices in the community. I read all the posts and removed those in support of politicians or political parties, focusing primarily on 11 postings or threads (posts and responses to those initial posts), also conducted a semi-structured interview with one member of the online community, Sooyi (pseudonym). I chose to interview Sooyi who emigrated from South Korea to the United States and was a daily user of the online community. Learning about her literacy practices and lived experiences as a transnational woman in the United States made it possible to contextualize this study by moving between online and offline spaces by interviewing her in person using our native language of Korean. I used the constant-comparative method (Glaser & Strauss, 1967) to identify themes of transnational women's literacy practices for change.

My focal participant, Sooyi, emigrated when she was in her twenties to live with her sister; she is now in her late fifties. At the time of the study, Sooyi had a full-time office job working with diverse others and used English in her workplace. Sooyi was asked about her experiences and literacy practices in the online community, such as why she participated and how she engaged in literacy practices online. I focused on how her social conditions and experiences generate "subjectivities and identities" (McRobbie, 1994, p. 193) and how she mobilized her literacy practices.

Mobilizing Transnational Literacies as Active Participants

Across posts, comments, and interviews, two themes emerged that showed how transnational women engaged in transnational literacy practices through an online community and how they mobilized their literacy practices. First, Korean American transnational women make meaning for social change by inviting their potential audiences to make an impact broadly and powerfully together. Their social change was not restricted to the virtual community or to individuals. The meaning-making process was multi-layered from the self to other communities across borders and multidirectional from the local to the global or vice versa. In the process, they negotiated decision-making or action processes by reading and sharing multiple resources, such as blog posts and news articles in Korean or English, videos from YouTube, broadcasts from South Korea or the United States, and posts from other communities or social networking sites that were usually shared by the first author of the posting. Then, other commenters or writers added more information and knowledge based on the first posting by describing their own related experiences or sharing outside of the community. They mobilized their transnational literacy practices to make their voices heard so that they could make an impact beyond the online community and at the societal level.

Second, participants negotiated transnational identities that mostly spanned two countries (i.e., South Korea and the United States) by engaging in discourse on social change in/for/between the two countries. It is noteworthy that these discourses demonstrated their concern for other minority groups, such as women, children, and other racial or ethnic groups and their issues, not only from the two countries but also those of people from other countries around the globe.

Making an Inward and Outward Impact

Not every post about social change imagined or targeted the online community alone. The potential impact of the writings in the community was broader than the online community itself. It the participants' aimed to extend their efforts toward social justice beyond themselves and other members of the community. For example, participants invited others to sign petitions to the South Korean government or to the White House such as a petition to reopen a 9-year-old case of a young actress' suicide after sexual abuse in South Korea, an effort that was stimulated by the #MeToo movement. A total of 35 posts shared this story, adding their voices by advancing the petition through posting related news articles, texts, a YouTube video, and photographs.

One member posted a message titled, "Me too . . ." (2/25/2018) in which she argued that this case should be remembered, and 33 members commented on the post. The third commenter said, "It is the first thing to solve" and two commenters asked whether there was a petition for the case to support the issue.

Other commenters also confirmed this sentiment and thanked the writer for sharing the story of the young actress. Later the same day, a petition related to the case was posted in the forum, and 35 members replied to the post by saying that they had signed the petition and added comments. For example:

Commenter 4:   I hope many of you make a petition.
Commenter 5:   I created a twitter account.
               🖕🖕🖕🖕 🖕🖕🖕🖕 🖕🖕🖕🖕 🖕🖕🖕🖕 🖕🖕🖕🖕 🖕🖕🖕🖕
               Please post this on the Entertainment forum!!!
Commenter 6:   And please post this several times even a day, so many Missies can participate!!!! Thanks to the person who posted this. Someone has done what needs to be done with courage!

The petition was shared several times afterward, and more than 200,000 people from the online community and outside of it eventually signed it. Finally, the South Korean government decided to reopen the case. Regardless of their current residence and citizenship, the Korean American women cooperated together in making social change happen by writing posts on social issues and asking for action to impact a broad audience beyond the community and the nation.

The #WithYou movement to support the victims that followed the #MeToo movement was also supported by transnational women in this community. A woman shared a post by one of her Facebook friends in the hope that the #MeToo movement can move society in a healthy direction (2/26/2018). The original writer highlighted this part with an underline: "The reason why we put #WithYou alongside #MeToo is because that not only one person should take the bullet but we should build a community together to change together." A commenter supported the post by saying, "From simple revelations to changing society!" Another post requested that a separate forum be made for the #MeToo movement in the community because she thought, "As a woman, it seems to be a matter of continuous and focused importance" (3/10/2018). The community members' literacy practices brought both local and international attention to cases of injustice for women by making efforts to support the victims and considering an opportunity to change society together.

Sooyi shared how her participation in the online community impacted her offline life. In her case, the virtual interactions with anonymous members of the online community extended to her other digital platforms and face-to-face interactions. She visited the online community almost daily to read about news and issues related to her local community, South Korea, the United States, and other parts of the world. She also contributed to the community by answering questions from other members based on her work and lived experiences because of her sense of the forum as a community. One day, Sooyi read a posting about the new Korean president's visit to the United States, and she commented on the posting that she was interested in attending a meeting to welcome the president. The conversation migrated to a mobile messenger and to face-to-face meetings among participants. As she showed me hundreds of unread messages in the KakaoTalk messenger on her smart phone, she said, "The talks are never finished even at midnight. People cannot sleep, there are time-zone differences. Some are in Alaska, some are in New York." I asked her why she joined the small group to support the Korean president and she replied, "Who will support the Korean Americans?"

These virtual interactions expanded to physical actions to support Korean Americans, including attending seminars on South Korea and relations between North Korea and the United States, meeting South Korean politicians to make suggestions, and calling Senators in the United States. Through active participation in online forums and offline interactions, Korean American women connected with one another to support their communities and others by reaching broader audiences. These efforts were intended to make social impact both inwardly within the online community and outwardly to those outside the community, both locally and globally.

Mobilizing Transnational Literacies Across Borders

The discursive impact of participants' literacy practices resulted in women on the site mobilizing their transnational identities as civic actors across borders. The topics they shared were wide-ranging, from news regarding a Korean woman in India to news about refugee women in Syria. The Korean American women showed how they cared about other minorities regardless of race, gender, ethnicity, and nationality, as well as social issues around the world by reflecting on their own experiences as transnational women in the United States. For example, a discussion group member shared a news article and screen captures of Twitter users' reactions to the news on discrimination toward African American men at a coffee shop in the United States. The incident was where two men came into the coffee shop but did not order because they were waiting for a friend so an employee of the coffeeshop called the police. The first commenter said that the staff member's actions reflected the company policy. Most of the other respondents agreed that it was an example of racial discrimination, however. A respondent to the first commenter questioned, "If he were a white man and not a black man, would the employee ever call the police?" The second commenter said, "Well, suddenly I'm afraid to go to [the coffee shop]. We're strangers, too." The third commenter responded, "[The coffee shop] provides reasons to boycott." The next commenter asked, "Can I get a refund on my balance at the mobile app?" The fifth commenter said, "It is really hard to live in America." Although the case involved a person of a different race, the Korean American women tried to understand the situation as immigrants of color and see that discrimination could happen to them. They not only expressed their empathy, but they also shared ideas about how to take action against discrimination.

Sooyi provided an additional example of engaging across borders, explaining the broad regions and other people in different contexts of concern to her. She reflected, "I identify myself as a humanist. We should care about all issues of social injustice." Then, she added, "I still care about South Korea very much. As a Korean American here, how South Korea is doing matters to me and people here." During the presidential scandal in South Korea, "I stayed up all night to watch the hearing in South Korea on YouTube. You know people here did the same thing for the presidential election in the United States." She stated that she paid the most attention to news from her local community where she currently lives. Sooyi's insights show how multi-localities are intertwined withier transnational literacies and identities and in her lived experience. As Sooyi and the online discussion forum elaborated, Korean American women's literacies and identities are not limited to their home or host countries or to groups of people with the same cultural and linguistic heritage.

Implications for Literacy Education and Cross-Disciplinary Fields

The ways in which transnational women make meanings together by broadening their impact and how they make sense of transnational identities by fostering empathy across borders illuminates how transnational women practice digital literacies and have implications for future scholarship. These women's digital literacies moved them to engage in multiple social actions across space and borders and gave them access to learn about and impact one another. These findings contribute to understandings of how transnational women engage in civic engagement through digital literacies and contribute to social change by supporting one another. These women mobilized their transnational literacy practices in the community and beyond as community members, readers, writers, thinkers, and social designers negotiating multiple texts and modes, languages, dynamic resources, and multi-layered audiences across nations.

The findings that Korean American women engaged in conversation online, expressed their voices together, and negotiated boundaries of national identities to effect social change in multiple ways are worthwhile to consider in contrast to the ways the literacy practices of transnational communities and women have been portrayed (e.g., Kumaravadivelu, 2003). For instance, these women's digital literacies complicate the traditional concept of transnational communities with limited ties to their home countries and evidence new digital literacies as social capital they shared and used to support each other. These findings challenge stereotypical perceptions of the role of Asian women in a global society and refutes the notion of their invisibility and characterization as passive and silent (e.g., Paek & Shah, 2003). These participants' transnational identities and actions were found to be dynamic and fluid as they reached out to address social issues across borders.

Moreover, these Korean American women's literacy practices in the online community have had an impact beyond that community, expanding from their past to their present and future lives. Their literacy practices help to show how transnational individuals and communities can build a community of social changers by sharing various cultures, histories, and lived experiences for a more equal society. The participatory culture in the transnational virtual community critically engages transnational women as societal change agents by expanding their opportunities to learn from one another. They make their learning resources available to others by sharing articles with the networked audience and inviting different ideas in multiple ways by interrogating the binaries between the local and the global. Transnational women engage in actions online, then bring those actions into their offline lives. Sometimes, the online community can spread their actions to other spaces. These multi-directional interactions and impacts can empower marginalized groups to mobilize their literacy practices and make their voices heard (Ito et al., 2013).

These women's digital literacies demonstrated how online literacy practices can be used to advance social action and change. This study demonstrated that women of color are critically engaging in meaningful literacy practices for themselves and for societal change. Educational researchers will need to conduct more comprehensive research on how transnational literacies can be mobilized to impact individuals' lived experiences connecting local and global communities (Parisi & Thornton, 2012). This research agenda may offer new possibilities for understanding and learning about diverse populations in terms of their history, contemporary issues, and cultures that transcend conventional notions and challenge stereotypes about under researched ethnic communities.

References

Appadurai, A. (1996). *Modernity at large: Cultural dimensions of globalization*. Minneapolis, MN: University of Minnesota Press.

Arisaka, Y. (2000). Asian women: Invisibility, locations, and claims to philosophy. In N. Zack (Ed.), *Women of color and philosophy: A critical reader* (pp. 219–223). New York, NY: Blackwell.

Brandt, D., & Clinton, K. (2002). Limits of the local: Expanding perspectives on literacy as a social practice. *Journal of Literacy Research, 34*(3), 337–356.

Brandtzaeg, P.B. (2017). Facebook is no "great equalizer": A big data approach to gender differences in civic engagement across countries. *Social Science Computer-Review, 35*(1), 103–125.

Buckingham, D. (2006). Defining digital literacy: What do young people need to know about digital media? *Nordic Journal of Digital Literacy, 4*(1), 263–276.

Freire, P., & Macedo, D. (2005). *Literacy: Reading the word and the world*. London, UK: Routledge.

Garcia, C., Standlee, A., Bechkoff, A., Cui, J., & Yan, C. (2009). Ethnographic approaches to the internet and computer-mediated communication. *Journal of Contemporary Ethnography, 38*(1): 52–84. doi: 10.1177/0891241607310839

Gee, J.P. (2010). A situated-sociocultural approach to literacy and technology. In E. Baker (Ed.), *The new literacies: Multiple perspectives on research and practice* (pp. 165–193). New York, NY: Guilford.

Glaser, B., & Strauss, A. (1967). *The discovery of grounded theory*. Chicago, IL: Aldine.

Grewal, I., & Kaplan, C. (Eds.). (1994). *Scattered hegemonies: Postmodernity and transnational feminist practices*. Minneapolis, MN: University of Minnesota Press.

Han, N. (2017, September 3). This is a response to the driver who almost ran me over this weekend – and then dared to yell out her window, "This is America" [Facebook video]. Retrieved from www.facebook.com/6abcNydiaHan/videos/10156752826863508.

Hansen, D.T. (2014). Cosmopolitanism as cultural creativity: New modes of educational practice in globalizing times. *Curriculum Inquiry, 44*(1), 1–14.

Hine, C. (2008). Overview: Virtual ethnography: Modes, varieties, affordances. In N.G. Fielding, R.M. Lee, & G. Blank (Eds.), *The SAGE handbook of online research methods* (pp. 257–270). London, UK: Sage.

Ito, M., Gutiérrez, K., Livingstone, S., Penuel, B., Rhodes, J., Salen, K., & Watkins, S.C. (2013). *Connected learning: An agenda for research and design*. Irvine, CA: Digital Media and Learning Research Hub.

Kumaravadivelu, B. (2003). Problematizing cultural stereotypes in TESOL. *TESOL Quarterly, 37*(4), 709–719.

Lammers, J.C. (2016). "The Hangout was serious business": Leveraging participation in an online space to design Sims fanfiction. *Research in the Teaching of English, 50*(3), 309–332.

Lee, S.J., Park, E., & Wong, J.H.S. (2017). Racialization, schooling, and becoming American: Asian American experiences. *Educational Studies, 53*(5), 492–510.

McRobbie, A. (1994). *Postmodernism and popular culture*. London, UK: Routledge.

Mayuzumi, K. (2015). Navigating orientalism: Asian women faculty in the Canadian academy. *Race Ethnicity and Education, 18*(2), 277–296.

New London Group. (1996). A pedagogy of multiliteracies: Designing social futures. *Harvard Educational Review, 66*(1), 60–93.

Paek, H.J., & Shah, H. (2003). Racial ideology, model minorities, and the "not-so-silent partner": Stereotyping of Asian Americans in US magazine advertising. *Howard Journal of Communication, 14*(4), 225–243.

Parisi, L., & Thornton, L. (2012). Connecting the local with the global: Transnational feminism and civic engagement. *Feminist Teacher, 22*(3), 214–232.

Pyke, K.D., & Johnson, D.L. (2003). Asian American women and racialized femininities: "Doing" gender across cultural worlds. *Gender & Society, 17*(1), 33–53.

Royster, J. (2007, September). Literacy and civic engagement. Keynote address presented at the Civil rights symposium: An interdepartmental and interdisciplinary conversation on civil rights reform, Albuquerque, NM. Retrieved from www.unm.edu/~wac/old_site/CurriculumResources/ROYSTER--Keynote%20Address--2007.pdf.

Stornaiuolo, A., & LeBlanc, R.J. (2016). Scaling as a literacy activity: Mobility and educational inequality in an age of global connectivity. *Research in the Teaching of English, 50*(3), 263–287.

Street, B.V. (1984). *Literacy in theory and practice*. Cambridge, UK: Cambridge University Press.

Street, B.V. (2006). Autonomous and ideological models of literacy: Approaches from New Literacy Studies. *Media Anthropology Network, 17*, 1–15.

16

DIVERSE MEN MAKING MEDIA

Creating Cultural (Re)Constructions of Gender and Race

Barbara J. Guzzetti

Despite recent attention to the topic (e.g., Bose, 2014; Guzzetti & Foley, 2017; Guzzetti & Lesley, 2015; Marshall & Rogers, 2016), there remains a paucity of research on adult men's literacy practices. Little is known about how men engage in literacy beyond their schooling years (Gustavson, 2002). The extant research on men's literacy practices, particularly for men of color, has focused on school-age males and their out-of-school literacy practices (e.g., Bean & Ransaw, 2013; Kirkland, 2013a, 2013b; Noll, 1998). Few studies or public sharing of men's literacy practices have highlighted men's writings, particularly Black men's writing, either for each other or for a wider audience (e.g., Smith, Moore, Laymon, & Green, 2013). Native American men have tended to share their stories through the generations orally rather than by writing (Wieser, 2017). Few descriptions exist of men of any race authoring in offline or online forms and forums. It is unclear why diverse men make media or how they participate in the new literacies, those literacy practices that are chronologically new and represent new socially recognized ways of communicating (Lankshear & Knobel, 2011). Therefore, not much is known about why men choose to write, what they write about, or the types of media they produce.

Yet, surveys have shown that men have kept pace with women in producing social media (Vermeren, 2015) or participatory media, those media that have interactive capabilities and allow for content creation, social interaction, collaboration, and deliberation (Jenkins, 2006). Social media include social networking platforms, such as Facebook or Instagram and blogs or microblogs like Twitter. Men have become active members of a participatory or do-it-yourself (DIY) culture (Jenkins, 2006) as they create new forms of print media, such as zines (self-publications) and as they use and create Web 2.0 technologies.

The silences on men's online and offline literacy practices in the current professional literature reflect the national trend in the United States of men becoming an underrepresented group, educationally and economically. Data from the U.S. Census Bureau and the National Center for Education Statistics indicate that men, particularly minority men, lag behind women in college enrollment (Niemi, 2017; Vedder, 2015). Fewer men than women complete Bachelors and advanced degrees (Lopez & Gonzalez-Barrera, 2014; Schow, 2016). Consequently, more women are now out earning men (Pianin, 2017).

One explanation for this gender disparity in academic and social achievement is that men, particularly men of color, have typically lacked mentors and role models of men pursuing education and engaging in literacy practices (Williams & Flores-Ragade, 2010). Such descriptions could provide vicarious role models for men of all ages who lack insight into the functions that literacy can serve in a man's life. Descriptive studies of how and why men engage in new media to represent themselves as men could raise men's awareness of new possibilities for self-representation and stimulate their engagement in new forms of literate expression.

My Purpose

The purpose of this case study (Stake, 2011) was to examine the literacy practices of an under-researched population – adult men of color. I focused on how diverse men crafted personal zines (perzines) and created social media to advance their agendas and represent themselves as men. I asked: Why do men of color compose media? How do diverse men produce media texts that represent their gender and racial identities?

Perspectives

A theory of writing as meaning-making informed this study (Andrews & Smith, 2011). In this view, writing is a way of making sense of the world and the self and a means to communicate. This perspective focuses on how writers develop, what functions writing plays in people's lives, and why people write. Studying why and how people write can assist others in developing their writing. This view is consistent with a sociocultural perspective underlying the new literacies or those literacy practices that are chronologically new and represent new ways of communicating, including an ethos of participation, collaboration, and distribution of content (Knobel and Lankshear, 2007). This perspective recognizes multimodal forms of text (Cope & Kalantzis, 2000) and semiotic constructions of meaning (Kress & van Leeuwen, 2006). A social-semiotic perspective focuses on making meaning through situated practices and interpretation, multiple modes, and representational features (Jewitt & Kress, 2010). Multiliteracies scholars consider all meaning-making as multimodal, requiring navigating multiple modes of communication (Kalantzis & Cope, 2012).

This study was also informed by theories of cultural constructions of masculinities and gender. Such theories recognize the nuanced and relational contexts of lived experience where men have agency to overcome hegemonic views of masculinity (Bean & Ransaw, 2013) and to challenge dominant notions of gender and literacy performance (Kehler, 2008; Kirkland, 2013a, 2013b). As a feminist qualitative researcher, I have subscribed to a feminist sociology (Stanley & Wise, 1993) by recognizing the influence of multiple subjectivities, including race, ethnicity, culture, and social class on the performance of gender that eschew essentializing or stereotyping, believing that men are worthy of study, particularly in their interactions with women.

Like other men, African American males may find relevance in their literacy practices in informal contexts where they are stimulated to tell their stories in alternative forms and formats (Kirkland, 2013a, 2013b). For African American men, the performance of masculinity is typically portrayed by the media as acting emotionally distant and hyper-masculine (Kirkland, 2013b). One-dimensional and stereotypical characters in films perpetuate misperceptions and negate the broader lived experience of Black men (Smith, 2013). These stereotypes affirm restrictive notions of masculinity, avoiding behaviors that are considered as feminine (Bean & Ransaw, 2013, like engaging in literacy practices (Archer & Yamashita, 2003). Resistance to literacy practices may for some African American males stem from the notion that engaging in academics is not acting "cool" (Bean & Ransaw, 2013).

Navajo men may have varying ideas of what it means to be a man yet tend to agree that men have a caring responsibility toward their families (Lee, 2013). Although contemporary Navajo are assimilating American notions and characteristics of what it means to be a man, responsibility to his family and people and his cultural knowledge still epitomize a Navajo man (Lee, 2013). The Navajo culture is one in which gender is fluid, recognizing more than two genders – feminine female, masculine male, feminine masculine, and masculine female (Fortino, 2011; Lee, 2013). Some Navajo believe in two spirits (male and female) that inhabit each person while others acknowledge five genders, including those who are transgender (Brayboy, 2017). These views have historically been oppressed by others from non-native cultures with dichotomous and restrictive views of gender and gender performance (Brayboy, 2017).

My Inquiries

Selecting the Participating Men

I focused on two men who produce zines, self-publications that are authored or edited and distributed as alternatives to commercial magazines by those who create them, referred to as "zinesters." I selected these men due to their diverse racial and ethnic backgrounds as Native American or African American. They each produced multimedia in print, visual, and digital forms, including their personal or perzines consisting of their own poetry, cartoons, comics, or prose and their supporting social and Internet media.

Collecting and Analyzing the Data

I observed and photographed these men discussing and distributing their zines at a national Zine Fest held in the southwestern region of the United States during a weekend in October 2016. I took field notes and conducted in-situ interviews with the men as they distributed and discussed their zines. I collected one issue of their zines at the symposium and other issues by mail. Each zinester completed a demographic questionnaire, asking their ages, ethnicities, socioeconomic statuses, educational and professional experiences, as well as their zines' purposes, messages, distribution, audiences, and readers' feedback

Following the zine festival, I conducted audio-recorded, semi-structured, and transcribed interviews with these men by Skype or telephone. The interview questions focused on the men's influences, inspirations, messages, zining trajectories, and how their related social media supported their zines. I conducted informal interviews with them by email to clarify and elaborate on their questionnaire responses. I examined their zines and related websites, blogs, and social media. In doing so, I followed the zinesters on their social media and became their Facebook friends, taking screenshots of their posts.

I conducted an inductive thematic analysis (Patton, 2015) in which I read, reread, annotated, coded, and categorized the data. Reoccurring categories across the data forms became themes. I also deductively coded and categorized the data for illustrations of constructs from the theoretical frameworks. Member checks (Lincoln & Guba, 1985) were conducted by returning interview transcripts and manuscript drafts to the men for their modifications, resulting in corrections to information that was unclear or incorrectly recorded or represented updates.

The Zinesters and Their Zines

Damon Begay

Damon Begay is a 25-year-old man born on the Navajo reservation who migrated with his family throughout the southwest while growing up, living last in Gallup, New Mexico before moving to Phoenix. Damon has a Bachelor of Fine Arts degree in graphic information technology and freelances in that industry while working in a factory. Damon considers himself to be middle class. He has been motivated to write and is influenced by his Navajo girlfriend who creates her own comic-book zines. With her encouragement and following her example, Damon attended his first zine symposium where he shared his three comic-book zines, including *Interstellar Comix* (2016), *Living Weapons* (2017), and *Spiral* (2017).

These texts serve as a catharsis for Damon's anger that he was not taught the Navajo language and mostly learned his cultural traditions in negative ways. Damon was often scolded by his elders for exhibiting behaviors that contradicted Navajo superstitions, such as moving in a dangerous counterclockwise direction instead of clockwise when participating in a ceremony or for tickling a baby's toes, a practice thought to stunt a baby's growth. He was warned not to whistle at night or look at snakes due to Navajo beliefs. Some childhood teachings were more positive, however, as Damon was told of Native American myths to explain the world, including the Lava myth regarding an area near Albuquerque with lava rocks that are supposedly present because twins were fighting the Lava Monster and their blood spill formed rocks. Damon remarked, "I liked those stories growing up and want to incorporate them in my zines."

Composing DIY media that represent Native Americans has stimulated Damon's independent discoveries about his culture as he consults online and offline resources, including a Navajo/English dictionary, Glosbe (www. glosbe.com/en.nv), his Navajo girlfriend, her father who is a medicine man, and a mentor Navajo man when conducting research for his stories. Using the knowledge he has gained from these sources, Damon creates perzines to represent Native Americans and their lived experiences in comic genres. Damon explained:

> My main goals are to learn about my culture and repurpose it into stories . . .
> I want to repurpose the folklore from my own Navajo culture. I grew up
> on the rez and want to show the life of a Navajo today. When I draw and
> create, I feel I have a purpose.

Creating Storylines

Damon was stimulated to create zines because he could not locate commercially published comic books written by Native Americans or find comics that included contemporary American Indians as characters with settings and plots that reflect Native American culture. His comic-strip zine, *Spiral* (coauthored with his Navajo girlfriend), advances his agenda of representing Native Americans in comic books with fictional storylines authored by a Native American. *Spiral* is a parody of a Japanese manga (comic), *Uzamaki*, but incorporates Navajo language, referred to as Dine Bizaad (Goossen, 1995), and Navajo characters and settings. The storyline reflects tales of Native Americans in modern life, incorporating traditional Navajo folklore with plots of action, adventure, romance, and fantasy.

Spiral conveys elements of Navajo folklore through a supernatural plot. The words in speech bubbles and the accompanying cartoons portray Damon leading his girlfriend away from numerous snakes and consulting with a medicine man who advises them to burn sage (known as smudging) while running and moving their hands in a clockwise circle to escape the surrounding rattlesnakes. This plotline alludes to Navajo myths regarding the dangers associated with looking at snakes and burning sage (called smudging) to eliminate negative energy. Damon and his girlfriend are finally assisted in escaping the snakes by giant robots who consume them, a device that updates traditional Navajo tales of monsters, advancing Damon's agenda of sharing cultural folklore with his readers.

Spiral's character development exemplifies the Navajo's belief in two sprits and four genders. Damon's girlfriend is portrayed in the story as a female character who is intuitive and sensitive, traits associated with femininity (Murray, 2001), acting as a feminine female. She is the first to notice ominous spirals in their surroundings at a coffee shop. Spiral shapes are evident in their wind chimes and cinnamon buns and are seen in vehicles and billboards in the streets, foreshadowing the danger to come of omnipresent snakes, spiraled into coils. Damon's girlfriend is a problem solver, cautioning Damon to stretch before running to escape the rattlesnakes so they would not experience muscle cramps. In these ways, she personified traits associated with masculinity as assertive and imitative (Murray, 2001), acting as a masculine female.

Damon is also portrayed in the story as expressing both feminine and masculine gender performances. Damon acquiesces to his girlfriend's wishes, assuming the posture of a feminine man. Yet, it is Damon who suggests they consult a medicine man for a solution to their dilemma and it is he who eventually leads them to safety, portraying the courage and strong will commonly associated with masculinity (Murray, 2001). His protective actions personify the Navajo tradition of men as caretakers. Hence, the storyline conveys cultural notions of women's and men's roles in contemporary Navajo life, demonstrating gender performance as fluid.

Sustaining a Living Language

Damon's stories incorporate cultural transmission of the Navajo language. In *Spiral*, Damon inserts Navajo terms as characters' exclamations. For example, the Navajo word, "Yiyah" (pronounced "yee-yah") is defined in a glossary preceding the story as "an expression that ranges in meaning from scary to dangerous and is often used in jest." The term carries the connotation that "something unpleasant will become of a behavior" and can be used as a less formal way to stop an action (http://navajoword.com/word/yiiah-yee-yah). This translation enabled readers to comprehend the medicine man's exclamation, "Yiyah!" in the story when he opened a door to attempt their escape only to be surrounded by more rattlesnakes (Figure 16.1).

Inclusion of these Dine terms assists Damon in keeping the Navajo language a living language, as it is in danger of extinction due to influences of English-only policies in public education in some regions and the influence of mass media (Benally & Viri, 2010; Miller, 2015)

FIGURE 16.1   The medicine man's exclamation.

Incorporating Navajo Art Forms

Damon crafted his comics not only to discover and reclaim his cultural heritage, but also to extend Navajo or Dine (meaning "the people") art forms. Damon's sequential drawings allow him to represent traditional Native American artistic devices in contemporary images. His sketches illustrating the setting and characters incorporate the strong geometrical shapes used in Navajo art. Damon explained, "Navajo art is geometric. It's based on shapes and colors." Consequently, many of Damon's illustrations incorporate circles, spirals, squares, rectangles, and arrows. Damon's images are strong enough to progress the storyline at strategic points and 7 of his 26 pages contain no words as only stark visuals emphasize the boldness of his designs and advance the plot. His drawings of robotic monsters consuming snakes to protect Damon and his girlfriend need no words of explanation. In producing these images, he draws his comics with India ink and scans them into his computer to bring them together into a pdf file that can be printed at many locations. This process and format allow him the freedom to experiment with images and forms and self-publish his creations.

Creating Community Through Internet and Social Media

Damon uses more online than offline resources to create community. Influenced by the competition among zinesters to create well-crafted zines, Damon produces zines to keep pace with his contemporaries, sharing excerpts, photographs, and videos of his zines' covers and pages on his social media. Like his friends, Damon migrated from DeviantArt to Facebook and Instagram where he promotes his comics and announces his appearances at events, including ComicCon and gallery showings.

Damon's social media support and extend his zines by allowing him to display photographs of his covers and pages in their original color, an artistic element that is prohibitively expensive to reproduce in hard copy. Damon uses social media to share and publicize his zines and to solicit and obtain feedback and questions from his readers. He dispenses and sells his zines at web-comic sites like Tapastic, renamed Tapas (https://tapas.io), and Gumroad (https://gumroad.com) and distributes hard copies at a local comic-book stores. His attendance at the zine fest allowed him to meet fellow zinesters who he had prior contact with online, including one who creates zines featuring Native monsters and superheroes. In these ways, Damon is enabled to fulfil his purpose in life – sharing stories and art reflecting his culture.

Lawrence Lindell

Lawrence Lindell (his pen name composed of his first and middle names), is a 30-year-old Black man who when I met him at age 28 was residing in Compton, California, a city like Los Angeles that some refer to as a "gang capital" with active members of the Crypts, Bloods, Mexican, and El Salvadoran gangs. Having earned a Bachelor of Fine Arts in digital-media illustration, Lawrence considers himself to be middle class, but as he observed, "probably lower-middle class because the middle class is shrinking." Lawrence once lived in London with his girlfriend and has worked for a fashion magazine as an event coordinator and videographer, covering Fashion Week in Los Angeles and London. He has been a punk-rock fan since he was a teenager, listening to hardcore punk tapes, attending punk shows, and was a performer playing drums in a punk-rock band. By age 17, he was wearing band shirts promoting Bane and Minor Threat, his favorite hardcore bands. Lawrence has provided a music and art program at an elementary school in west Los Angeles and currently teaches comic-book classes to children in Grades 1–5. He has attended zine festivals in Los Angeles, San Diego, San Francisco, Minneapolis, and Phoenix. Lawrence has created two cartoon perzines he distributed at these festivals, *Color N Stuff* (2016) and *Romance N Stuff* (2016).

Confronting Racial and Gender Stereotypes

Color N Stuff is a collection of characters, life experiences, and autobiography. Some of it centers on his experiences with Tinder, a dating App, and his friends' experiences with it. Writing this zine assisted him in processing the disconnect between his self-representation of identity as a Black man and others' expectations for how he should enact his race and gender. Lawrence found that his musical interests and his lifestyle choices influenced how others perceive him as a Black man:

> I am not like other Black guys from Compton or not like you see on TV and in the movies with Black men engaged in fighting and gangs. I am not like the Black guys portrayed on TV and movies that come from Compton; the characters lack the emotion and complexity of what it's like to be Black in a neighborhood deemed as "unlivable and violent." Some people who don't know me assume I am rough. There are those elements of me because I grew up around violence. White people in the punk community have told me I am cooler than Black people and Black kids have told me I am a Black who wants to be White. So, the theme in this zine is a celebration of people of color. It's a celebration of common things, like what we do that most people don't think we do. I am into punk, but I am considered not Black enough for Black people who don't know me and not White enough for Punk. It's not a place most Black people find themselves in, like being fans of punk or metal.

Lawrence's comments allude to the fact that African American men have been more associated with rap and hip-hop music (Kirkland, 2013a, 2013b) than with punk or hardcore. These associations have served, as Kirkland (2013b) observed, to "cast Black males into almost monolithic nodes" (p. 138). Lawrence grew up listening to rock and hardcore music. Consequently, he was "not really considered to be Black" – both by members of the punk scene and by other Blacks in his neighborhood (Figure 16.2).

Inspired by his and others' experiences like these, Lawrence crafted his zines to offer counternarratives to stereotypical notions of African American men.

FIGURE 16.2 Lawrence's cartoon.

Lawrence's cartoons raise awareness of how language can impact others' perceptions of the performance of Black masculinity. For example, a cartoon chronicled Lawrence's friend's date with a woman who was half White and half Filipino who told him he was "not like other Black guys" because he did not use "Black speak."

Lawrence's friend spoke "proper" English due to his education, defying constraining notions of how a Black man should be and act.

Lawrence's zine also gives a voice to African American women, conveying comparable stories of essentializing or stereotyping race and gender, refuting notions that all Black women are alike. One cartoon depicts a Black woman reflecting on her date with a man she met on Tinder, complaining, "I can't believe he said I'm not your average Black girl! As if there is anything average about being Black." Through cartoons like this, Lawrence's zines interrogates dominant ideologies. While opening possibilities for transforming social scripts of race and gender, Lawrence finds commonalities among differences with other Black men:

We cannot be put into a box and Compton, as well as Black people, are so widely diverse that there is not one type of Black. The same guys you see on the corner also like video games and comics like I do, but sometimes they were not offered the same opportunities I was or maybe they were, and a series of circumstances landed them where they are (you don't know until you ask). I say I am like the other Black guys in Compton because we are Black and the only reason we are looked upon as different is because people have taken the time to get to know me because I am an artist and musician and I make sure my voice is heard. There are plenty of Black guys in Compton that listen to punk and are into alternative stuff and there are Black guys in Compton that sell drugs and gangbang, and there are some that do both. I say all that to say that we are not limited and we all share that same ancestral history and roots, making us the same.

Lawrence's remarks reflect on his social class, life experiences, and interpersonal relationships that have affected his performance of masculinity as a Black man. His remarks allude to individuality and possibility for the performance of gender and race within a shared community.

Writing for Emotional Catharsis

Lawrence crafted his zine, *Romance N Stuff*, to process the painful dissolution of a six-year relationship, writing and drawing as an outlet for his feelings. Lawrence reflected: "I wrote that zine more for myself as a release, to express myself. I shared feelings in that space that I would not talk about outside the zine space. Writing was like therapy for me." Lawrence's cartoons helped him process the emotional turmoil he experienced after his break up, emotions associated with beginning to date again. His writings and drawings spoke to uncertainty ("She's cute, but she has a backpack on . . . she could be a high school student"); apprehension ("So, this is Tinder . . . nah, I'm good; I'm just going to rewatch Buffy") and romance ("let's learn each other so when we touch the stars align"). In ways like these, Lawrence's zining allowed him to reveal his innermost sensitivities in a safe space. He wrote in a genre of emotionality that is atypical for men and considered to be a feminine practice (Weaver-Hightower, 2003). Men do not usually write of romance and when they do, they tend to publish under a feminine or gender-neutral pseudonym (Naughton, 2012).

Creating Complementary Art Forms

Lawrence's medium complements his message. Cartoons with their alternative messages are drawn in an alternative artistic style that deviates from the design principles he was taught in his academic education, a practice he had been criticized for earlier in his career. His cartoon figures are constructed with large heads and tiny bodies, lending the notion that beliefs and ideas are more important than appearances.

Lawrence creates his graphics through an artistic style of sharp shapes and angular forms that complement his confrontational writing. He draws attention to his cartoon characters through bright colors and bold patterns that are consistent with his direct messages addressing gender and racial stereotypes. It is therefore understandable why when Lawrence was asked what zining meant to him, he replied, "Freedom . . . [of] form; power and function in my own words." His textual forms with their no rules format allow Lawrence the autonomy to represent his lived experience and to critique and transform hegemonic social scripts and their enactments.

Forming Online and Offline Community

To support his zines, Lawrence uses Internet and social media. Lawrence maintains a website (www.lawrencelindellstudios.com) to post his artist dates and tours, directing site visitors to follow him on Tumblr. His website chronicles his numerous appearances at zine festivals to promote his zine and network with other zinesters. Lawrence uses Instagram more than other social media because he finds it visual and instant, allowing him to post the process of making a zine from the first drawing to the entire zine and to post his "behind the scenes" processes and sketches. He finds Instagram particularly useful for artists, considering it an online portfolio that people can follow. Lawrence remarked, "I use Instagram every day . . . It's like a form of journaling." He has reached a larger audience by selling most of his zines on Instagram.

Lawrence is a facile "produser" (Bruns, 2016) who both produces and uses multimedia through social media. Lawrence posts his photographs of his zine's pages on Facebook and Twitter, sending tweets announcing his public appearances. He advertises and distributes his cartoon zines on these sites as well, allowing him to reach a wider audience than those on Instagram. These participatory media assist Lawrence in accomplishing his goal – to raise awareness of issues faced by Black people – or in his words, "the things we deal with that people don't think about," attempting to create consciousness regarding the range of gender and racial performance that can exist in the everyday lives of Black men and women.

Implications for Literacy Education and Cross-Disciplinary Fields

This study lends insight into why adult men write past their schooling years with implications for adolescent and adult-literacy educators or others who foster men's literacy. These men each authored perzines to represent their gender, racial, and ethnic identities. Both men produced counternarratives to hegemonic masculinities and stereotypical enactments of gender and race through their writing genres, of poetry and fiction and by the topics they took up of race and gender performances. Their stores serve as illustrations of new images of contemporary performance of masculinities for Native American and African American men, and how zines can be written to discover, repurpose, and preserve a cultural heritage and to confront racial and gender stereotypes. Each produced multimodal texts (visual, digital, and print) to celebrate diversity, to advance a social cause, to promote their work, and to form community. Their social and Internet media served as portfolios, audience outreach, teaching devices, and archives of new textual representations of gender and culture. These men's zines and supporting media serve as examples for other men of the functions that literacy can have in a man's life and how multimodal texts can be created to author identity and self-representation.

This study also advances a theory of zine-making as masculine pedagogy and practice with implications for those in such fields as women's and gender studies, English, and communication. Although much has been written on zines as females' literacy practice or as a feminist experience (e.g., Clark-Parsons, 2017; Piepmeier, 2009), little attention has been paid to men who create zines and their related media. These zinesters demonstrated how men can write with emotionality in forms and genres that defy gender stereotypes and offer men permission to do so. By writing and self-publishing media in online and offline forms and forums men can be enabled to construct, celebrate, and share diverse performances of masculinity, race, and culture.

References

Andrews, R., & Smith, A. (2011). *Developing writers: Teaching and learning in the digital age.* New York, NY: Open University Press.

Archer, L., & Yamashita, H. (2003). Theorizing inner city masculinities: "Race," class, gender and education. *Gender and Education, 15*(2), 115–132.

Bean, T.W., & Ransaw, T. (2013). Masculinity and portrayal of African American boys in young adult literature: A critical deconstruction and reconstruction of this genre. In B.J. Guzzetti & T.W. Bean (Eds.), *Adolescent literacies and the gendered self: (Re)constructing identities through multimodal literacy practices,* (pp. 22–30). New York, NY: Routledge.

Benally, A., & Viri, D. (2010). Dine bizaad [Navajo language] at a crossroads: Extinction or renewal? *Bilingual Research Journal, 29*(1), 85–108.

Bose, L. (2014, January 23). Are zines making a comeback, too? *OC Weekly.* Retrieved from www.ocweekly.com/music/are-zines-making-a-comeback-too-6429146.

Brayboy, D. (2017). Two spirits, one heart, five genders. *Indian Country Today.* Verona, NY: Indian Country Media Network. Retrieved from https://indiancountrymedianetwork.com/news/opinions/two-spirits-one-heart-five-genders.

Bruns, A. (2016). Prosumption, produsage. In B. Jensen, C. Klaus, R.T. Pooley, D. Jefferson, & E.W. Rothenbuhler (Eds.), *The international encyclopedia of communication theory and philosophy.* London, UK: John Wiley & Sons.

Clark-Parsons, R. (2017). Feminist ephemera in a digital world: Theorizing zines as networked feminist practice. *Communication, Culture & Critique, 10,* 1–17.

Cope, B., & Kalantzis, M. (2000). *Multiliteracies: Literacy learning and the design of social futures*. New York, NY: Routledge.

Fortino, S.S. (2011, May 10). Four genders in Navajo culture. *Newspaper Rock*. Retrieved from http://newspaperrock.bluecorncomics.com/2011/05/four-genders-in-navajo-culture.html.

Goossen, I.W. (1995). *Dine bizaad: Speak, read, write Navajo*. Flagstaff, AZ: Salina Bookshelf.

Gustavson, I.C. (2002). Zine writing, graffiti and turntablism: The creative practices of three youth. *Dissertation Proquest*. AA1304881. Retrieved from http://repository.upenn.edu/disserttions/AA1304881.

Guzzetti, B.J., & Foley, L. (2017). *Rad dad*: A Chicano man reconstructing masculinity and fatherhood through zines. In E. Ortlieb & E. Cheek (Eds.), *Addressing diversity in literacy instruction* (pp. 89–114). Bingley, UK: Emerald Press.

Guzzetti, B.J., & Lesley, M. (2015). Surviving: An African-American man reconstructing masculinity through literacy. In T. Ransaw & M. Majors (Eds.), *Emerging issues and trends in education* (pp. 57–85). International Race and Education Series, Volume 3. East Lansing, MI: MSU Press.

Jenkins, H. (2006). *Convergence culture: Where old and new media collide*. New York, NY: New York University Press.

Jewitt, C., & Kress, G. (2010). Multimodality, literacy and school English. In D. Wyse, R. Andrews, & J. Hoffman (Eds.), *The Routledge international handbook of english, language and literacy teaching* (pp. 342–353). Abingdon, UK: Routledge.

Kalantzis, B., & Cope, M. (2012). *Literacies*. Port Melbourne, Australia: Cambridge University Press.

Kehler, M. (2008). Masculinities and critical social literacies practices: The read and mis-read bodies of high school young men. In R.F. Hammet & K. Sanford (Eds.), *Boys, girls and the myths of literacies and learning*. Toronto, Canada: Canadian Scholars Press.

Kirkland, D.E. (2013a). *A search past silence: The literacy of young Black men*. New York, NY: Teachers College Press.

Kirkland, D.E. (2013b). Inventing masculinity: Young black males, literacy and tears. In B.J. Guzzetti & T.W. Bean (Eds.), *Adolescent literacies and the gendered self: (Re)constructing identities through multimodal literacy practices* (pp. 131–139). New York, NY: Routledge.

Knobel, M., & Lankshear, C. (2007). *A new literacies sampler*. New York, NY: Peter Lang.

Kress, G., & van Leeuwen, T. (2006). *Reading images: The grammar of visual design*. New York, NY: Routledge

Lankshear, C., & Knobel, M, (2011). *New literacies: Everyday practices and classroom learning*. New York, NY: Open University Press/McGraw Hill.

Lee, L.L. (2013). *Dine masculinities: Conceptualizations and reflections*. CreateSpace Independent Publishers.

Lincoln, Y.E., & Guba, I.V. (1985). *Naturalistic inquiry*. Newbury Park, CA; Sage.

Lopez, M.H., & Gonzalez-Barrera, A. (2014). Women's college enrollment gains leave men behind. *Factank: News in the Numbers*. Retrieved from www.pewresearch.org/facttank/2014/03/06/womens-college-enrollment-gains-leave-men-behind.

Marshall, E., & Rogers, T. (2016). Shouting from the street: Youth, homelessness and zining practices. In T. Rogers, K. Winters, M. Perry, & A. LaMonde (Eds.), *Youth, critical literacies, and civic engagement: Arts, media and literacy in the lives of* adolescents (pp. 20–52). New York, NY: Routledge.

Miller, J. (2015, March). Most native tongues of the west are all but lost. *High Country News*. Retrieved from www.hcn.org/issues/47.4/most-native-tongues-of-the-west-are-all-but-lost.

Murray, T.R. (2001). Feminist perspectives. In T. Murray (Ed.), *Recent theories of human development* (pp. 237–260). Thousand Oaks, CA: Sage.

Naughton, J. (2012, June). Yes, Virgil, there are men writing romance: Focus on Romance 2012. *Publishers Weekly*. Retrieved from www.publishersweekly.com/pw/by-topic/new-titles/adult-announcements/article/52473-yes-virgil-there-are-men-writing-romance-focus-on-romance-2012.html.

Niemi, N.S. (2017). *Degrees of difference: Women, men and the value of higher education*. New York, NY: Routledge.

Noll, E. (1998). Experiencing literacy in and out of school: Case studies of two American Indian Youths. *Journal of Literacy Research*, *32*(2), 206–232.

Patton, M.Q. (2015). *Qualitative evaluation and research methods* (4th ed.). Newbury Park, CA: Sage.

Pianin, E. (2017, May 23). Data shows millennial women are dominating the current job market. *Fiscal Times*. Retrieved from www.thefiscaltimes.com/2017/05/22/Millennial-Women-are-Surging-Ahead-Men-Job-Market.

Piepmeier, A. (2009). *Girl zines: Making media, doing feminism*. New York, NY: New York University Press.

Schow, A. (2016, September 19). Women earning more doctoral and master's degrees than men. *Washington Examiner*. Retrieved from www.washingtonexaminer.com/women-earning-moredoctoral-and-masters-degrees-than-men/article/2602223.

Smith, D.T. (2013). Images of black males in popular media. *Huffington Post*. www.huffingtonpost.com/darron-t-smith-phd/black-men-media_b_2844990.html.

Smith, M.D., Moore, D.L., Laymon, K., & Green, K.M. (2013). Black men writing to live: Brothers' letters. *Feminist Wire*. Retrieved from www.thefeministwire.com/2013/black-men-writing-to-live-brothers-letters.

Stake, R.E. (2011). Qualitative case studies. In N.K. Denzin & Y.E. Lincoln (Eds.), *Handbook of qualitative research* (pp. 443–467). Newbury Park, CA: Sage.

Stanley, L., & Wise, S. (1993). *Breaking out again: Feminist ontology and epistemology*. New York, NY: Routledge.

Vedder, R. (2015, May 4). The disappearing college male. *Forbes CCAP*. Retrieved from www.forbes.com/sites/ccap/2015/05/04/the-disappearing-college-male/#355d3a234d3c.

Vermeren, I. (2015, January 28). Men vs women: Who is more active on social media? *Broadband Watch*. Retrieved from www.brandwatch.com/blog/men-vs-women-active-social-media.

Weaver-Hightower, M. (2003). The "boy turn" in research on gender and education. *Review of Educational Research*, *73*(4), 471–498.

Wieser, K.G. (2017). *Back to the blanket: Recovered rhetorics and literacies in American Indian studies*. Norman, OK: University of Oklahoma Press.

Williams, R., & Flores-Ragade, A. (2010). The educational crisis facing young men of color. *Diversity & Democracy: Association of American Colleges & Universities*, 13, 3. Retrieved from www.aacu.org/publications-research/periodicals/educational-crisis-facing-young-men-color.

17

READING FATHERHOOD

The Importance of Fathers in Children's Literacy Development

Theodore S. Ransaw

Fathers are not often thought of as involved in their children's literacy practices. Nevertheless, fathers' involvement in their children's literacy development has a positive influence on literacy independently from the mother (Pancsofar, Vernon-Feagans, & The Family Life Project Investigators, 2010; Sims & Coley, 2016). The misidentification of a father as an important part of a child's literacy development has many detriments including educators and policy makers neglecting to implement father-friendly reading policies. Fathers love to read to their children (Nord & West, 2001) and frequently do so despite the obstacles.

Obstacles to fathers participating in their children's literacy development include fathers being on the road, working during the day and going to school at night, long hours at the office, and having two jobs (Saracho, 2010). A father's literacy interactions are also related to his employment status. Despite scheduling barriers, Clark's (2009) study found that 19% of unemployed fathers read to their children every day while 15% of employed fathers read to their children some of the time every day. Swain, Welby, and Brooks (2009) argue that a father's support of his children's literacy may be hampered by issues of gender stereotypes that see school and reading support relegated to women.

The behaviors that support or inhibit childrearing collaboration between mothers and fathers are called maternal gatekeeping (Allen & Hawkins, 1999). Since a gate opens two ways, a maternal gatekeeper can have both a positive and negative effect on a father's involvement with his children. This is especially important since the mother of a father's children can significantly influence his participation in his children's upbringing, thus defining his fathering role and the extent to which he can provide homework assistance, regardless of the parents' marital status (Ransaw, 2017). Mothers also play a role in a father's belief in himself to be a good parent. As Tomas Moniz shared in Guzzetti's and Foley's

(2017) research, a father becomes frustrated when told that he holds, "his baby incorrectly or had not dressed his child properly – or by women who would not speak with him at all at parks and playgrounds" (p. 102).

Gender identity can also be a barrier to a father's educational involvement with his children. For example, Karther (2002) asserts that fathers may defer to their wives as the primary reading teacher to children at home because of both gender expectations, and because of their own low reading achievement in school. Ortiz and Stile (1996) found that even fathers who were involved in their children's literacy development often found themselves unsure how to start reading activities with their children. Another obstacle to a father's literacy involvement with their children is that literacy practices may not be as valued for men as for women (Fletcher & Daly, 2002). The belief that fathers cannot play an influential role in their children's literacy development is surprising as well as unproductive since fathers can have a substantial influence on their children's ability to read, their levels of interest in reading, as well as their reading choices (Lloyd, 1999). Fathers read with children (Vandermaas-Peeler, Sassine, Price, & Brihart, 2012), choose texts for children (Ortiz, Stile, & Brown, 1999), and engage in literacy development with children differently than women do in ways that improve reading outcomes independently from mothers (Pancsofar et al., 2010; Sims & Coley, 2016). Many fathers use their literacy fathering practices unconsciously, drawing on their natural instincts (Swain, Cara, & Mallows, 2017). Parents are their children's first teachers, and fathers are parents, too. People need to know that fathers can positively influence their children's literacy outcomes so that gender stereotypes about men and reading can be reframed in ways that support and encourage fathers to read to their children. According to Compton-Lilly (2002), fathers make great teachers!

Overview

Contrary to popular thought, fathers do indeed value literacy learning (Karther, 2002). According to Swain et al. (2017), 78% of the fathers in their study reported they wanted to help their child to do well at school and wanted to help their child learn how to read. Intrinsic motivation to help their children get ahead in school and a desire to help them learn to read is important because the time a father spends reading with his child is crucial. In fact, a father reading with his children can be the most consistent predictor of their positive literacy outcomes (Brooks, 2002).

The fact that fathers like to read to their children seems to be consistent across ethnic groups and across income levels (Cabrera, Hofferth, & Chae, 2011). Duursma, Pan, and Raikes' (2008) assert that among low-income families, 25% of fathers said that they read daily to their toddlers or preschool children. Additionally, when work hours are taken into consideration, there is no difference between mothers' and fathers' time spent reading to their children

(Peters, Seeds, & Goldstein, 2008). Not only do fathers enjoy reading to their children, they also like to sing to them (Sims & Coley, 2016). One early childhood longitudinal study found that 71% of fathers in their study told their children stories at least once a week, and 89% had fathers who sang songs to them at least once a week (Nord & West, 2001). Singing to children is also a way to increase children's literacy development, especially bilingual children (Nord & West, 2001).

Fathers and Reading Outcomes

Although most prior research focuses largely on a mother's input into children's literacy development (Duursma, et al., 2008; Patterson, 2002), a father's involvement in his children's literacy should not be overlooked since a father's influence on his children's literacy development is just as important as the mother's input (Sims & Coley, 2016). In fact, a father's vocabulary use during picture-book time is associated with early language skill development for low-income children independently from a mother's vocabulary use (Pancsofar et al., 2010). Morgan, Nutbrown, and Hannon (2009) suggest that fathers play four key roles in their children's literacy development: providing literacy *opportunities*, showing *recognition* of their children's achievements, *interacting* with their children through literacy activities, and being a literacy user *role model*.

In addition, Nord, Brimhall, and West(1997) showed that fathers from two-parent families, who participated in schooling activities at a moderate or high level, had children who usually achieved high marks, enjoyed school, and never repeated a grade. Low-income families that had fathers who were involved in their child's school and read to their 24- and 36-month-old children had children with more developed cognitive skills.

The literature on fathers' contributions to their children's literacy development does not suggest that a father is more important than a mother. Mothers and fathers *both* contribute to their children's literacy experience (Nord et al., 1997). Gendered or gender-stereotypical expectations of parenting duties should shift from being more welcoming and inclusive to a father's input and methods, especially how they engage in literacy practices with their children.

Fathers and Reading Involvement

In general, fathers spend less time with their children than do mothers. As a result, fathers often use more complex language and different reading styles when interacting with their children to maximize their time with them (Lamb & Tamis-LeMonda, 2004; Swain et al., 2017). For example, some research supports the phenomena that fathers and mothers do use language differently and consequently play different roles in children's language experiences that potentially influence later language development and impact children's social-cognitive understanding (LaBounty, Wellman, Olson, Lagattuta, & Liu, 2008; Magill-Evans & Harrison, 2001).

In addition, fathers tend to be the main readers to their daughters, and mothers the main readers to their sons (Vandermaas-Peeler et al., 2012). Fathers similarly tend to read longer to their daughters than to their sons. Milliard (1997) noted that boys seeing a father read can have a positive impact on their literacy education since a father is a role model who can encourage his children's reading habits. Wragg, Wragg, Haynes, and Chamberlain's (1998) research asserts that fathers act as role models, often relating their own practices and experiences as they read to their children, and even adapting reading strategies according to the time of day and their children's mood (Vandermaas-Peeler et al., 2012).

While both mothers and fathers can model literacy practices, fathers are more likely to use multimodal texts with their children. Fathers tend to use alternative texts, such as photographs, newspapers, letters, magazine stories, newspapers grocery bags, fruits, plants from their garden, comic strips (Karther, 2002) comic books, and even zines or self-publications (Guzzetti & Lesley, 2017). Ortiz et al.'s (1999) study revealed that fathers are also more likely to participate in informal literacy activities, such as reading aloud and reading road signs, logos, and billboards together with their children.

Sharing fun-time activities like reading helps to define and balance a father's work schedule and the parenting time of a modern-day father (Swain, et al., 2017). The intrinsic motivation of a father's desire to want to be involved with their child's literacy practices and the positive outcomes that come from that interaction cannot be overstated. For example, Naber, Van IJzendoorn, Deschamps, Van Engeland, and Bakermans-Kranenburg (2010) found that a father's desire to play with their children increases with their involvement. When fathers play with their children, they become more engaged with them. As involved fathers learn more about their children, and as children learn more about their fathers, parental sensitivity increases (Brown, Mangelsdorf, & Neff, 2012). Fathers, like any good parent, have the capacity to learn how to become better parents the more they practice.

Fathers readily adapt to parenting in multiple ways, adjusting their job schedules, using multiple literacy platforms, and developing unique strategies based on their children's personalities. These parenting strategies supporting their children's literacy development seem to be consistent across income levels, race, and educational attainment. It seems that fathers share a commonality in finding creative ways to connect to their children through literacy practices as a performance of their masculinity.

Masculine Theory

This study used Connell's (2002) theory of masculinity as a lens from which to examine fathering involvement and education outcomes. Connell developed her theory on hegemonic masculinity while researching class structure and education inequities, two issues specifically pertinent to masculinity. Connell views hegemonic masculinity as two-way and simultaneous, a practice that forms and is formed by structures that are appropriated and defined (Connell, 1995). Put another way, hegemonic masculinity is a practice that is being recreated under constantly changing conditions (Wedgwood, 2009), and is not a fixed biological behavior (Bean & Harper, 2007). Connell's hegemonic masculinity is suitable as a frame to study the interrelated issues of male's parenting styles, including literacy development strategies.

My Procedures

A phenomenological qualitative interview process was adopted as a research methodology for the present study. Qualitative studies analyze social productions, practices, and perspectives of small sets of participants more so than do large data sets used in quantitative research (Denzin & Lincoln, 1994). Phenomenological research designs typically consist of interviews with about ten or so participants as the aim is to understand a phenomenon from the participants' perspective (Hein & Austin, 2001). The aim of this study was to investigate the practices that African American fathers employ to help their children achieve in school. The relationship of fathers' literacy strategies to educational outcomes was an unexpected finding.

Participants

Since African Americans typically attend Black churches (Wilcox & Gomex, 1990), fliers were posted and disseminated across religious institutions in southwest Nevada, and mid-Michigan. The fliers targeted biological African American fathers or African American stepfathers who were at least 18 years old. Each participant was given a pseudonym based on African American male authors. A total of 12 African American fathers were interviewed to examine their parenting strategies to help their children get ahead in school. The 12 fathers who participated in the study ranged in age from 31 to 58, had incomes ranging from less than 25,000 a year to more than 100,000 a year, 9 of the 12 had college degrees, and 4 reported reading to their children four or more hours a week.

While all the participant fathers indicated that they enjoyed reading to their children, 11 of the fathers identified specified reading strategies or the approximate length of time they spent reading to or with their children. The average length of time spent reading to or with school-age children was 2.3 hours a week, reading to about two children per week.

All the fathers indicated that they enjoyed reading to their children and that they read to their children almost every day, but not all the fathers were able to estimate an exact amount of time. The time spent reading to their children was based on the father's estimated average time they fathers spent reading to their children when they were school age. The fathers did not distinguish between biological or step-children when identifying homework assistance strategies.

Measuring Fathers' Involvement in Children's Literacy

There is only one known fathering involvement scale, developed by Rubin and Rubin in 2005. Fathering involvement comprises three components: (1) direct interaction (or engagement) with the child in the context of caretaking, play, or leisure; (2) accessibility (or availability), being physically and/or psychologically available to the child; and (3) responsibility, assuming responsibility for the child's welfare and care, including organizing and planning his or her life (Lamb, Pleck, Charnov, & Levine, 1985). This model is presently the most widely accepted definition of father involvement, as it focuses on a father's feelings and society's perceptions of masculinity (Pleck & Pleck, 1997). An adaptation of the scale was used to help formulate discussion questions. The data collection instrument used in this study was Ransaw's (2013) African American Fathering Involvement Qualitative Questionnaire (FIQQ). The FIQQ uses the three components of Rubin and Rubin's (2005) quantitative scale based on the three categories of engagement, accessibility, and responsibility.

My Findings

Fathers Use Different Reading Approaches

Consistent with Morgan et al.'s (2009) research, the fathers in this study used alternative texts in their fathering literacy activities. For example, Dumas reads both newspapers and books to his children. Du Bois used the Bible in his literacy practices with his children and Ellison employed books, dictionaries, and a thesaurus, while Woodson, Haley, and Dumas used smartphones, cellphones, and apps for literacy support. Also, one of Larry's children did not think in abstract terms, so his strategy was to draw pictures with her to help her understand difficult concepts. Some studies suggest that parents using the Bible in their children's literacy practices can have a positive effect on family life (Palkovitz & Palm, 1998) and using alternative text, including religious texts, is a common practice that fathers who practice literacy strategies employ (Guzzetti & Lesley, 2017; Karther, 2002).

Fathers Teach their Children How to Overcome Learning Frustrations

Dunbar encouraged his daughter to "get out of her comfort zone" and try new things by disrupting his daughter's natural tendency to resort to the familiar.

Baldwin also liked to help his children operate at their frustration level with reading homework assistance, confiding "frustration is a good thing with regards to children's learning." Swain et al. (2017) posit that fathers may have an intuitive ability to recognize and implement literacy practices. Helping students to be comfortable outside of their comfort zone, i.e., their frustration level, has been known to increase reading comprehension (Roberts, 2006). Fathers who teach their children to read at or through their frustration level was an unexpected finding.

Fathers Are Adaptive

Both Haley and Dumas reported that they used different strategies to teach their sons and daughters. Both said they "differentiate" their sons' learning by using sports analogies. Differentiation can occur when a teacher understands that all children learn differently and adjusts teaching strategies to accommodate those differences (Smit & Humpert, 2012). Dunbar tried to relate his readings to his daughter to what was happening in their lives at the time. Ellison reported that he employs different strategies for each of his daughters that are specifically aligned with their personalities. One of his daughters is more focused, but also more emotionally needy, and calls and texts him often. His other daughter is "more strong willed," so he and his ex-wife would often check whether she did her homework at all. Ellison had different times of the day that he read to his daughters. This differentiation was another unexpected finding from this study but was also consistent with Swain et al.'s (2017) findings.

Fathers Find Reading Opportunities

During the summer, Woodson took his children to the library, had them read to him and took them to tutoring at church. Johnson took his children to the theater, the arts center, and different events outside of school during the summer months. Hughes gave his children schoolwork during the summer. Du Bois bought his children a Spanish book, as well as high school proficiency books. Washington encouraged his son to read whatever book he wanted to, and also gave his children money at book or book fairs and let them pick out what they want to read. Coates only let his son listen to NPR on the radio when he drove him to school in the morning. These findings are consistent with other research that suggests that fathers often create opportunities for literacy development of their children (Morgan et al., 2009).

Fathers Model Reading and Use Play

Dumas stated that he makes time to ensure that his children see him sit down and read every day, just so that they "can see that learning can also be for fun." Haley also modeled good reading habits, stating that, "I have an education, and they can see it. I want them to like learning." He aimed to show his children that reading is fun. Fun seems to be a key component to both the way fathers engage with literacy practices with their children and why they like reading to or with their children. Fathers in this study used play when interacting with their children in many different ways, including literacy practices where they use their inherent playfulness when reading to their children as both a bonding tool and a teaching tool. Both Haley and Baldwin stated that they used "play to talk about everything" including reading to their children, especially during story time. More than unintentional and happenstance, play is an integral part of the learning process that is "a mix of physical, social, emotional, and intellectual rewards at all stages of life" (Eberle, 2017, p. 217). Role modeling can be a form of play, thus the reason why these two overarching themes were placed together, fathers modeling reading is consistent with the literature of Morgan et al.'s (2009) research.

Implications for Literacy Education and Cross-Disciplinary Fields

The father participants in this study implemented the following approaches with their children; different reading approaches, at or through frustration level, adaptation, providing literacy opportunities, modeling reading, and Dad play.

These fathers' literacy practices were consistent with three of the four fathering literacy practices noted by Morgan et al. (2009): using alternative texts, providing literacy opportunities, and modeling reading. An argument can be made, however, that the third category found in that study – fathers interacting with their children – is similar to this study's findings of teaching at or through frustration level and using differentiation. These findings were consistent across income levels for the fathers in this study. These findings are similar to findings from Cabrera et al.'s (2011) study, which reported no significant difference across degree attainment, income, and race in a father's verbal strategy or verbal stimulation in their children's literacy development. Therefore, hegemonic masculinity was a suitable framework with which to approach this study since it looks at both hegemonic and non-hegemonic masculinity and how males, in this case fathers, continually adapt to their situations (Connell, 1995, 2002). Fathers in this study had similar practices to promote their children's literacy development as did other fathers regardless of ethnicity, income level, and degree attainment.

What Can Fathers Do to Help Their Children with Literacy Development?

Radical Fathering

Radical fathering is based on the premise that a father can be an active parent in their children's upbringing and education (Guzzetti & Foley, 2017).

The single most important thing that a father can do to help their children's literacy outcomes is to realize that fathers may do things differently, and that it is okay for them to do so. Since fathers typically are not represented in the media in a favorable way, they can turn to online communities and online or print resources, such as zines, which focus on fatherhood for support. Zines are do-it-yourself publications that are typically created using cut-and-paste methods, use multi-modal text, and are personal in nature (Guzzetti & Foley, 2017). There are also many YouTube video channels supporting fathers, including: the Dad Network, Fatherhood Institute, DadLabs, Richard Jaramillo's self-titled channel, and the Just Us Guys channel for gay fathers.

Reimagine Parenting

When mothers open themselves up to the possibility that fathers can be involved and effective parents, they become more inclusive and supportive of fathers' unique parenting styles. The positive influence a mother has when she encourages the father of her children to be involved cannot be overstated. For example, when a mother helps a man improve his image as a capable father, he tends to become more involved. Research also reveals that when fathers play with their children, they want to engage with their children even more (Naber, et. al, 2010; Raeburn, 2014). As involved fathers learn more about their children, and as children learn more about their fathers, parental sensitivity increases (Brown et al., 2012).

Where Can Social Workers Look for Empirical Methods that Include Fathers?

Thinking of Parenting as a Dynamic

Family system theory (FST) views family as interrelated complex and dynamic (Cox & Paley, 2003). One member in a family can affect the relationships of the other members in the family. This is especially relevant to fathers since fatherhood is studied from either the perspective of the father alone or how a mother allows or prevents a father from being included in parenting – *gatekeeping*. Rarely are there discussions of how children can influence a father's interactions or how a mother's *and* father's unique personalities and distinctiveness influence a father's involvement as a whole. FST allows exploration of family dynamics in its entirety.

Acceptance

Accepting that fathers have different communication styles with independent outcomes than mothers is an important step in the process of including men in the definition of a good parent. Fathers often have different approaches in which they interact with their children, ask more abstract questions, and have more outcome-based interactions with their children (Keizer, Lucasses, Jaddoe, & Tiemeier, 2014). Consequently, a father's involvement in their children's lives has been shown to encourage toddlers to talk more, use a more diverse vocabulary, and produce longer utterances when interacting with their fathers (Rowe, Cocker, & Pan, 2004).

While there is more that can be done to support fathers' literacy engagement with their children than radical fathering, reimagining parenting, thinking of parenting as a dynamic, and employing family system theory, it is the hope of this author that readers consider joining the "Fathers Are Important to Education" revolution. While we are far from the 1950s when men were arrested for being in their wives' delivery rooms, we are still far from thinking that fathers are just as important as mothers when it comes to teaching children to read. Please support and include fathers in the literacy development of their children. *Parenting without inclusivity is tyranny.*

References

Allen, S.M., & Hawkins, A.J. (1999). Maternal gatekeeping: Mother's beliefs and behaviors that inhibit greater father involvement in family work. *Journal of Marriage and the Family, 61,* 199–212.

Bean, T.W., & Harper, H. (2007). Reading men differently: Alternative portrayals of masculinity in contemporary young adult fiction. *Reading Psychology, 28*(1), 11–30.

Brooks, G. (2002). *What works for children with literacy difficulties? The effectiveness of intervention schemes.* London, UK: DfES Research Report no. RR380.

Brown, G.L., Mangelsdorf, S.C., & Neff, C. (2012). Father involvement, paternal sensitivity, and father–child attachment security in the first 3 years. *Journal of Family Psychology, 26*(3), 421–430.

Cabrera, N.J., Hofferth, S.L., & Chae, S. (2011). Patterns and predictors of father–infant engagement across race/ethnic groups. *Early Childhood Research Quarterly, 26*(3), 365–375. doi: 10.1016/j.ecresq.2011.01.001

Clark, C. (2009). *Why fathers matter to their children's literacy.* London, UK: National Literacy Trust.

Compton-Lilly, C. (2002). *Reading families: The literate lives of urban children.* New York, NY: Teachers College Press.

Connell, R.W. (1995). *Masculinities.* Cambridge MA: Polity Press.

Connell, R.W. (2002). *Gender.* Cambridge, MA: Polity Press.

Cox, M.J., & Paley, B. (2003). Understanding families as systems. *Current Directions in Psychological Science, 12*(5), 93–196. doi: 10.1111/1467-8721.01259

Duursma, E., Pan, B.A., & Raikes, H. (2008). Predictors and outcomes of low-income fathers' reading with their toddlers. *Early Childhood Research Quarterly, 23,* 351–365. doi: 10.1016/j.ecresq.2008.06.001

Denzin, N.K., & Lincoln, Y.S. (1994). *Handbook of qualitative research.* London, UK: Sage.

Eberle, S.G. (2017, March). The elements of play: Toward a philosophy and a definition of play. *American Journal of Play, 6*(2), 214–233.

Fletcher, F., & Daly, K. (2002). *Fathers' involvement in their children's literacy development*. Newcastle, New South Wales: Family Action Centre, University of Newcastle, Australia.

Guzzetti, B.J., & Foley, L. (2017). Rad dad: A Chicano man reconstructing masculinity and fatherhood through zines. In E. Ortlieb & E. Cheek (Eds.), *Addressing diversity in literacy instruction* (pp. 89–114). Bingley, UK: Emerald Press.

Guzzetti, B.J., & Lesley, M. (2017). An African-American man reconstructing masculinity through literacy. In T.H. Ransaw and R. Major (Eds.), *Emerging trends and issues in education* (pp. 57–85). East Lansing, MI: Michigan State University Press.

Hein, S.F., & Austin, W.J. (2001). Empirical and hermeneutic approaches to phenomenological research in psychology: A comparison. *Psychological Methods, 6*(1), 3–17.

Karther, D. (2002). Fathers with low literacy and their young children. *The Reading Teacher, 56*, 184–193.

Keizer, R., Lucasses, N., Jaddoe, V., & Tiemeier, H. (2014). A prospective study on fathering involvement and toddlers' behavioral and emotional problems: Are sons and daughters differently affected? *Fathering, 12*(1), 38–51.

LaBounty, J., Wellman, H.M., Olson, S., Lagattuta, K., & Liu, D. (2008). Mothers' "and" fathers' use of internal state talk with their young children. *Social Development, 17*, 757–775.

Lamb, M.E., Pleck, J.H., Charnov, E.L., & Levine, J.A. (1985). Paternal behavior in humans. *American Zoologist, 25*, 883–894.

Lamb, M.E., & Tamis-LeMonda, C.S. (2004). The role of the father. In M.E. Lamb (ed.), *The role of the father in child development* (pp. 1–31). Hoboken, NJ: John Wiley & Sons.

Lloyd, T. (1999). *Reading for the future: Boys' and fathers' views on reading*, London, UK: Save the Children.

Magill-Evans, J., & Harrison, M.J. (2001). Parent–child interactions, parenting stress, and developmental outcomes at 4 years. *Children's Health Care, 30*, 135–150.

Milliard, E. (1997). Differently literate: Gender identity and construction of the developing reader. *Gender and Education, 9*, 31–49.

Morgan, A., Nutbrown, C., & Hannon, P. (2009). Fathers' involvement in young children's literacy development: Implications for family literacy programmes. *British Educational Research Journal, 35*, 167–185.

Naber, F., VanIJzendoorn, M.H., Deschamps, P., VanEngeland, H., & Bakermans-Kranenburg, M.J. (2010). Intranasal oxytocin increases fathers' observed responsiveness during play with their children: A double-blind within-subject experiment. *Psychoneuroendrcrinology, 35*(10), 1583–1586.

Nord, C.W., Brimhall, D., & West, J. (1997) Fathers' involvement in their children's schools. *NCES 98–091; ED 409 125*. Washington, DC: US Department of Education, National Center for Education Statistics. Retrieved from http://files.eric.ed.gov/fulltext/ED409125.pdf.

Nord, C.W., & West, J. (2001). *Fathers' and mothers' involvement in their children's schools by family type and resident status* (NCES 2001-032). Washington, DC: U.S. Department of Education, National Center for Education Statistics.

Ortiz, R., & Stile, S. (1996, February). *A preliminary study of fathers' reading activities with their preschool-age children from three academic programs: Head Start, developmentally delayed, and gifted*. Paper presented at the meeting of the New Mexico Federation of the Council for Exceptional Children, Albuquerque, NM.

Ortiz, R., Stile, S., & Brown, C. (1999). Early literacy activities of fathers: Reading and writing with young children. *Young Children, 54*, 16–18.

Palkovitz, R., & Palm, G. (1998). Fatherhood and faith in formation: The developmental effects of fathering on religiosity, morals & values. *Journal of Men's Studies, 7*, 33–51.

Pancsofar, N., Vernon-Feagans, L., & the Family Life Project Investigators. (2010). Fathers' early contributions to children's language development in families from low-income rural communities. *Early Childhood Research Quarterly, 25*, 450–463.

Patterson, J.L. (2002). Relationships of expressive vocabulary to frequency of reading and television experience among bilingual toddlers. *Applied Psycholinguistics, 23*, 493–508. doi: 10.1017/S0142716402004010

Peters, M., Seeds, K., & Goldstein, A. (2008) *Parental involvement in children's education*. Research Report. DCSF RR034.

Pleck, E.H., & Pleck, J.H. (1997). Fatherhood ideals in the United States: Historical dimensions. In M.E. Lamb (Ed.), *The role of the father in child development* (3rd ed., pp. 33–48). New York, NY: Wiley.

Raeburn, P. (2014). *Do fathers matter? What science is telling us about the parent we've overlooked*. New York, NY: Scientific American.

Ransaw, T. (2013). The impact of television portrayals of fatherhood and its influence on Black masculinity: Video clip reflection responses of five African American fathers in southern Nevada. *Journal of Black Masculinity, 3*(1), 147–173.

Ransaw, T. (2017). Cool papas: How six fathers in mid-Michigan use sports as a tool for engagement, accessibility and responsibility to increase the educational outcomes of their children. *Spectrum: A Journal on Black Men, 6*(1), 1–31.

Roberts, T. (2006). "Frustration level." Reading in the infant school. *Educational Research, 19*(1), 41–44.

Rowe, M.L., Cocker, D., & Pan, B.A. (2004). A comparison of fathers' and mothers' talk to toddlers in low-income families. *Social Development, 13*(2), 278–291.

Rubin, J., & Rubin, I. (2005). *Qualitative interviewing*. Thousand Oaks, CA: Sage.

Saracho, O.N. (2010). A culturally responsive literacy program for Hispanic fathers and their children. *Journal of Hispanic Higher Education, 9*(4), 281–293. doi: 10.1177/1538192710374234

Sims, J., & Coley, R.L. (2016). Independent contributions of mothers' and fathers' language and literacy practices: Associations with children's kindergarten skills across linguistically diverse households. *Early Education and Development, 27*(4), 495. doi: 10.1080/10409289.2016.1091973

Smit, R., & Humpert, W. (2012). Differentiated instruction in small schools. *Teaching and Teacher Education, 28*(8), 1152–1162. doi: 10.1016/j.tate.2012.07.003

Swain, J., Cara, O., & Mallows, D. (2017) "We occasionally miss a bath but we never miss stories": Fathers reading to their young children in the home setting. *Journal of Early Childhood Literacy, 17*(2), 176–202.

Swain, J., Welby, S., & Brooks, G. (2009) *Learning literacy together: The impact and effectiveness of family literacy on parents, children, families and schools*. (Executive summary October 2009). Coventry, UK: Learning and Skills Improvement Service.

Vandermaas-Peeler, M., Sassine, B., Price, C., & Brihart, C. (2012). Mothers' and fathers' guidance behaviours during storybook reading. *Journal of Early Childhood Literacy, 12*(4), 415–442.

Wedgwood, N. (2009). Connell's theory of masculinity: Its origins and influences on the study of gender. *Journal of Gender Studies, 18*(4), 329–339.

Wilcox, C., & Gomex, L. (1990). Religion, group identification, and politics among American Blacks. *Sociological Analysis, 51*(3), 271–285.

Wragg, E.C., Wragg, C.M., Haynes, G.S., & Chamberlain, R.P. (1998). *Improving literacy in the primary school*. London, UK: Routledge.

ABOUT THE CONTRIBUTORS

Donna E. Alvermann is an Appointed Distinguished Research Professor at the University of Georgia, focusing on young people's digital literacies and use of popular media.

Maria-Antonieta Avila is an Independent Consultant and has been an educator for over 20 years. Through her work with parents, teachers, and students she advocates for access to equitable education highlighting the need to support bilingual and bicultural resources.

Pamela Baer is a PhD candidate in Curriculum Studies and Teacher Development at the Ontario Institute for Studies in Education where her focus is in applied theatre, LGBTQ+ family experiences, and arts-based, youth-led methodologies.

Thomas Bean is a Professor of Reading/Literacy and the Rosanne Keeley Norris Endowed Chair at Old Dominion University, Darden College of Education, Department of Teaching and Learning.

Jacob Cassidy is an elementary school teacher on Vancouver Island in Campbell River, British Columbia, whose research focuses on multimodal literacy, superhero fiction, gender, and masculinities.

Judith Dunkerly-Bean is an Assistant Professor of Literacy in the Department of Teaching and Learning, Darden College of Education, at Old Dominion University, where she directs the Literacy Research and Development Center.

Sarah Evis teaches Grades 7 and 8 in the Toronto, Canada District School Board where her teaching focus is on indigenous worldviews, social justice, and critical thinking.

Ben Gallagher is a PhD candidate in Curriculum Studies and Teacher Development at the Ontario Institute for Studies in Education, where his research focuses on poetry, the environment, and informal learning spaces.

Elisabeth Gee is a Professor and the Delbert and Jewell Lewis Chair in Reading and Literacy in the Mary Lou Fulton Teachers College at Arizona State University.

Barbara J. Guzzetti is a Professor in the New College of Interdisciplinary Arts and Sciences and Affiliated Faculty with the Mary Lou Fulton Teachers College and the Center for Gender Equity in STEM at Arizona State University.

benjamin lee hicks is a PhD candidate in Curriculum Studies and Teacher Development at the Ontario Institute for Studies in Education, whose main research focus is teacher education in relation to trans identities and queering school space.

Kathleen A. Hinchman is a Professor of Reading and Language Arts at Syracuse University, who explores teachers' and adolescents' perspectives toward literacy and instruction.

Erik Jacobson is an Associate Professor in the Early Childhood, Elementary, and Literacy Education Department at Montclair State University and the Project Coordinator for Write on Sports, an educational program that teaches sports writing to middle school students.

Jin Kyeong Jung is a PhD student in Literacy, Culture, and International Education at the University of Pennsylvania, whose research interests include digital literacies, multilingual learners' practice of multiple literacies, and global teacher education.

Kate E. Kedley is an Assistant Professor of Language, Literacy, and Sociocultural Education at Rowan University in Glassboro, New Jersey, who researches education in Honduras and secondary English Language Arts classrooms.

Michael Kehler is a Research Professor of Masculinities in Education at the Werklund School of Education, University of Calgary and has research interests including boys, literacies, homophobia, male body image, counter-normative practices, heteronormativity, men as agents of social change, activism, and #MeToo.

Jacqueline Lynch is an Associate Professor in the School of Education and Human Development at Florida International University whose research interests include social and cognitive influences on early literacy development, family literacy, and teachers' professional learning.

Shelly Melchior is a PhD student in Instructional Leadership and Social and Cultural Studies at the University of Alabama and a former English Language Arts teacher.

sj Miller is a trans*+–disciplinary scholar and Coordinator of the Joint Masters in Secondary English Education and English Language Learning (ELL) Teacher Certification Program at the University of Wisconsin-Madison, whose research emphasizes policy and schooling practices about gender identity.

Julia Morris is a doctoral candidate in Literacy Education at Old Dominion University who serves as the Rosanne Keely Norris Graduate Assistant and studies curriculum and instruction and literacy.

Priyanka Parekh is an Assistant Professor of education at Transylvania University in Lexington, Kentucky.

Rebekah Piper is an Assistant Professor of Literacy at Texas A&M University San Antonio.

Tracey Pyscher is an Assistant Professor of Secondary Education at Western Washington University where she researches the social and cultural experiences of children and youth with histories of trauma and domestic violence, critical literacy and learning, and what praxis means to/for teacher education.

Theodore S. Ransaw is Curriculum Specialist and Affiliated Faculty member of African American and African Studies in the James Madison College at Michigan State University, who studies gender and educational outcomes.

Stephanie Anne Shelton is an Assistant Professor of Qualitative Research in Psychology, Research Methodology, and Counseling at the University of Alabama.

Rob Simon is an Associate Professor at the Ontario Institute for Studies in Education of the University of Toronto, whose scholarship explores critical literacy and participatory research.

Jenna Spiering is an Assistant Professor in the School of Library and Information Science at the University of South Carolina, where she researches school libraries, literacy, and literature for youth.

Shirley R. Steinberg is a Research Professor of Youth Studies in the Werklund School of Education at the University of Calgary, whose work is grounded in social theory, critical pedagogies and literacies, and community activism.

Ty Walkland is a high school English teacher and a PhD candidate in Curriculum Studies and Teacher Development at the Ontario Institute for Studies in Education, where his research focuses on collaborative inquiry and educational labor.

Karen E. Wohlwend is an Associate Professor of Literacy, Culture, and Language Education and Affiliated Faculty in Learning Sciences at Indiana University, where she studies young children's play as an embodied literacy by creating action texts with toys, popular media, and digital technologies.

INDEX

Pages in *italics* show illustrations